Drugs

Dilemmas and Choices

By a Working Party
of the Royal College of Psychiatrists
and the Royal College of Physicians

Gaskell, London

Gaskell is an imprint and registered trade mark of the Royal College of Psychiatrists, 17 Belgrave Square, London SW1X 8PG.

The Royal College of Psychiatrists is a registered charity (no. 228636).

Cover illustration by Ivan Allen of the Inkshed, London.

British Library Cataloguing-in-Publication Data.
A catalogue record for this book is available from the British Library.
ISBN 1-901242-44-7

The Joseph Rowntree Foundation has supported this project as part of its programme of research and innovative development projects, which it hopes will be of value to policy makers and practitioners. The facts presented and views expressed in this report, however, are those of the author and not necessarily those of the Foundation.

Printed by Bell & Bain Limited, Thornliebank, Glasgow.

Drugs
Dilemmas and Choices

Contents

Introduction

Drugs are contentious and attitudes to them are polarised. To many people they are alarming and dangerous, and their effects on the lives of people they know, or at least know about, are usually damaging and sometimes catastrophic. To others, particularly those under the age of 30, the drugs they and their friends have tried in the past, and perhaps still use occasionally, seem no more dangerous than alcohol, and they know that their psychological effects are at least as beneficial and enjoyable as those of either alcohol or tobacco. The first group's views are largely based on what they have read and heard. The younger generation's views are largely based on personal experience, or at least on the experience of their friends. Neither group can understand why the other can be so misguided.

The conflict is partly generational, and a consequence of the profound changes that have taken place since the 1950s, both in attitudes to 'drugs' and in the prevalence of drug use. Anyone who has witnessed the profound social and economic changes that have taken place in Britain in the last 30 years cannot fail to be aware that the use of drugs is far more common and the associated social ills far more obvious now than they were 30 or 40 years ago. In the 1950s, a few 'beatniks' and students smoked 'pot', others took amphetamine, and middle-aged people quietly became dependent on the sedatives prescribed for them by their doctors, and that was all, or nearly all. Now drug taking impinges, sometimes disastrously, on the lives of many families and most communities. Drugs can be obtained not just in big cities but in every market town. School children experiment with them from an increasingly early age, many teenagers and young adults take ecstasy and other stimulants almost as a matter of course most weekends, and tens of thousands of others have become dependent on heroin and resort to shoplifting, prostitution and burglary in order to pay for the drug they can no longer do without.

Despite these alarming changes, and a strong impression of a problem spiralling out of control, successive governments continue to insist that there is no alternative to the control policies they are already pursuing. The media report dramatic events – like the death of a happy, attractive teenager after taking a single ecstasy tablet – with increasing frequency, and novels and films like *Trainspotting*, depicting the glamour and squalor of heroin addiction, attract widespread interest. Almost never, though, is there any serious discussion of the underlying causes of the alarming increase in drug taking, or of the alternative and possibly more effective policies that might be available to our own and other governments in their attempts to bring the epidemic under control and to reduce its harmful consequences. Worse still, anyone who attempts to raise these issues is usually accused of being 'pro-drugs' or in favour of widescale legalisation.

This book was conceived and written against this background. A working party was set up by two medical Royal Colleges – the Royal College of Physicians and the Royal College of Psychiatrists – with a formal brief "to provide an authoritative review of the medical and social effects of drug use in the UK, and the historical and cultural setting in which this has developed, as a means of stimulating a widespread and well-informed debate, and thereby influencing public policy". This necessarily involved discussing the reasons why many substances are illegal while others that are equally dangerous, like alcohol and tobacco, are not, and the social and economic consequences of this distinction.

Unlike most Royal College reports, which are on highly technical subjects and intended for a largely medical readership, this book was explicitly aimed from the beginning at a general readership. It is for anyone in any walk of life who is concerned about the 'drug problem', puzzled by the widespread appeal of these illicit substances and interested to know what alternative strategies there might be for dealing with them, or what help is currently available to those who become dependent on drugs.

The 14 members of the working party were originally chosen for having open minds as well as for their expertise. We inevitably came to firm conclusions on a number of issues. Most of these conclusions appear as recommendations – mainly to the UK government or our own professions – in the summary of each chapter. Reaching conclusions and making recommendations was not, however, the central purpose of this book. Our main purpose was to make as wide a readership as possible aware of the historical evolution and the complexity of our current drug problem, and of the advantages and disadvantages of the various strategies and policies that might be adopted for tackling it. There are, in our view, no easy answers or simple solutions. For one thing, our national drug problem can only be tackled in the context of the much wider international problem, and the government's freedom of manoeuvre is seriously constrained by international agreements. Our aim is to stimulate a better informed and more intelligent public discussion of what we believe to be deeply important issues for the health and stability of our society and many of its young people.

Acknowledgements

The two Royal Colleges' working party was supported by the Joseph Rowntree Foundation. This support included a grant that enabled us to employ as a research worker Sarah Mars, who, in addition to seeking out many of the facts contained in the report, played a major part in its drafting and editing. The membership of the working party is shown in Appendix I. Several are doctors professionally concerned with the treatment of drug misusers – psychiatrists, physicians and a general practitioner (GP). However, the membership also included a chief education officer, a social scientist, a lawyer with a deep interest in social policy, an eminent American authority on drugs, and the Chief Executive of the Standing Conference on Drug Abuse. We met on 13 occasions over a period of over two years. During that time, several distinguished people, including a social historian, a senior civil servant, a health economist, a police superintendent, a criminologist and a pharmacologist, very nobly gave up their time to talk to us and answer our questions. So too did several Australian, British and American psychiatrists and social scientists involved either in the planning and provision of services for drug misusers or in research into drug misuse. We are deeply grateful to all these experts, and they influenced our thinking in many ways. Their names are listed in Appendix II, though they bear no responsibility for the views expressed in this book.

We also had a valuable meeting, and more informal discussions, with Viscountess Runciman and other members of the Independent Inquiry into the Misuse of Drugs Act 1971, set up by the Police Foundation with the assistance of The Prince's Trust. We would also like to record our gratitude to Professor Griffith Edwards, Sallie Robins and Charlie Lloyd who all took the trouble to read the draft text of this book for us and give us the benefit of their comments, and to Andrea Woolf who provided invaluable administrative support to the Working Party. Finally, we would like to thank for their help Dr David Ball, John Corkery, Professor Neil McKeganey, Joy Mott, Dr Jussi Simpura, Dr Adam Winstock, John Witton, and colleagues at the Institute for the Study of Drug Dependence and the National Addiction Centre, London.

Chapter 1. The main drugs

SUMMARY

People take a large number of psychoactive substances which can produce a wide range of different effects. Some are legal, others are not, and the law does not consistently reflect the relative risks of using them. Legally marketed alcohol and tobacco are used by many more people than are drugs and of these people, tens of thousands die prematurely each year from their adverse effects. In contrast drug use is less common and responsible for far fewer deaths. These substances vary in their capacity for creating dependence, with heroin and nicotine the most addictive. Injecting drugs can spread disease, such as HIV and hepatitis B and C. Cannabis, the most widely taken illicit substance, produces relaxation and can impair judgement, slows reflexes and can lead to accidents. Ecstasy is regularly taken in tablet form by thousands of young people at clubs and parties, with few apparent ill effects. While the risks of many substances are well-understood, it is too early to predict the long-term toll of ecstasy taking and cannabis smoking.

INTRODUCTION

The use and misuse of drugs (the term is defined in the glossary) is such a complex topic that most people find it difficult to comprehend. In order to try to understand the subject, it is necessary to appreciate what effects drugs have on mind and body; both effects which are sought-after and those which are unwanted and sometimes harmful. This chapter outlines the salient facts about misused substances in order to give users, non-users, parents and authorities a concise indication of the main medical and psychological effects of substance misuse. There are many ways in which drugs can be described and listed. The order chosen here is simply alphabetical. Because the effects produced, frequency of use and risks to health vary considerably, these are summarised for the main substances in Table 1.1.

Most drug users do not limit themselves to one of the drugs described here. They tend to have an experimental approach and will try other substances to find a range that they can use at different times or in different circumstances when they are available. The term 'polydrug use' describes the simultaneous use of more than one drug or the frequent use of several drugs.

People who regularly attend parties and other events where drugs are taken generally establish their own repertoire of substances and the order in which they take them, so as to sustain or modify the 'high' and ease the 'come down'. Sometimes, the thinking behind this kind of polydrug use is based on sophisticated scientific understanding of the drugs' chemistry and their effects. On the other hand, some frequent polydrug users have chaotic lifestyles and will use whatever substance is available or whatever they can afford, often as an accompaniment to regular heroin or methadone use. When considering drug use today, the place of individual substances within drug repertoires needs to be borne in mind.

Although the possession, sale and use of alcohol and tobacco are not controlled by the Misuse of Drugs Act 1971, legal controls are exercised over both. They are both addictive, and both have considerable implications for health. They are included here so that they can be considered in context with illicit substances. Where the information is available, figures for use across the population is provided. Certain other drugs available on prescription or over the counter (such as diuretics and laxatives) are also misused by some patients, to control their weight rather than for a psychological effect. These are not considered here.

Most, although not all, of the psychoactive substances that are widely misused are addictive; that is, they are drugs of dependence. Before the 1970s, addiction or dependence was regarded, and defined, largely in pharmaco-logical terms. Its hallmarks were increased tissue tolerance (implying that a substantially larger dose was needed to achieve a given psychological effect) and, above all, unpleasant withdrawal effects if drug use ceased abruptly. People addicted to alcohol, for example, can drink far more than inexperi-enced drinkers without appearing drunk, but are liable to epileptic fits or delirium tremens (DTs) if they suddenly stop drinking. Likewise, heroin addicts often take daily doses of heroin that would kill a normal person and experience very unpleasant symptoms ('cold turkey') if they try to stop abruptly, or even miss a couple of doses. Viewed in these terms, tobacco and cocaine were not obviously addictive, yet it was clear that smoking and taking cocaine were extremely difficult habits to break. Initially, attempts were made to deal with this dilemma by distinguishing between physical and psy-chological dependence and assuming that only the former was associated with withdrawal symptoms, but this highly questionable distinction was eventually replaced by a new more broadly based concept of dependence. This emphasised the importance of the subject's strong desire, or sense of compulsion, to take the drug, and their increasing difficulty controlling their substance-taking behaviour, a difficulty that was often revealed in a progressive neglect of alternative pleasures or interests and an inability or failure to give up despite clear evidence of overtly harmful consequences.[1]

Table 1.1. Comparisons of toxicity of licit and illicit substances with approximate numbers of deaths each year in Britain from acute and chronic toxicity.

	Prevalence of use (% of population)	Acute toxicity	Acute deaths (n/year)	Chronic toxicity	Total deaths (n/year)	Addictive	Withdrawal symptoms
Alcohol	90	+++	100	+++	30 000	+++	+++
Amphetamine	5	++	10	++	10	++	++
Cannabis	15	+	0	++	NK	++	+
Cocaine	NK	+++	NK	+++	NK	+++	++
Ecstasy	NK	++	10	NK	10	NK	+
Heroin	NK	+++++	200	+	200	+++++	++++
LSD	NK	++	NK	+	NK	0	+
Methadone (diverted)	NK	++++	400	+	NK	+++	+++
Temazepam[i] (diverted)	NK	++	100[ii]	+	100	++	++
Tobacco	35	+	0	+++++	120 000	++++	++
Solvents	NK	+++	100	++	100	+	+

Key

+++++, very high; ++++, high; +++, moderate; ++, low; +, very low.

NK, not known.

i Temazepam is the most widely used benzodiazepine.

ii Overdose death from temazepam alone, although a recognised phenomenon, is rare. Most deaths involving temazepam involve a combination of substances (such as opiates or alcohol).

This more behavioural concept of dependence is the basis of contemporary definitions and clearly embraces smoking. Indeed, viewed in this way tobacco is as addictive as heroin. It is important to appreciate, too, that dependence is not something that is present or absent. It can be present to varying degrees and often develops slowly and insidiously as regular drug use continues. Different drugs also vary markedly in their liability to induce dependence. A few weeks' use of heroin or a couple of packets of cigarettes smoked by a teenager will, more often than not, result in a lifelong habit. Heavy drinking, on the other hand, may not result in significant dependence even when sustained for several years. Indeed, it is common for young men to drink excessively from their late-teens to their mid-twenties and then, often after marrying and acquiring other responsibilities, to reduce their consumption substantially without difficulty.

ALCOHOL

Alcohol is a central nervous depressant, and although it may appear to stimulate conversation and sociability, this is because of its depressant effect on brain function. It impairs judgement, reduces inhibitions and slows reflexes in proportion to blood alcohol levels. Large doses may reduce inhibitions to the extent that people become argumentative, aggressive and violent – typical signs of drunkenness. A large dose of alcohol alone (about a bottle of spirits in people who are not regular drinkers) can cause deep coma and death. Regular users become tolerant and may be able to 'hold their drink' so that they appear relatively sober after taking amounts of alcohol that would make another person very drunk. Alcohol slows reactions and can lead to errors of judgement and accidents. Twenty per cent of drivers who die in road traffic accidents are above the legal limit for driving. Even walking and crossing roads while under the influence of alcohol can be dangerous – 20% of pedestrians killed in road accidents have blood alcohol levels which are over the legal limit for driving a motor vehicle.

There is considerable controversy about so-called 'safe' drinking levels. On the one hand, it has been shown that the regular consumption of small amounts of alcohol can protect against coronary heart disease in men over the age of 40 or women past the menopause, but it is also clear that excess consumption can lead to illness, disruption of a person's life and even death.[2] The Health Education Authority warns that there is increasing risk to health for men who drink twenty-one or more units per week or for women who drink 14 or more units per week and this was agreed in a joint report from the Royal Colleges of Physicians, General Practitioners and Psychiatrists. (A unit is about 8 g of alcohol – the quantity in half a pint of beer, a small glass of wine or a single pub measure of spirits.) Alcohol is well-known to be addictive, the risk increasing with regular consumption of large amounts (normally over 50 units a week in men or 35 in women). People who rely on alcohol for support on social occasions or for the relief of stress may gradually increase the dose until they become dependent. The development of dependence on alcohol is one way of defining an alcoholic.

Contrary to common belief, dependence can develop insidiously without a person ever experiencing drunkenness. Sudden withdrawal from alcohol, or even a reduction of intake in a person who is severely dependent, can lead to anxiety and tremors; more serious but rarer withdrawal symptoms include paranoid feelings, hallucinations and fits. Once dependence is established, the alcoholic has to ensure that a supply of alcohol is constantly available to prevent withdrawal symptoms. Heavy intake of alcohol can cause liver cirrhosis and liver cancer. The heart and brain can also suffer from toxic effects of alcohol, leading to irregular heartbeats or heart failure or to alcoholic dementia. Indeed, if it is drunk in sufficient quantities for long enough, alcohol is toxic to almost every tissue in the human body, and so contributes to a very wide range of disorders. As a result, alcoholics are much more likely to die prematurely – mainly from cirrhosis of the liver, accidents of various kinds and suicide. A 'foetal alcohol syndrome' can also occur in the children of mothers who drink heavily during early pregnancy, with the child suffering mental retardation and having a characteristic facial appearance. More minor forms of the syndrome, producing learning difficulties, but without the physical signs, may also occur.

Alcohol is our most commonly used drug, with only 7% of men and 13% of women in the general population describing themselves as non-drinkers. Like drug use, the heaviest drinking occurs among young adults (aged 16–24). Among 15–16-year-olds, 94% reported that they had ever drunk alcohol, and 79% had been drunk. Women drink much less than men, even taking into account the different levels for 'safe' drinking, but their consumption is rising.

AMPHETAMINE

The amphetamines constitute a large group of chemicals related to adrenaline, and here the term 'amphetamine' refers to both amphetamine itself and methamphetamine, which is more widely used in the USA. Amphetamine is a stimulant which increases wakefulness and suppresses appetite. It was widely used during the Second World War by combatants from all the main powers as a means of keeping exhausted men awake and vigilant, and has also been used by students trying to stay awake before examinations. However, although it keeps people awake, it does not increase accuracy but impairs judgement and reduces learning ability. Amphetamine and related drugs have also been prescribed as appetite suppressants in order to help weight reduction. Because these drugs improve athletic performance, they were among the first to be banned in sport. Today, amphetamine is the second most commonly used drug in England and Wales: 20% of 16–29-year-olds and 10% of the general population (those aged 16–59) have tried it. Across the UK, 13% of 15–16-year-olds have tried it.

Amphetamine is misused because it causes a 'buzz' with increased alertness and energy. It can be taken by mouth, sniffed as a powder, smoked or injected. After using the drug for several hours, the user tends to fall into an exhausted sleep and to wake extremely hungry. Depression and anxiety characteristically follow such amphetamine binges. Its ability to suppress appetite temporarily is attractive to some of the drug's female users. Addiction is not common but does occur. Psychotic reactions indistinguishable from acute paranoid schizophrenia are common following heavy use of amphetamine.

ANABOLIC STEROIDS

Many drugs, of which the anabolic steroids are the best known, are used to enhance athletic performance.[3] They comprise a group of synthetic drugs closely related to natural hormones such as testosterone, and their main property is to promote protein-building by the body. Their main medical use is to help the body recover from debilitating illnesses, but they are misused by athletes for their body-building properties and also because they increase aggression and competitiveness during training. These substances are banned in competitive sports, and heavy use can lead to aggressive behaviour with outbursts of violence ('roid rage') and also depression and atrophy of the testicles. Other unwanted physical effects include acne and breast develop-ment in men. They can cause premature accumulation of fats in the arteries, and death can occur from these unwanted effects on the heart and blood vessels. For those who inject steroids, rather than take them orally, all the accompanying dangers apply. One per cent of 16–29-year-olds have taken steroids, rising to 3% among 20–24-year-old males, and 1% of men and women aged 16–59. Their use is common among body-builders.

BARBITURATES

The barbiturates were widely used as sedatives in the early part of the 20th century but were largely replaced by the benzodiazepines when these drugs became widely available in the 1970s. Phenobarbitone, a member of this group, is still commonly used to control epilepsy. Barbiturates, which are addictive, have potential for misuse because they can produce an alcohol-like state of intoxication. Withdrawal can produce severe reactions including epileptic fits. The misuse of these drugs by injecting polydrug users in the 1970s and their wide use for suicidal overdose by patients prescribed barbiturates led to them falling from favour among prescribers. At one stage in the 1970s, there were 2000 deaths each year in Britain from this cause. Surveys of drug use do not usually ask about barbiturates nowadays since their use has become rare.

Benzodiazepines

Benzodiazepines is the technical name for a group of tranquilliser drugs which include diazepam (Valium), nitrazepam (Mogadon), temazepam, lorazepam, and several others. There are some benzodiazepine-like chemicals in plants such as valerian which are used as sedatives, but modern synthetic benzodiazepines are not derived from plants. The prescription of these drugs had a wide vogue in the 1960s and 1970s because of their sedative and anti-anxiety effects. However, it eventually became apparent in the 1980s that many people had become dependent on benzodiazepines; there are still one to two million people who remain on benzodiazepine sleeping tablets in Britain at the present time because they are dependent. These drugs are now only recommended for short-term use (up to two weeks) in specific circumstances for the relief of anxiety or promoting sleep, or occasionally as muscle relaxants. They are also legitimately prescribed to counteract the symptoms of alcohol withdrawal and in the treatment of epilepsy. In elderly patients, benzodiazepines can cause confusion and unsteadiness and doctors are advised not to prescribe them to these patients.

However, benzodiazepines were rarely misused by drug users until temazepam came on the market in the early 1980s. This drug was originally sold in egg-shaped capsules, and injecting drug users discovered that they could get a feeling of intoxication from injecting the contents of the capsules. Attempts were made to produce uninjectable formulations, which led to further problems (see Chapter 3).[4] Temazepam is now only sold in tablet form in the UK, which has helped to reduce problems due to injection. Even today, of the millions of tablets prescribed every year, only a very small proportion end up in the hands of misusers.

Temazepam and other benzodiazepines are still frequently used as a constituent of drug cocktails, for example to diminish the 'come down' after the use of stimulant drugs such as ecstasy and cocaine, as a supplement to opiates or for the 'buzz' they produce on their own. Overdose of benzodiazepines can cause prolonged sleep, coma, impairment of breathing and possibly death, particularly if combined with other sedative drugs such as alcohol or heroin. Three per cent of English and Welsh adults have tried tranquillisers which had not been prescribed to them, most of which will be temazepam.

Cannabis

Cannabis (known as marijuana in the USA) is a product of the cannabis (Indian hemp) plant. It is used in three main forms: the leaves (grass, pot) resin (hash) and liquid (cannabis oil). In the 1960s, the average cannabis plant contained about 0.5% tetrahydrocannabinol (THC), the main active substance in cannabis, but because of selective growing, the THC content now averages 5%. Intensive forced growing under greenhouse conditions produces 'skunk' – a yellowish cannabis plant with a distinctive smell, which can contain 10–30% THC.

It has long been smoked or ingested in a number of tropical cultures and is the most widely used drug in the UK, most of Europe and the USA at the present time. In England and Wales, 25% of those aged 16–59 report that they have tried it at least once and five per cent had used it in the last month. Across the UK, a startling 42% of 15–16-year-olds have tried cannabis.

Cannabis is usually smoked as dried plant material often mixed with tobacco in the form of a large cigarette ('joint' or 'reefer') but it can be eaten, and has been known to be injected. It produces a pleasurable feeling of intense relaxation and detachment. 'Stoned' is a term often used to describe this state. However, some people can feel depressed or experience panic attacks when they use cannabis. It also slows reactions – smoking a single joint can slow reactions for 24 hours, thus affecting the ability to drive, operate machinery, make decisions or study for that length of time. It also raises pulse rate and blood pressure in the short term, and causes the whites of the eyes to go pink for a couple of hours. While cannabis can depress the cells which maintain the immune system, there is no evidence that it predisposes to infections in humans.

Heavy use can lead to an acute psychosis which resolves as the cannabis is eliminated by the body. Elimination is slow because cannabis dissolves in fatty tissues and is only gradually released. There is evidence from psychological tests that memory and learning processes are impaired by cannabis use, and the degree to which this can be reversed by stopping its use is uncertain.[5]

Cannabis has also been linked with schizophrenia. In individuals already affected by the condition, it can exacerbate the symptoms, but whether cannabis can cause schizophrenia is uncertain. In one Swedish study, the incidence of schizophrenia was found to be six times higher in men who had used cannabis on 50 occasions or more, at the time when they had been recruited into the army 10 years earlier, than in those who had never used cannabis. It is not clear from this whether cannabis causes schizophrenia or whether the personality characteristics which predispose adolescents to use cannabis are also linked to schizophrenia, but the relationship is obviously a cause for concern.

A further problem with smoking cannabis is that it may increase the risk of lung cancer and cancers of the head and neck, and there is some evidence that these cancers may occur at a younger age than in cigarette smokers. However, because most people smoke cannabis and tobacco together, it is difficult to differentiate their effects. Cannabis has also been shown to reduce sperm production and probably decreases fertility in men. Babies born to cannabis-smoking mothers are smaller than normal and tend to be hyperactive and to have a reduced attention span. Contrary to popular belief, dependence on cannabis is common among daily users, although withdrawal symptoms are generally mild.[5]

There is considerable controversy concerning the possible medicinal uses of cannabis. It may relieve symptoms in conditions such as severe pain, glaucoma, multiple sclerosis and AIDS, and many people have argued that it should be available on prescription.[6] There are certainly established medical uses for some of the substances contained in the cannabis plant; the medical preparation nabilone is a synthetically produced cannabinoid related to THC, which is available on prescription for the relief of the vomiting caused by treatment with some anti-cancer drugs. Another cannabis-related drug, dronabinol, is being used experimentally in pain relief and can already be prescribed on a limited basis. These and other uses for cannabis are now being actively researched. The harmful and potential therapeutic uses of cannabis are discussed in more detail in Chapter 10.

Cocaine

The coca plant has been used for centuries as a mild stimulant by Latin–American Indians who chewed the leaves. However, it was discovered in the

19th century that cocaine hydrocholoride (its full chemical name) could be extracted from the plant material, and the drug became widely popular, being included in drinks (even Coca Cola until 1903). Later it was found that a euphoriant effect could be produced by inhaling the powdered drug ('snorting'). More recently, cocaine hydrochloride has been further refined into a form known as 'crack', which is smoked by playing a flame on a crystal of the drug and directly inhaling the smoke containing the vapour. There are arguments about whether cocaine or crack is more addictive.

Cocaine produces a powerful stimulant effect owing to its ability to increase the amount of a chemical called dopamine at nerve terminals in the central nervous system. It also increases the amount of noradrenaline at these sites, which leads to a fast heart rate and a sharp and severe rise in blood pressure when the drug is taken. Its other main chemical property is that it acts as a powerful local anaesthetic, and it is still used for this purpose in ear, nose and throat surgery.

When cocaine is taken, there is a brief, intense 'high' which tends to be followed by a 'come down' or 'crash'. Many users try to extend the high by taking repeated doses, but eventually they come down feeling exhausted, anxious and hungry. Cocaine tends to be addictive, and the craving can last for many months after the last dose. A number of medical problems can be associated with cocaine use. Like amphetamine and other stimulants, paranoid feelings and psychosis can occur. The nasal passages can also be damaged by snorting, leading to nosebleeds and perforation of the septum of the nose; intravenous use carries all the health risks associated with injecting. Smoking crack can cause chest pain, black spit and lung damage, and sometimes the user develops paranoid ideas. Long-term use of cocaine can cause the coronary arteries to 'fur up' with fatty deposits, leading to heart attacks early in life within a few years of regular use.

In the general population cocaine use is relatively rare, with 6% of 16–29-year-olds having tried cocaine powder and only 1% reportedly having tried crack. In the general population of England and Wales aged 16–59, it was slightly less common, with figures at 3% for cocaine and 1% for crack. Among 15–16-year-olds in the UK as a whole, 3% have taken crack and cocaine.

Ecstasy

Ecstasy, whose chemical name is 3,4-methylenedioxymethamphetamine (MDMA), is closely related to amphetamine and has broadly similar effects on mind and body, but also causes a feeling of well-being and of closeness to others. Because of the amphetamine-like surge in energy and the feeling of empathy and meaningfulness produced by this drug, it has become popular as a dance drug at parties, clubs and raves. It is taken by mouth in tablet form, and users often need to increase the dose from one or two to several tablets over a period of two or three months. In an interesting parallel to the cannabis story, scientific research is currently underway into potential psychological benefits of ecstasy as a medication for terminal cancer patients and sufferers from post-traumatic stress disorder.

Ecstasy use is mostly confined to 16–29-year-olds, of whom 1 in 10 has tried it, whereas only 4% of those aged 16–59 had taken it in England and Wales. Taken together with Scotland and Northern Ireland, 8% of 15–16-year-olds have tried ecstasy. Estimates of use in Britain vary widely, but some people have suggested that there may be as many as half a million tablets taken each week.

Under the stimulant effect of the drug, many people have carried on dancing for several hours without replacing fluid or resting, and some have died from overheating of the body.[7] By contrast, a number of others have been taken ill from drinking too much fluid without exerting themselves by dancing; some of these cases may have been the result of publicity urging ecstasy users to drink fluids to avoid dehydration. The problem is that ecstasy causes a surge in blood levels of antidiuretic hormone,[8] so that those who drink excess water when they take ecstasy are unable to pass it out through the kidneys. The consequence of this is that the brain may swell and cause illness. A small number of people have suffered from other problems after taking this drug – liver damage, strokes and psychological effects such as panic attacks, paranoid psychosis and depression. The true extent of ecstasy-related mental illness is unknown. Although dependence will occur if ecstasy is taken on a daily basis, there have been no reports of individuals using the drug frequently enough for this to occur.

One of the more important problems with MDMA is that it is toxic to a crucial type of nerve ending (serotonin terminals) in the brain. This has been demonstrated in animal studies – and there is evidence that this may also occur in humans.[9] The doses taken by clubbers and ravers are similar to those which cause permanent damage to serotonin terminals in animals. In monkeys, the damaged nerve terminals regrow locally, like the branches of a tree which sprout from the points where they were cut, but never regain their original shape.

Sophisticated brain scanning techniques have now demonstrated that the balance of serotonin is impaired in the brains of some ecstasy users, although this does need confirmation.[10] Other recent studies have demonstrated subtle memory loss that is greater in those who have used ecstasy the most and, because memory naturally declines with age, it is possible that what are currently subtle deficits might become increasingly pronounced as time goes by. Users may also be at increased risk of developing depressive illness in middle or old age as a result of serotonin depletion.

Further indication that ecstasy is having deleterious effects on the brain comes from the usual experience of ecstasy users that the sought-after effects of the drug decrease the more often it is taken.[11] These effects are not due to tolerance and do not disappear after the initial period of abstinence. This is particularly alarming for Britons, who take ecstasy in higher doses and more frequently than reported elsewhere. It has also been reported recently that ecstasy taken in early pregnancy may be associated with an increased risk of congenital abnormalities. Although all these studies point in the same direction, they should be interpreted with caution because of the other drugs taken by users, the selection of users and controls studied and the difficulties in measuring the dose of drugs where 'purity' varies.

Many people have been concerned that ecstasy tablets may contain other substances put there by illicit drug manufacturers in order to increase the effect and thus raise their profitability. There is little evidence that the ill effects of ecstasy are a result of 'contaminated' tablets of this kind.

GHB

Gamma-hydroxybutyric acid (GHB) is present in the body in small amounts. It has been used medically as an anaesthetic and also in treating alcohol withdrawal. Body-builders have used it to increase muscle bulk, and more recently it has become a misused substance. It is available as a colourless liquid tasting like seaweed, and sometimes as powder or capsules. Users drink small quantities of the liquid until they achieve a euphoric 'high'. However, this sometimes occurs just before they lose consciousness, partly because it is difficult to get the dose right and partly because the strength varies. Most users feel high for 24–48 hours followed by feeling low for a few days afterwards. GHB is a central nervous system depressant with effects similar to those of alcohol. Its potency is therefore increased when it is taken with alcohol. Users may experience symptoms including vomiting, headache, confusion and muscle tremors. Severe intoxication can result in deep coma and breathing difficulties, and deaths have been reported.

HEROIN AND OTHER OPIATES

The opiates consist of a large number of natural and synthetic drugs including heroin, morphine, codeine, methadone and a number of others which are most commonly used for pain relief, but which are also taken to suppress coughing and control diarrhoea. Morphine and codeine are derived from the opium poppy. Heroin (diacetylmorphine or diamorphine) was introduced over a hundred years ago in the mistaken belief that it could act as a non-addictive substitute for opium.

It is only used as a medicinal drug in Britain and Belgium where it is widely prescribed for the treatment of severe pain, including that caused by heart

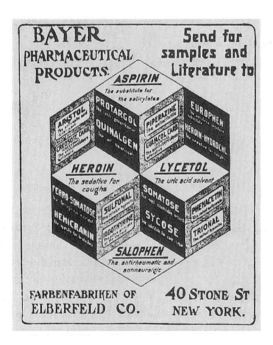

Figure 1.1.   In the early 20th century, heroin could be bought as a medicine like aspirin without prescription. Image reproduced with kind permission from Corbis/Bettmann UK.

attacks. In all other countries, heroin is not used medicinally, and morphine is the preferred strong pain reliever. Apart from medical use, fewer people have taken heroin than cocaine – about 1% of adults. The figure for school children across the UK reached 2%.

Heroin acts quickest when given intravenously, rapidly entering the brain and producing immediate euphoria and pain relief. Its ability to produce euphoria is the reason why it is misused, most commonly by intravenous injection. However, it can also be snorted as a powder or placed on silver foil, heated with a cigarette lighter and inhaled as vapour – described as 'chasing the dragon' (see Figure 1.2).

Heroin is highly addictive. Repeated use for 2–3 weeks leads to tolerance, which means that a much larger amount of drug (often tenfold or more) is required to produce the same effect. Sudden withdrawal leads to anxiety, nausea, muscle pains, diarrhoea and goose flesh ('cold turkey'). The withdrawal illness can last for up to 10 days, but is immediately relieved by taking more of the drug. Thus although users may start by seeking euphoria, they continue, not only because they want to obtain the euphoric 'rush', but

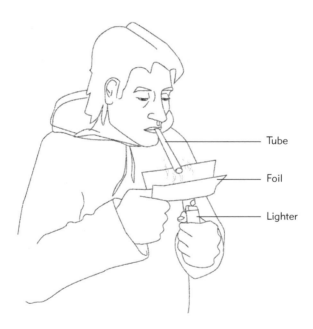

Tube

Foil

Lighter

Figure 1.2.   Inhaling the heated vapours of heroin or 'chasing the dragon'.

also because they need to avoid withdrawal symptoms. Apart from these effects and the problems associated with intravenous drug use, there is little evidence that long-term use of heroin is damaging to health. However 'chasing the dragon' can, rarely, lead to severe and sometimes fatal brain damage.

Overdose of an opiate drug produces drowsiness, slowing of respiration and coma. It can easily be fatal if breathing becomes too slow to meet the body's demand for oxygen. One of the more serious problems about heroin addiction is that the body's tolerance – its increased capacity to deal with the drug – is lost after about 2–3 weeks of abstinence. Therefore, the usual dose required by the regular user is reduced to a very low dose after withdrawing from the drug. If somebody who has withdrawn from heroin takes their previous high dose, they may die within minutes. Every year there are about 200 deaths from heroin overdose in Britain; some due to accidental overdose, many because of loss of tolerance, and a few due to intentional overdose. Almost all of these deaths occur before the victim reaches hospital because he or she usually stops breathing within minutes of injecting too high a dose. About half of all long-term heroin users have seen a fellow addict die, and there is a case for teaching addicts resuscitation techniques, and possibly for providing them with an antidote to be used if necessary. There might be many more deaths from heroin overdose if it were not for the availability of a powerful but short acting antidote to opiates (naloxone; 'Narcan'), which can immediately reverse heroin toxicity if injected. Accident and emergency departments dealing with a likely overdose of opiates may use it if the respiratory rate is too slow or the patient is deeply unconscious. However, the effects of naloxone are short-lived, and the patient must be kept under observation in case further doses are required.

Methadone is a synthetic opiate which relieves pain and which, like other opiates, is potentially addictive. However, it is eliminated slowly from the body, and if given by mouth once a day will prevent opiate withdrawal symptoms (whereas heroin needs to be taken up to four or five times a day to prevent withdrawal symptoms). It therefore reduces crime committed in obtaining money to buy heroin and reduces injecting, thus helping to prevent the spread of HIV and hepatitis B and C. Because of this, methadone has become the most widely used drug to treat heroin addiction; over 200 000 people in the European Union are currently receiving methadone treatment for opiate addiction. It may cause drowsiness, and overdose can be fatal. A person who is not tolerant to heroin and who takes a high dose of methadone may die within an hour or after 2–3 days as drug levels build up in the body. At present there are about 400 deaths each year from methadone. Part of the problem is that methadone itself is subject to misuse, and may be sold on by the person for whom it was prescribed. The British Crime Survey found that, among adults under the age of 30, 1% had tried non-prescribed methadone, as had 2% of 16–19-year-olds. Of course, being prescribed methadone replacement does not prevent the user from taking other substances or from injecting heroin as well.

KHAT

Khat is an evergreen shrub growing in parts of East Africa and the Middle East. Local names vary: kuat, kat, chaat, mriaa, tschut, tohat. In many countries, its use has social and cultural significance, and it is also used as a traditional remedy for a number of illnesses. However, it is most widely used as a social stimulant in informal groups and at weddings and other cel-ebrations. Heavy use and dependence are a problem. In Britain, where it is currently not an illegal substance, it is sometimes misused by the indigenous population, but is more widely used by Middle Eastern and East African expatriates. It is harvested and transported to the UK by air, moistened and wrapped in banana leaves to preserve its potency. Where possible the plant is chewed fresh as the potency deteriorates within 1–3 days. When used, the amount of plant material varies, but usually about two ounces of leaves or stems are chewed for about two hours with the plant material being kept in the cheek. The juice, which has a highly astringent taste, is swallowed. Since the drug induces drying of the mouth, large amounts of liquid are also consumed. The main psychoactive substances in khat are cathine and cathinone, which are closely related to amphetamine. Extracts of khat have been sold in Britain, and methcathinone, a synthetic compound related to cathinone, has a powerful effect on the mind similar to that of cocaine. Effects commence within 15 minutes of chewing, and usually persist for two hours or more after chewing has ceased. The normal effect is talkativeness and mild euphoria. However, aggressive verbal outbursts or hallucinations may occur. So too may nausea, vomiting, abdominal pain, headache and palpitations. Long-term use can lead to lack of appetite, migraine and sometimes to psychotic behaviour.[12] Constipation is common and stomach ulcers are a frequent finding in regular users.

LSD (LYSERGIC ACID DIETHYLAMIDE)

LSD is the best-known hallucinogen. The effective dose is extremely small (50–150 micrograms) and it is usually administered on paper squares about a quarter of the size of a postage stamp. It is almost always taken by mouth. The effects commence within 30 minutes and may last up to 12 hours depending on the dose. It produces distortions in shapes and colours which generally tend to be pleasant and enjoyable, but which may appear extremely menacing and unpleasant ('bad trip'), but it is not addictive. The LSD user may occasionally be threatening and violent, usually because of paranoid delusions about his or her surroundings. Bad trips are more common when LSD has been taken unknowingly or by a person who has not taken the drug before, but they can also occur spontaneously in people who have taken the drug without problems on previous occasions, particularly if a stressful event occurs during the LSD experience. Rarely 'flashbacks' – an unwanted recurrence of a previous hallucinatory experience – can occur days or months after use, usually unpredictably. LSD may also precipitate relapses in people already susceptible to schizophrenia.[13] Deaths from the direct effects of overdose are unknown, but injuries and accidental fatalities can occur in people under the influence of the drug.

About 5% of the English and Welsh population aged 16–59 have tried LSD. It is commonly used with the dance drugs ecstasy and amphetamines by young people, with 14% of 15–16-year-olds having tried LSD or other hallucinogens across the UK as a whole.

NITRITES

Amyl nitrite ('poppers') used to be inhaled to relieve acute angina attacks but now is seldom used medically. Poppers derive their name from the sound made when the glass ampoules containing the drug are crushed prior to use. They now more commonly contain butyl or isobutyl nitrite, and are usually packaged as a yellowish-gold liquid in brown bottles, with exotic names such as 'gold', 'Hi-tech', 'locker room' and 'rush', and are not controlled under the Misuse of Drugs Act. They are used in clubs and at parties, and are also used by the homosexual community because they relax the muscles of the anus. They have a fruity odour and pungent aromatic taste. The vapour from the liquid is sniffed either directly or by soaking on a cloth. Effects are immediate and last only a few minutes. The skin becomes flushed, blood pressure falls and the heart rate accelerates as the user experiences a euphoric rushing sensation. Fainting and loss of balance, headache and nausea can occur. The skin around the nose and lips may be affected by dermatitis. Swallowing poppers can lead to a blue colour of the skin, difficulty in breathing, convulsions and unconsciousness; a few deaths have been reported. Tolerance can develop after 2–3 weeks' continuous use, but this disappears if the user stops for a few days, and these drugs do not appear to be addictive. Some surveys have found quite common use of poppers among young people with 16% of 16–29-year-olds having tried them and 7% of the general population (aged 16–59) in England and Wales.

PSILOCYBE MUSHROOMS

Psilocybe mushrooms (the best-known species is *Psilocybe semilanceata*), commonly known as 'magic mushrooms' or 'liberty caps', are widely used in Britain with one in ten young people (16–29 years) in England and Wales having tried them. They are small mushrooms with a thin white stalk and a brownish cap 5–10 mm in diameter, and contain two substances, psilocybin and psilocin. Possession of the mushrooms themselves is not against the law, but if extracts are made from the mushrooms, this is illegal. They are usually harvested in the autumn and may be eaten raw or cooked, sometimes after being preserved or deep frozen, or even made into tablets. It usually takes about 30–50 mushrooms to produce a hallucinogenic experience similar to that obtained with LSD. This occurs between 30 minutes and four hours after ingestion and can last up to 12 hours. As with LSD, flashbacks are known to occur. Apart from the hallucinogenic experience, users may experience nausea, vomiting and dizziness. They may have a flushed face, dilated pupils and a rapid heart rate. Occasionally, the user may experience paranoid feelings or be violent.

SOLVENTS (VOLATILE SUBSTANCES)

Solvents are commonly misused by school-age children ('glue sniffing').[14] Many of the substances used are commonly found in the home; they include certain types of glue, dry cleaning fluids, petrol, paint strippers or thinners, butane gas cigarette lighter refills and aerosols which contain a large amount of propellant, such as deodorants or hair sprays.

Butane in cigarette lighter refills is inhaled by the user clutching the plastic nozzle between the teeth and the gas is then breathed in directly, giving an immediate 'high'. There is intense cooling which can be severe enough to cause a reflex slowing or stopping of the heart and frostbite in the mouth and throat. Butane is the commonest solvent to cause death among solvent misusers.

Glue is usually poured into a plastic bag and vaporises slowly. The vapour is then inhaled ('sniffed') by the misuser in order to obtain a state of giggly intoxication, which can be maintained by further inhalations from the bag. This process is less likely to cause sudden death than butane inhalation, but death may occur due to accidents because of the more prolonged intoxication. Sudden exercise or fright can cause the heart to stop. Users can also lose consciousness and die through choking on vomit. There is also a danger from suffocation if the plastic bag is placed over the head to inhale the vapour.

Solvent misusers usually experience an immediate euphoria with confusion, unsteadiness and lack of coordination. The immediate onset of the effect may be one reason why solvent abuse is common among children. Coughing, sneezing, salivation, flushing and vomiting are common. Following heavy inhalation, distorted perception, delusions and hallucinations can also occur. These effects are usually short-lived with the misuser recovering fairly rapidly. However severe intoxication can lead to coma and death. Long-term use can lead to damage to the brain, liver, kidneys and bone marrow. Six per cent of 16–29-year-olds have used solvents at least once and 2% of 16–59-year-olds in England and Wales. However, the picture varies greatly across the regions, and there is disagreement across the major surveys with one reporting as many as 1 in 5 15–16-year-olds trying solvents.

TOBACCO

Tobacco smoking is the cause of several types of cancer (of which lung cancer is merely the most common), chronic lung disease and heart attacks, resulting in around 120 000 premature deaths each year in Britain alone. By the age of 13, 19% of children are smoking daily. Twenty-nine per cent of 16–19-year-olds are current smokers, and 28% of all adults (aged 16 and over). More encouragingly, 32% of men and 20% of women who used to smoke regularly have now given up. Regular smoking is most common among 20–24-year-olds (39%).

It is beyond doubt that smoking is the greatest single cause of preventable illness and premature death in the UK. The active substance in tobacco, nicotine, is highly addictive, perhaps as addictive as heroin. It is primarily a stimulant and its pharmacological actions are similar to those of cocaine and amphetamine. Indeed, when given intravenously its subjective effects are almost indistinguishable from those of these drugs. Smoking aids concentration and suppresses appetite. It also helps people relax, but it is not clear how much this is simply because of relief of the craving for nicotine.

The highly addictive nature of nicotine is well-known by those who have tried to stop smoking. Medical aids to smoking cessation include nicotine chewing gum and nicotine skin patches, which aim to help the user to break their habit in a controlled fashion. Withdrawal symptoms include irritability, craving, increased appetite and weight gain. Advocates of smoking point out that Parkinson's disease and ulcerative colitis are less likely to occur in smokers, but the adverse effects far outweigh any benefits. Cigarette smoking also affects the foetus: babies born of smoking mothers are likely to have a lower birth weight and are slightly more likely to be stillborn.

CONCLUSION

This brief review of some of the more widely misused substances illustrates some of the complexities of drug use. It is not just the substances themselves which cause problems: there are also the problems associated with injecting, accidents and other indirect effects. When drugs are injected into the body, usually into a vein, in order to increase their effect on the user, numerous complications may result. The most important of these are infective illnesses transmitted from another user.

Hepatitis B has long been known to be transmitted by needles previously used to inject another person suffering from the illness or carrying the virus. The amount of blood required to transmit the infection is minute and invisible; the only way of preventing transmission is to discard all used injecting equipment or to sterilise any equipment that is going to be shared. Several other types of hepatitis are also transmitted this way, particularly hepatitis C, which often leads to a chronic progressive form of hepatitis. Injecting drug use accounted for most cases of HIV infection in cities such as Edinburgh and Brighton during the early years of the epidemic.

Other infective complications resulting from intravenous infections with dirty needles include abscesses, septicaemia and heart valve infections. Contaminants which are not soluble, such as talcum powder, may also end up in the lungs and can lead to an inflammatory reaction. Accidental injection of a drug into an artery instead of a vein does not usually cause a major problem unless there is insoluble material present which can block the blood vessels and may cause gangrene, with the loss of a limb.

The drugs in this chapter are discussed in more detail in the following publications:

Advisory Council on the Misuse of Drugs (1995) *Volatile Substance Abuse: A Report by the Advisory Council on the Misuse of Drugs*. London: HMSO.

British Medical Association (1997) *Therapeutic Uses of Cannabis*. Amsterdam: Harwood Academic Publishers.

Glass I. B. (ed.) (1991) *International Handbook of Addiction Behaviour*. London: Routledge.

Liska, K. (1994) *Drugs and the Human Body with Implications for Society*. 4th edition. New York: Macmillan Publishing Company.

Cho, A. K. & Segal, D. S. (eds) (1994) *Amphetamine and its Analogs. Psychopharmacology, Toxicology and Abuse*. San Diego, CA: Academic Press Inc.

Hammer, R. P. (ed.) (1995). *The Neurobiology of Cocaine: Cellular and Molecular Mechanisms*. Boca Ratons, FL: CRC Press Inc.

Nahas, G. G. & Burks, T. F. (eds) (1997) *Drug Abuse in the Decade of the Brain*. Netherlands: IOS Press.

World Health Organization (1997) *Cannabis: A Health Perspective and Research Agenda*. Geneva: WHO.

British Medical Association (1998) *New Guide to Medicines & Drugs* (ed. J. A. Henry). London: Dorling Kindersley.

Chapter 2. Drugs and society – the historical background

SUMMARY

The psychological effects of alcohol and of a variety of other naturally occurring drugs were discovered at an early stage in human history and monarchs and parliaments have been faced for thousands of years with the need to make difficult decisions about these potent substances. All have been forced to place restrictions on their use, but few have ever sought to ban them completely. Characteristically, each culture accepts the use of one or two of these substances, usually those with which it is most familiar. Their beneficial effects are prized, and their ill effects are simultaneously glossed over and minimised by laws or customs that restrict their use to particular individuals, situations and occasions. However, alien substances, brought in from other cultures by foreigners or traders, are character-istically viewed with suspicion and harsh penalties inflicted on those who introduce or use them. The last 500 years have seen many attempts, successful and unsuccessful, to prevent the importation and use of alien drugs. There have also been several striking reversals of opinion and policy whereby a prohibited alien drug wins acceptance, or an accepted drug is subsequently banned. Technological developments, such as the manufacture of cigarettes and the extraction of cocaine from coca leaves, have altered the effects of these substances both on the user and society. New drugs continue to be developed, some specifically for recreational use. Current international legislation reflects the cultural traditions and economic interests of the politically dominant countries of Europe and North America: alcohol and tobacco are accepted and international trade is encouraged; opiates, cocaine and cannabis are banned and international trade prohibited.

INTRODUCTION

Britain at the turn of the millenium is not the first society to be uncertain how to respond to the widespread use of psychoactive drugs by its citizens, or to find itself confronted by strongly held and conflicting opinions about the benefits and dangers of these tantalising substances. Alcohol and psychoactive drugs are woven into the fabric of human history, and monarchs and parliaments have repeatedly had to decide whether to sanction their use or to proscribe them, and whether to decree that some of these substances should be banned while others were tolerated or even revered. At first sight, this history is a bewildering kaleidoscope of cultures and drugs, of attitudes, customs and laws, of cycles of acceptance and prohibition, and of perplexing contradictions. But on closer acquaintance some recurring themes emerge, and it is apparent that there are important lessons to be learnt.

Homo sapiens is a unique species in many ways and we are probably unique in our predilection for psychoactive substances. Under laboratory conditions, dependence on alcohol, barbiturates, opiates or cocaine can be induced quite easily in a wide range of other species and, once dependent, a rat or guinea pig will work single-mindedly to obtain further doses of the drug, often ignoring rival attractions like food, water and sex. Dogs kept as regimental mascots have been known to develop a similar dependence on the alcohol they were given day after day in an officers' or a sergeants' mess. But although the leaves of the coca plant are readily accessible to llamas and alpacas, and gorilla troops have been seen visibly intoxicated after eating overripe fruit, mankind is the only species that actively seeks out and ingests the psychoactive substances in its environment.

THE ORIGINS OF DRUG USE

For most human societies, alcohol has been the most important of these psychoactive substances, simply because of its wide availability. Airborne yeasts readily lead to fermentation in sugary juices from grapes, fruits or berries if they are exposed to warm air for a few days, and most preliterate peoples learnt the intoxicating effects of such juices and how to facilitate the fermentation process. Many also learnt how to convert cereals like maize to alcoholic brews by chewing and then spitting the cereal into water, which allows an enzyme in saliva to convert the starch to sugars, which yeasts then convert to alcohol.

As a result, alcoholic beverages were produced by most early civilisations. Prescriptions for beer were written on clay tablets by Sumerian physicians more than 4000 years ago, and by 1500 BC the papyri of Egyptian doctors included beer or wine in many of their prescriptions. The Hindu Ayurveda, which dates from about 1000 BC, describes the use of alcoholic beverages and also the consequences of both intoxication and habitual intoxication. The oldest surviving code of laws, that of Hammurabi which dates from about 1770 BC, regulated Babylonian drinking houses, and the Semitic cuneiform literature of the pre-Biblical Canaanites contains numerous references to the many religious and household uses of alcohol. Opium from the immature fruits of the opium poppy, cannabis from the Indian hemp plant, cocaine from the leaves of the South American coca plant, nicotine from the leaves of the tobacco plant and mescalin from the peyote cactus were similarly identified in the local vegetable environment, extracted and utilised. But because each of these psychoactive substances was only produced by a single species of plant, or a few related species, none has obtained such widespread use or exerted so ubiquitous an effect on human history as alcohol.

Because of its remarkable effects on behaviour and mood, the use of alcohol and other psychoactive substances was strictly controlled in most cultures, either by custom or law, from an early stage. Indeed, these substances were generally reserved for use by the priesthood, or by the population as a whole at particular religious ceremonies, or in medicines, which were usually prepared and administered by priests. Wine and beer were both widely used as offerings to deities, and as a means of enabling priests and shamans to achieve a state of ecstasy or frenzy, and evidence of misuse emerged at an early stage. The Hebrew prophet Isaiah, for example, was driven to complain: "Priest and prophet are addicted to strong drink and bemused with wine; clamouring in their cups, confirmed topers, hiccuping in drunken stupor; every table is covered with vomit".

Despite Isaiah's strictures, however, wine retained its sacerdotal role in the Hebrews' religion and subsequently for Christianity too. Both equating red wine with blood and the symbolic drinking of wine in the Christian Eucharist arose out of a long tradition that still has many parallels in other cultures and religions. Indeed, the role of wine was just as prominent in the religion of the ancient Greeks and their Roman successors as it was for the Hebrews. Drinking and drunkenness are recurring themes in Greek mythology and the worship of Dionysus or Bacchus, the wine god, played a prominent part in the life of the peoples of the Mediterranean for a thousand years. The god's female devotees, the Maenads, worshipped him in drunken orgies and the name of his festival, the Bacchanalia, still survives as a contemporary term for a drunken orgy.

Historical records suggest that it was the religious uses of alcohol which first generated uncontrolled intoxication and drunkenness, and it generally fell to religions to control the dangerous excesses to which alcohol gave rise. Islam in the seventh century AD chose total prohibition. The Qur'ān condemned the use of wine, and the disciples of Muhammad ensured that this taboo was respected in all the lands they conquered. A similar process was repeated a thousand years later when a number of ascetic Protestant sects, first in northern Europe and then in North America, made abstinence a fundamental tenet, derived in their eyes from Biblical ideology just as that of the Muslim was derived from the Qur'ān. Similar sequences of events took place in other parts of the world. The devout adherents of the Buddhist religion, which arose in India in the fifth and sixth centuries BC and spread across southern and eastern Asia, have abstained from alcohol ever since, and Hindu Brahmins have done the same. Indeed, on a global scale, it is striking how nearly all the successful attempts to control the misuse of alcohol have been based on religious tenet rather than on secular decree. The history of China, whose main religions never proscribed the use of alcohol, includes several abortive attempts at control or prohibition. Only the pre-Columbian Indians of North America, the Melanesian and Polynesian peoples of the Pacific, and the Aboriginal peoples of Australia remained immune to these conflicts and dilemmas, for only they and a few scattered groups elsewhere did not discover the secret of fermentation, which is probably why the distilled spirits or 'firewater' to which the Europeans introduced them had such disastrous effects.

COEXISTENCE AND CONDEMNATION

Anyone familiar with mankind's long and complicated relationship with psychoactive substances cannot fail to be struck by two things. The first is our capacity for finding and then systematically eating, drinking, chewing or smoking vegetable products with stimulant, sedative, euphoriant or intoxicating properties. Tens of thousands of plant species are available to us, yet we and our ancestors have generally only thought it worthwhile to drink infusions of the leaves or fruit of the tiny number of plants which contain stimulant drugs – tea leaves and coffee beans (which both contain caffeine), the Latin–American drink maté, made from the dried leaves of *Ilex para-guariensis* (which also contain caffeine), and cocoa beans (which contain the related drug, theobromine).

The second, equally striking aspect of mankind's relationship with psychoactive substances is the strong feelings and opinions, both laudatory and condemnatory, which human societies characteristically develop towards these intriguing substances, particularly on first encountering them. Tobacco was introduced to Western Europe from the Americas in the second half of the 16th century, and in England in particular the smoking habit began to spread rapidly towards the end of that century. Robert Burton described it thus: "Tobacco, divine, rare, super excellent tobacco, which goes far beyond all their panaceas, potable gold, and philosopher's stones, a sovereign remedy to all diseases". His King, James I, however, took a different view. He condemned smoking as "A custom loathsome to the eye, harmful to the brain, dangerous to the lungs, and in the black stinking fume thereof, nearest resembling the horrible Stygian smoke of the pit that is bottomless".

Similarly contradictory views have been expressed, by many different cultures at many different times, about alcohol, opium, cannabis and cocaine, and the reasons are fairly obvious. All of these substances are capable of inducing pleasurable subjective states of various kinds. If that were not so no one would have taken any interest in them. Many of them, although not all, are capable of inducing states of dependence in regular users. Most, and perhaps all, have other overtly harmful effects, either medical (to the health of the user), or social (by inducing irresponsible or antisocial behaviour of various kinds), or both. All, in other words, have potential attractions at least to their users and most, if not all, hold dangers for their users or the society to which they belong. And the subjective attractions are invariably more immediately apparent than the long-term ill effects. It is not surprising, therefore, that human societies, confronted for the first time with users of one of these substances, have sometimes been uncertain whether to approve or to disapprove.

It is clear from the history of the last 500 years that the early users of a novel substance, like Robert Burton and his tobacco, are characteristically uncritical admirers of their new drug, while the secular and religious authorities, personified in Burton's case by his King, usually seek to stamp out the alarming new habit, or else to restrict it to their own class or social circle. An alternative, more sophisticated response is to impose a special tax on users of the new drug, thereby both raising revenue and restricting the spread of a potentially disruptive social phenomenon. Indeed, within a few years of delivering his famous 'Counterblaste to Tobacco' King James himself imposed a tax of 6 shillings and 8 pence on every pound of tobacco imported to his kingdom on top of the standard customs duty of 2 pence a pound. He was also politically astute enough to draw a distinction between "persons of good calling and quality" who took the drug only as a "physic to preserve their health" and a "number of riotous and disordered persons of mean and base condition" who spent their time and money on tobacco "not caring at what price they buy their drug".[1]

It has to be admitted, too, that it is characteristic of physicians to declaim upon the virtues or dangers of newly introduced psychoactive substances with all the authority of their profession, and that with hindsight their views simply reflect the assumptions and prejudices of their society and rank rather than revealing any deep insight into the pharmacological properties of the drug in question. In the early years of the 19th century, several physicians wrote diatribes against 'that most deadly poison' tea, and recommended 'nourishing beer' instead. Even in the 20th century, two eminent physicians described habitual coffee drinkers in these terms in their textbook: "the sufferer is tremulous and loses his self command; he is subject to fits of agitation and depression. He loses colour and has a haggard appearance...

As with other such agents, a renewed dose of the poison gives temporary relief, but at the cost of future misery".[2]

Incongruous medical opinions such as these illustrate an important, indeed almost universal, characteristic of cultural attitudes to psychoactive substances. Apart from the inhabitants of environments that are too harsh to support plants containing psychoactive drugs, almost all human societies tolerate the use of at least one of these drugs. For hundreds of years Europeans tolerated alcohol, the Indian subcontinent tolerated the smoking of opium and the ingestion of cannabis, Peruvian Indians chewed coca leaves, and Mexican Indians indulged themselves with the hallucinogen mescalin in the peyote cactus. In each case, use of the drug was circumscribed and controlled by custom or law. Just as adolescents slowly learn to drink alcoholic beverages without vomiting or getting drunk, so cultures slowly learn to use their chosen drug in a way that enables them to enjoy the benefits with a minimum of social disturbance and morbidity. Traditions and rituals develop which have the effect of restricting use of the drug to a few well-defined occasions or places, and preventing use by children, and thereby serve to minimise potential ill effects. Moreover, because the psychological effects of the drug are prized, and the drug itself acquires symbolic importance, the ill effects that do still occur are glossed over, or attributed to the short-comings or folly of the individual user, rather than to the inherent dangers of the drug itself. In contemporary Britain, the young man who vomits or falls downstairs, or gets involved in a brawl after downing eight pints of beer, is dismissed as an idiot who 'can't hold his drink'. Even if he is found dead in bed after drinking a bottle of gin for a bet, he is dismissed with a sad shake of the head as a young fool. Whatever the precise explanation, blame is attributed to the drinker or to circumstances rather than to our favourite drug, ethyl alcohol.

ALIEN DRUGS

Attitudes to other less familiar substances, to the foreign drugs introduced by travellers or traders, are quite different, however. These are usually regarded with intense suspicion and any ill effects resulting from their use are regarded as proof of their intrinsic dangers. If a teenager dies after taking cocaine or ecstasy at a party, or is found dead in a tenement beside an empty syringe of heroin, this is evidence not of his folly or bad luck but of the intrinsic dangers of these alien substances. At the same time, savage penalties are often inflicted on those who import or use the alien drug in an attempt to stamp out the dangerous new habit. In 17th century Europe, for example, many princes made even more determined attempts than King James to eliminate the new habit of smoking. In Russia, the Czar Mikhail Federovitch executed anyone on whom tobacco was found, and his successor Alexei Mikhailovitch decreed that anyone found in possession of tobacco should be tortured until he or she revealed the name of the supplier. In Turkey the nose of a tobacco smoker was pierced through with the stem of his pipe and he or she was made to ride through town on a donkey, and in the German principality of Luneberg the death penalty for smoking remained in force until 1691.

While European kings and emperors denounced the American drug tobacco and punished its users with the utmost severity, their American counterparts denounced alcohol and meted out dire punishments to those who dared to drink it. According to Calderon Naraez, the pre-Hispanic emperor of Mexico addressed his people thus immediately after his election:

"This is the wine known as 'octli', which is the root and source of all evil and of all perdition, because octli and drunkenness are the cause of all this discord and strife, and all the rebelliousness and restlessness among the people and Kingdoms; it is like a whirlwind that stirs up and smashes everything; it is like a tempest in hell that brings everything bad with it. Drunkenness is the cause of all the adulteries, rapes, corruption of virgins, and fights with relatives and friends; drunkenness is the cause of all the thefts and robberies and banditry and violence; it is also the cause of cursing and lying and gossip and slander, and of clamouring, quarrels, and shouting."

Drunkenness in Mexico was therefore treated very severely and savagely punished:

"If a young man appeared in public in a drunken state, or if he was found in possession of wine, or if he was found lying in the street, or singing, or in the company of other drunkards, this young man, if he was a plebeian, was punished by being beaten with clubs until he was dead, or he was garrotted in the presence of all the young men, who were gathered together so that this would serve as an example for them."

European and North American governments currently regard opiates, cocaine and cannabis in much the same light as the 16th century Mexican emperor and many contemporary Moslem governments regard alcohol. These are alien drugs whose use and importation are forbidden and rigorously proscribed. Indeed, in popular usage, and above all in the British tabloid press, a 'drug' is always alien and dangerous, and references to alcohol or tobacco as drugs are commonly received either with perplexity or anger. As Griffith Edwards has observed, the word itself has magical powers to dictate our thinking and conjures up a host of shadowy, menacing images. 'Drugs' are assumed to involve a Faustian pact: access to pleasures beyond the range of normal experience, but at the price of inevitable moral degradation.[3]

Regardless of the substance or the culture involved, most of the arguments put forward by established authority for the rigorous proscription of alien drugs emphasise not the risks to health but the near certainty of moral degradation, corruption and unbridled sexuality. The Mexican emperor condemned alcohol and drunkenness as "the cause of all the adulteries, rapes and corruption of virgins and fights..." in his kingdom. Four-hundred years later in the 1950s, the United States Commissioner on Narcotics condemned marijuana (cannabis) in equally lurid terms:

> "Marijuana is only and always a scourge which undermines its victims and degrades them mentally, morally and physically... A small dose taken by one subject may bring about intense intoxification, raving fits, criminal assaults... It is this unpredictable effect which makes marijuana one of the most dangerous drugs known... the moral barricades are broken down and often debauchery and sexuality result... where mental instability is inherent, the behaviour is generally violent... Constant use produces an incapacity for work and a disorientation of purpose. The drug has a corroding effect on the body and on the mind, weakening the entire physical system and often leading to insanity after prolonged use."[4]

The penalties for using these drugs were appropriate to the threat they were assumed to pose to society: judicial execution in 16th-century Mexico for drinking alcohol; up to 40 years in prison in post-war America for possession of marijuana.

Attitudes do change, however. Although it is characteristic of most cultures to sanction the use of one or two drugs whose ill effects are minimised or glossed over, and to regard other people's chosen drugs with intense suspicion and usually to forbid their use, these prejudices are not always immutable. A drug that is tolerated and widely used in one era may be banned a couple of generations later; and a drug that was once condemned as evil and dangerous may within a single lifetime come to be accepted and used openly and legally. Indeed, British views and habits have changed in both directions. In the 16th and early-17th centuries, in Britain as in most of Europe, smoking tobacco was regarded with grave suspicion, and its associations with dissolute behaviour were well-illustrated by the use of a clay pipe as the symbol of a brothel in Elizabethan London. But within a generation, tobacco was accepted by both parliament and people and, by the middle of the 20th century, the majority of the adult population of Britain were smoking throughout their waking hours.

Until the second half of the 19th century, both opium and cannabis could be bought perfectly legally and even advertised, not only in Queen Victoria's Indian domains, but in Britain itself. Indeed, they could be bought not only from chemists but even from grocers' shops as easily as aspirin is now. In the mid-19th century, laudanum, an alcoholic extract of raw opium, was one of the most widely used of all medicines, taken for fevers, for colic, for nervous exhaustion and even for fun. Nearly 100 000 lb (43 351 kg) of opium were imported every year, mainly from Turkey, and opium poppies were legally grown as a cash crop in Norfolk. Fretful babies were calmed throughout the land with Mother Bailey's Quietening Syrup and unwanted infants were quietened forever with laudanum by desperate women in urban slums. Indeed, when Parliament passed the Pharmacy Act in 1868, its main intention was to ensure that only pure opium was sold, and only by qualified pharmacists, rather than seriously to restrict access to the drug.[5]

PROGRESS TOWARDS INTERNATIONAL LEGISLATION

The origins of current international legislation on so-called narcotic drugs are particularly illuminating. Towards the end of the 19th century, public opinion in England was becoming increasingly aware of the dangers and addictive properties of laudanum, and more concerned about the wisdom of allowing the Queen's Indian subjects to use opium and cannabis, and about the morality of the opium trade with China. With characteristic Victorian energy and seriousness of purpose formal commissions were set up to advise the government. The seven-volume report of the Indian Hemp Commission, published in 1894, concluded that there was little cause for concern:

> "Viewing the subject generally, it may be added that the moderate use of these drugs is the rule, and the excessive use is comparatively exceptional. The moderate use practically produces no ill-effects... The excessive use may certainly be accepted as very injurious, though it must be admitted that in many excessive consumers the injury is not clearly marked. The injury done by the excessive use is, however, confined almost exclusively to the consumer himself; the effect on society is rarely appreciable. It has been the most striking feature in this enquiry to find how little the effects of hemp drugs have obtruded themselves on observation. The large number of witnesses of all classes who professed never to have seen these effects, the vague statements made by many who professed to have observed them, the very few witnesses who could so recall a case as to give any definite account of it, and

the manner in which a large proportion of these cases broke down on the first attempt to examine them, are facts which combine to show most clearly how little injury society has hitherto sustained from hemp drugs."

Not only were the observable ill effects of cannabis rather modest and inconspicuous, but they were also, at least in the eyes of Indian witnesses, much less prominent than the ill effects of the alcoholic drinks introduced to their country by their European rulers. A Hindu Maharajah, for example, told the Commission that:

"The use of the aforesaid indigenous drugs appears to me to be preferable to the use of ardent spirits and wines so rapidly replacing them to the great injury of the moral and material well-being of our people."

The report of the Royal Commission on Opium, also in seven volumes and published only a few months after the report of the Indian Hemp Commission, was equally reassuring:

"Our conclusions, therefore, are that the use of opium among the people of India in British Provinces is, as a rule, a moderate use, and that excess is exceptional, and condemned by public opinion... We have no hesitation in saying that no extended physical or moral degradation is caused by the habit."

Although the conclusions of the Royal Commission may well have been coloured by a concern to preserve the substantial revenues derived by the government of India from the opium trade with China, they were consistent with the views of both the rulers and the ruled in India itself, and with much public opinion in Britain. That public opinion was slowly changing, though, both in Britain and the USA. The activities of the Society for the Suppression of the Opium Trade and concern about opium smoking by the Chinese communities in the docklands of London and Liverpool, and similar moral concerns in America about the spread of opium to the Philippines and the damaging effects that the West's opium traders were having on China, led, within a generation, first to the Far Eastern regulations discussed at Shanghai in 1909 and then to the worldwide controls envisaged by the 1912 Hague Convention and to the American Harrison Act of 1914. In wartime Britain, concerns about the effects of drunkenness, and to a lesser extent about the effects of opium and cocaine on the war effort, led to the stringent and comprehensive controls enacted under the provisions of the Defence of the Realm Act. When the Great War was over, controls on the familiar, traditional drug alcohol were relaxed somewhat but those on opium and cocaine were retained and formalised in the 1920 Dangerous Drugs Act, which was consciously modelled on the Harrison Narcotics Act.

All subsequent international regulations and policies have been derived from this Anglo-American legislation. The Geneva Conventions of the League of Nations established in international law strict worldwide controls on trade in opium and cocaine, and in 1925 these were extended to include cannabis on the strength of its supposed association with insanity in Egypt. This comprehensive legislation was inherited by the United Nations in 1946 and confirmed by the 1961 Single Convention on Narcotic Drugs and the Vienna Convention of 1988, and the League's Permanent Central Opium Board was replaced by the International Narcotics Control Board. As a result, international trade in opium and its derivatives and analogues, in cocaine and in cannabis is still either banned completely or limited to strictly medical or scientific purposes. International trade in alcoholic beverages and tobacco, on the other hand, remains legal and unrestricted, and the controls on trade in dependence-producing pharmaceuticals like barbiturates and benzodiazepines (imposed by the United Nations' Convention on Psychotropic Substances in 1971) are modest and quite separate from those on 'narcotics'. Trade in 'narcotics' is condemned as 'trafficking' and subject to formidable penalties. International trade in alcohol and tobacco is actively encouraged and cannot be hindered without contravening the General Agreement on Tariffs and Trade.

This distinction between licit and illicit substances is not based on any scientific assessment of their social and medical benefits and dangers, of their capacity to produce dangerous intoxication or dependence, or of their long-term toxic effects. It is based largely on the assumptions, prejudices, customs and above all the economic interests of the Western European and North American nations who were the dominant influence on the League of Nations in the 1920s and 30s, and who determined the attitudes and policies of the United Nations in the aftermath of the Second World War. Alcohol and tobacco were then widely used by the citizens of the nations of Western Europe and North America. The most powerful of these countries – the USA, the UK and France – also had a huge economic investment in both of these drugs, and their cultural and economic dominance allowed them to export their attitudes, their customs and their chosen drugs to the rest of the world, and to earn handsome profits in the process. Opium, cannabis and cocaine, on the other hand, were the favoured drugs of less influential cultures and less powerful nations in Asia, the Middle East and Latin America. Their voice was barely heard in the international conferences which laid the foundations for binding international treaties and, until recently, their economic interests could not compete with the power of the industrialised West. If China, India and the Moslem world had been the dominant world powers at the time when international attitudes to psychoactive substances and international regulations governing trade in those substances were first determined, the lists of substances which are freely used and traded, and of those which are proscribed and traded only by criminals might look rather different.

TECHNOLOGICAL INNOVATIONS

Thus far, this discussion has been restricted to naturally occurring psychoactive substances of vegetable origin which have been extracted and used by man. Until quite recently all psychoactive substances were obtained in this way, although means were often found of increasing the concentration of the active ingredient, or of getting it to the brain faster. The introduction of distillation, first by the Chinese in the 8th century BC and the Arabs in the 10th century AD, but most effectively by the Dutch in the 17th century, made it possible to produce drinks with a much higher alcohol content than wines and beers. The development of cigarettes (tubes of paper filled with finely shredded tobacco leaves) and then of flue-cured tobacco in the middle of the 19th century, whose smoke could be inhaled, made it possible to get nicotine to the brain faster and in a higher concentration than by smoking coarsely shredded leaves in a pipe or rolled leaves in a cigar. Extracting the active principle, cocaine, from coca leaves made it possible to achieve much more intense psychological effects. And, of course, the development of the hypodermic syringe made it possible to inject morphine and a wide range of other drugs directly into tissues and veins.

In the early-20th century, minor modifications started to be made to the active substance itself, again to increase its potency or speed of effect. Heroin was manufactured from morphine, the most potent of the opiates in raw opium, and then 'crack' (a form of the drug that could be inhaled as smoke) was manufactured from cocaine hydrochloride.

The next development was that some of the synthetic drugs produced by the increasingly powerful and sophisticated pharmaceutical industry as conventional medicines began to be diverted for recreational use, or were unexpectedly found to produce states of dependence. The barbiturates and the benzodiazepines, originally developed as sedatives to relieve insomnia and anxiety, and a series of allegedly non-addictive synthetic morphine analogues developed as powerful analgesics to relieve pain, were all found to produce dependence. For each of these substances, a non-therapeutic demand slowly

Figure 2.1. In the West, opium has been superceded by morphine and heroin, but it is still smoked in several Asian countries. Image reproduced with kind permission from J. Jaffe.

developed, generated partly by former patients who had inadvertently become dependent and partly by younger people seeking novel subjective experiences from the outset.

The amphetamines and LSD became illicit substances in a similar way. Amphetamine and its analogues are synthetic stimulants which were manufactured and widely used by all the main combatants in the Second World War to enable exhausted men to remain awake and alert. LSD was first synthesised in the 1930s, found by chance to have hallucinogenic properties and used briefly in the 1950s and 60s in the treatment of mental disorders. Both subsequently came to be used for purely recreational purposes and amphetamines are now more widely used in the UK than any drug, other than cannabis.

The most recent development is the deliberate synthesis, in clandestine laboratories in Europe or North America, of psychoactive substances that are intended to be used for recreational rather than therapeutic purposes. Ecstasy and LSD are currently the most well-known and widely used of these substances, but there will undoubtedly be more of them, including novel compounds ('designer drugs') deliberately synthesised to evade national and international controls on manufacture and trade. A powerful youth culture has made the international market for recreational drugs so huge and so lucrative, and understanding of human neuropharmacology is developing so fast, that this is virtually inevitable. These new synthetic drugs may be entirely novel, as LSD was, but they are more likely to be modifications of known psychoactive substances, as MDMA was of amphetamine.

CONCLUSION

What conclusions can be drawn from this long and complex history? As with any other aspect of human history, there is no single interpretation. Here, as elsewhere, different historians will emphasise different relationships and draw rather different conclusions. But a few pre-eminent themes and conclusions stand out so clearly that they seem beyond challenge. All psychoactive drugs hold attractions and dangers either for the individual user or for the society to which he or she belongs, but despite these dangers no society with access to one or more of these substances has ever turned its back on them for long. Most cultures tolerate the use of one or two of them but reject, or at least regard with grave suspicion, those used by other alien cultures. Familiar, institutionalised drugs are often highly esteemed; their use is circumscribed by ritual, and their ill effects tend to be glossed over. Foreign drugs, on the other hand, are characteristically regarded as a threat to public order, morality and health – in that order – and their use is often subject to savage penalties.

It is clear from the historical record though that, sometimes within one or two generations, alien drugs may win acceptance and, less commonly, that familiar institutionalised drugs may cease to be tolerated. When these reversals occur, however, they are usually driven by powerful political, ideological or economic forces rather than by any dispassionate assessment of the pharmacological properties and toxic effects of the drugs themselves. This will probably continue to be the case in the future as the number of psycho-active drugs available, and the extent of their use, increases from one decade to the next. The one exception to this general principle is the declining use of tobacco and slowly changing attitudes to smoking in Western industrial countries in the last 40 years. This has been driven largely by increasing public recognition of the hazards to health, and from that we take some comfort.

Chapter 3. The rise of drug use in the UK

SUMMARY

Over the 20th century, the UK has seen a huge rise in the number of people using drugs and in the range of substances taken. Although the tide of drug use has been rising steadily for the last 40 years, different drugs and methods of use flow in and out of popularity. Investigation of the 'drug problem' in the 1920s revealed that most of the tiny number of opiate addicts were either health professionals or patients whose addiction had developed during the course of treatment. These 'therapeutic addicts' were not seen as any significant threat to society, and doctors were allowed to prescribe them opiates if they were unable to give up. It was not until the 1950s that clearly hedonistic use began to spread among young people. As in the past, drug taking in the young aroused much greater concern, particularly over morality and public order, than use of the same drugs by 'respectable' middle-aged addicts. The 1960s saw its continued growth, with some drug taking, such as cannabis and LSD, becoming associated with political dissent. New treatment facilities were brought in to deal with the growing opiate problem and to prevent supplies passing from prescription to the black market. Legislation was also introduced to control drug use. Since the 1960s, other drug epidemics have appeared, some remaining and continuing to grow, and others, such as barbiturate misuse, all but disappearing.

INTRODUCTION

Since the 1960s, the UK and most of the industrialised world have experienced a remarkable growth in drug use, particularly among young people. An illustration of this is that while only 5% of 14- and 15-year-olds had ever been offered a drug in 1969, more than 40% had been by 1994 (see Figure 3.1). The majority of the new drug users have probably only tried a drug a few times, but some have become more involved, and their behaviour has been influenced by the various drug 'epidemics' that the 20th century has witnessed. These epidemics, bringing new drugs, new ways to take them, or reviving old patterns of use, make up the ebb and flow of the 'drug problem', constantly in flux, while the larger tide of drug use continues to rise. Legislation and other actions aimed at tackling these changes at particular times during the century have sometimes succeeded in improving the situation. At other times, they have had little impact, and, occasionally, have led to unforeseen problems. This chapter charts these trends in drug use and attempts at control.

A distinctive feature of many of these epidemics has been the central role of drugs with which society was already familiar and with which it had already developed an apparently stable relationship. This is well-illustrated by amphetamines and benzodiazepines. In the post-war years, amphetamines were widely used as antidepressants, to reduce appetite, and as a general tonic to counter tiredness and lethargy, being mainly prescribed for adults in their middle or later years. Then in the late 1950s and early 60s, elements of the new youth culture began to use these same drugs for somewhat different purposes – for example, giving themselves extra energy and the ability to stay awake and dance at all-night clubs. This use of the same drugs in a different context, for different purposes and by a different section of society, led to expressions of outrage from the press and public, and indeed this was one of the first of the modern drug problems to be encountered in the UK.

A variant of this phenomenon can be seen with benzodiazepines (sedative drugs such as diazepam, Valium). Prescription of these drugs increased enormously through the 1960s and 70s and they were hailed, correctly, as far safer than previous sedative drugs such as the barbiturates, which not only carried a dependence potential but were also much more dangerous in

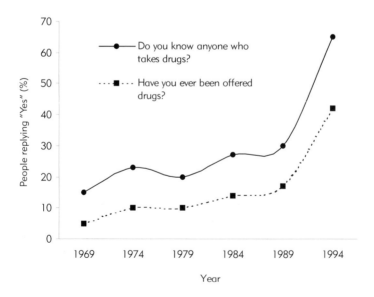

Figure 3.1. Changes over 25 years in "yes" responses to two questions about taking drugs. Source: Wright, J. D. & Pearl, L. (1995) Knowledge and experience of young people aged 14–15 regarding drug misuse, 1969–1994. *British Medical Journal*, **310**, 20–24.

overdose. However, concern about the dependence potential of oral benzodiazepines grew from the early 1980s onwards, and then, in the late 1980s, a new problem of intravenous misuse of benzodiazepines, particularly temazepam, which was available as a liquid-filled capsule, developed in many UK cities and provoked major concern among the general public, drug experts and many drug users themselves. Thus, the same drug can be viewed in very different ways – not only according to the ways in which it is used, but also according to the context and section of society using the drug.

While special attention is paid in this chapter to the arrival and spread of drugs within UK society in the 20th century, the continued presence of two legal substances – alcohol and tobacco – whose use was already widespread should not be overlooked. Having risen substantially in the 1960s and 70s, national per capita alcohol consumption remains high in the UK, with 14% of women and 27% of men currently drinking at levels above the limits recommended by the medical Royal Colleges.[1] Cigarette-smoking, which has shown an encouraging reduction over the last 25 years, is rising again among young people – especially women. Indeed, the proportion of 15-year-old girls who were regularly smoking increased by a third between 1982 and 1996 – from 25% to 33%.[2] While drugs are probably responsible for a substantial number of deaths per year, of the order of one to two thousand, and warrant major concern, alcohol and tobacco are respectively associated with around 30 000 and 120 000 premature deaths per year in the UK.

1916–1926

The defining Rolleston Report

The first domestic change in legislation affecting the use of opiates and other drugs since the 1860s was prompted not by concerns over opium, but by the use of cocaine by British soldiers while on leave, amid rumours of sex and drug use with prostitutes during the early stages of the First World War. The detailed regulations enacted in 1916 under the provisions of the Defence of the Realm Act made it illegal to possess cocaine unless prescribed by a doctor, and these restrictions were extended a few years later in the Dangerous Drugs Acts of 1920 and 1921 to include morphine and heroin.

While it is easy to think of the youth drug problems of recent years as a new phenomenon, the drug problem of the early-20th century in the USA was widespread and there were public concerns similar to those expressed today: the erosion of standards and sexual excesses; the particular dangers to young people; the association with delinquency and crime; and the alleged but often poorly substantiated involvement of unpopular ethnic minority groups. Heroin did not particularly concern Americans at the time as morphine and cocaine were the drugs mainly used and injecting methods among hedonistic drug users differed from those of today, but many of the other features were remarkably similar to the late-20th century.

Unlike the UK, where most opiate addicts were middle-class and had become dependent through medical prescribing, hostility rather than sympathy was aroused in America by these young, predominantly working-class, and sometimes criminal users. Nowhere else in the world at that time were so many young people using cocaine and opiates for pleasure, and the public and its leaders responded quite differently to these circumstances.

Simultaneously, substantial international pressure was exerted by the USA for strengthening of the international controls against the world trade in these drugs. Those seeking stricter domestic controls in the USA took the opportunity to press for similar domestic legislation supporting America's lead on the international stage. Campaigners and policy-makers portrayed users as deviant people whose behaviour was unacceptable and should be punished rather than treated.

The resulting compromise, the 1914 Harrison Act, was not intended to prevent doctors prescribing opiates, but was nonetheless used by government officials a few years later to prevent heroin prescription, whether to addicts or for patients with some other more orthodox requirement like the relief of severe pain. At first, physicians and law enforcement officers tacitly permitted the dwindling numbers of therapeutic addicts to continue to receive medical supplies of their drugs, but an increasingly strong line was taken against recreational addicts, and the prohibitionist approach became firmly rooted.

Subsequently, the UK Government established a committee under the leadership of Sir Humphrey Rolleston, President of the Royal College of Physicians, to examine the extent of the opiate problem in the UK and to advise accordingly. After examining the evidence, the Rolleston Committee concluded in 1926 that there was very little opiate addiction in the UK. It mainly involved the use of injectable morphine by a population who were virtually all middle-aged or elderly, many of whom were either doctors, pharmacists, dentists or nurses or therapeutic addicts – patients whose addiction had developed from being prescribed morphine in the course of treatment for a medical condition. Consequently, in contrast to the criminalisation of opiate addiction in the USA, the Rolleston Committee recommended that opiate-addicted individuals should be managed as patients for whom detoxification should be provided. If they were unable to re-establish stable lifestyles after withdrawal of the drug, continuing supplies of it might be prescribed to these addicts to maintain the stability of their lifestyles.

The Rolleston proposals are sometimes mistakenly credited with having dealt successfully with a major opiate epidemic in the UK, but it was rather the lack of any substantial problem, and perhaps the 'respectability' of the small number of addicts, and the origin of their dependence, which prompted this response. Nevertheless, the effect of the Rolleston Report was to create a fundamental difference in policies between the UK and the USA.

THE 1930S AND 40S

The quiet years

Over the next few years, the non-problem continued at a low level with only a few hundred opiate addicts across the whole of the UK in any given year, the majority of these addicts being either 'therapeutic addicts' or those working in the professions allied to medicine. Occasionally an outbreak of more explicitly USA-style use of heroin occurred, as it did in a small wealthy set in London in the 1930s who used illicit supplies of heroin, but these small outbreaks seem to have been completely extinguished by early action from Customs and the police.

THE 1950S AND 60S

A new drug sub-culture

In the post-war years, America witnessed a spread of use of cannabis amongst jazz musicians and their audiences. This coincided with the emergence of youth movements and was accompanied by a wider, and often repeated, fear of drug use by minorities. These new youth groups, with their own ideology and music, came to dominate the new drug-using populations that appeared in the early 1960s, and these developments in America spread, albeit to a lesser extent, to the UK. The rise in convictions for cannabis use through the 1950s and 60s, a useful, though imperfect index of increasing use, is shown in Figure 3.2.

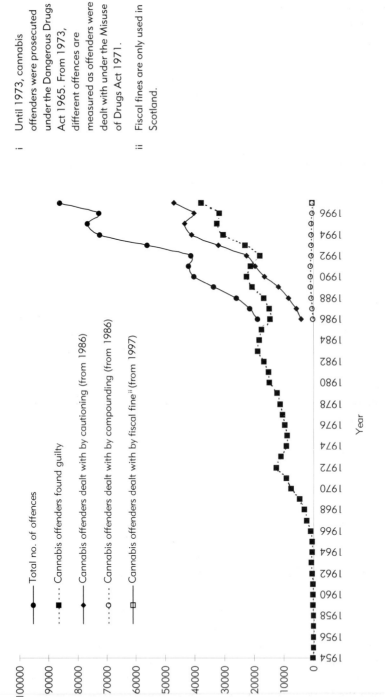

i   Until 1973, cannabis offenders were prosecuted under the Dangerous Drugs Act 1965. From 1973, different offences are measured as offenders were dealt with under the Misuse of Drugs Act 1971.

ii Fiscal fines are only used in Scotland.

— Total no. of offences

■ · · · Cannabis offenders found guilty

— Cannabis offenders dealt with by cautioning (from 1986)

· · ◇ · · · Cannabis offenders dealt with by compounding (from 1986)

—☐— Cannabis offenders dealt with by fiscal fine[ii] (from 1997)

Figure 3.2.   Convictions for cannabis offences in the UK, 1954–1997[i]. Data from Hawks, D. (1967) The dimensions of drug dependence in the UK. In *Drugs and Drug Dependence* (eds. G. Edwards, M. A. H. Russell, D. Hawks, *et al*). Farnborough, Hants: Saxon House; and Lexington, MS: Lexington Books. Information also from Home Office Drug Seizures Bulletins and personal communication (John Corkery, 1999).

In addition to the appearance and gradual spread of cannabis use in jazz clubs in London during the 1950s, amphetamine tablets ('uppers') began to appear, diverted from prescribed use, supplied from chemist break-ins, or in the form of over-the-counter preparations for nasal congestion, one of which in particular (the Benzedrine inhaler) contained an amphetamine impregnated cotton wool wad. These amphetamines were adopted by new sections of the youth attending all-night discos and by members of the scooter-riding 'mods' or motor-cycling 'rockers'. For these adolescents and young adults in the early 60s, this exposure to cannabis 'reefers' and amphetamine pills was the first contact of this age group with drugs. For the first time in the UK, young people were looking to hedonistic use of drugs as part of their own distinctive behaviours and identity.

THE 1960s

Cannabis as a symbol of protest

Of the drugs that were part of 1960s drug use, cannabis predominated. Often its use accompanied other aspects of alternative lifestyles and political statements, such as shoulder length hair for men, the new rock music and, particularly in America, involvement in the bitter protests against the USA's involvement in the war in Vietnam. While other drugs had their significant effects (see later sections on LSD and heroin, for example), cannabis became widely associated with the new values and behaviour of the emerging youth generation. Even today, 30 years on, the symbolic significance of cannabis colours the views held by middle-aged people and their contributions to the debate about cannabis policy in a way not seen with attitudes towards heroin or LSD (see later discussion of cannabis policy in Chapter 10).

Amid the debate of the late 1960s, the Advisory Committee on Drug Dependence, an early version of the Advisory Council on the Misuse of Drugs, set up an expert inquiry headed by Baroness Wootton of Abinger to consider cannabis. The resulting report concluded that the dangers of moderate use of cannabis had been exaggerated, while emphasising that cannabis was not free from risk. It explicitly recommended against legal-isation of the drug, but suggested that penalties for small scale possession should be reduced. Although recognised in retrospect for its rigorous scientific review of the evidence and balanced, independent approach to the subject, the Wootton report was at the time wildly misrepresented by both parliament and press. Yet despite the Government's rejection of its main recommendation, when drawing up the Misuse of Drugs Bill the Labour Government introduced a new distinction between the (less serious) offences relating to cannabis and (more serious) offences involving opiates and cocaine. This move was supported by the subsequent Conservative Government and became law in 1971. Today imprisonment for cannabis possession is rare and usually dealt with by police caution (see Chapter 7, Figure 7.10).

LSD and psychedelia

The hallucinogenic LSD first appeared on the drug scene in the mid-1960s – rather suprisingly from the universities of the USA. This extraordinary drug had originally been developed by Albert Hoffman in 1938 in the course of his work for a pharmaceutical company. He accidentally discovered its hallucinogenic effects in 1943 and later became an advocate for its use. From that date, it was tested with a mixture of fascination and fear by psychiatrists, who proposed its use in treating mental illness, and by the military, apprehensive of its potential as a chemical weapon. Concerned about its potency and capacity to distort perception and interfere with behaviour, the US Central Intelligence Agency (CIA) secured supplies of the drug and, in addition to conducting its own experiments on military personnel, provided LSD to American university departments for laboratory study. Out of the experiences of the volunteer students in these American universities the psychedelic revolution was born. Former lecturers, such as Timothy Leary, and volunteer subjects, such as Ken Kesey, author of *One Flew Over the Cuckoo's Nest,* embraced the new drug and travelled across the USA on a proselytising mission to convert American youth to LSD and the counter-culture – to 'turn on, tune in and drop out'. The exploits of this original group of LSD-promoting 'merry pranksters' are vividly chronicled in Tom Wolfe's *Electric Kool-Aid Acid Test.* LSD then became intimately woven with the hippy movement and the youth protest movement and, over the course of just a few years, spread to other parts of the Western world, including the UK. Despite the introduction of new laws against its use, black market production and distribution of LSD became widespread, culminating in major police arrests in the early 1970s.

The new opiate problem

In 1951, a new group of heroin addicts came to the attention of the UK Government's Inspectorate of Pharmacies. The system of maintenance prescribing for addicts endorsed by the Rolleston report in 1926 was starting to be abused: generous prescribing by a small number of London doctors slowly led to the emergence of a 'grey market', with diverted supplies of prescribed opiates finding their way into the hands of others than the intended recipients. By the mid-50s one or two London doctors found their prescribing habits scrutinised by the Home Office; and over the next few years there was a five-fold increase of known heroin addicts from 62 in 1958 to 342 in 1964 (see Figure 3.3), and also in the number of doctors with worrying prescribing habits.

Lady Isabella Frankau, a psychiatrist in Wimpole Street, gained the greatest notoriety in the early 1960s with prescribing that was described as 'lunatic generosity'. In general, very few doctors were willing to take on the care of drug users, but of the few who did, a small minority, mostly in London, prescribed extraordinary amounts of heroin and cocaine.

These new opiate addicts were different from the previous addict population in the UK. In 1960, for the first time ever, a heroin addict under the age of 20 came to the attention of the authorities. Seven years later, there were 381

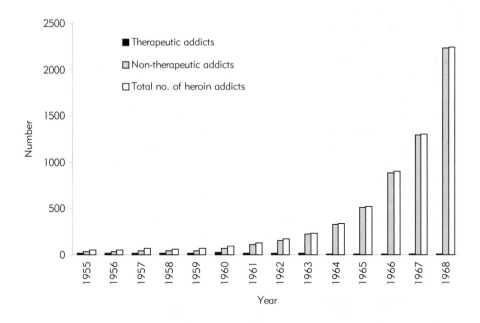

Figure 3.3.   UK heroin addicts known to the Home Office, 1955–1968. Data from: Hawks, D. (1967) The dimensions of drug dependence in the UK. In *Drugs and Drug Dependence* (eds. G. Edwards, M. A. H. Russell, D. Hawks, *et al*). Farnborough, Hants: Saxon House; and Lexington, MS: Lexington Books.

known cases of heroin addiction under the age of 20, and a further 827 aged between 20 and 34. The new heroin outbreak was occurring mainly among young men who were injecting themselves intravenously. Over a 10-year period, the number of heroin addicts in the UK grew from about 50 to a figure of 1299 in 1967. The increasingly forceful calls from the press and in parliament for a new response, with curbs on the prescribing doctors, now demanded some form of action.

Responding to the new drug problem

Urgent action was required. A government committee, under the chairman-ship of Sir Russell Brain, President of the Royal College of Physicians, was hastily reconvened and prepared its recommendations of a broad-based response to the new drug problem, which they saw as a 'socially infectious' condition. The recommendations from their 1965 report were implemented largely unaltered in the form of the 1967 Dangerous Drugs Act: new special addiction treatment centres were to be set up (especially in London) for the first time; the power of medical practitioners to prescribe heroin or cocaine to addicts was to be restricted to doctors working in these new treatment centres; a new system of compulsory notification of addiction (along the lines of infectious diseases notification) was to be introduced; and various aspects of government machinery to advise on the drug situation were to be established. Health remained a key concern, but the new approach emphasised abstinence rather than maintenance for addicts.[3]

By 1968, the new clinics had been opened and a more disciplined approach to prescribing of heroin and cocaine had been introduced. Patients were frequently required to pick up their supplies of drugs a day at a time, and checks were made on the quantity actually needed. The changes both guarded against surplus drugs being sold on the black market, and drug users taking several days' supply at once and then resorting to black market supplies until their next prescription.

The new clinics attempted to walk a 'prescribing tightrope' so as, on the one hand, to provide sufficient drug supplies to the addict, drawing them into treatment and away from the black market, and, on the other hand, to build motivation to come off the drug. Within this new variant of the 'British System' the new clinics were to operate with the twin goals of treatment of the individual and control of the drug problem. To a considerable extent, this curtailed the surplus prescribed heroin feeding the black market so that, in the words of one addict at the time, "the heyday was over".[4]

The apparently exponential growth of the youth heroin problem was dampened, but not entirely stopped. Over the following years, the problem largely moved out of the public limelight, but it did not disappear. Year on year, the number of addicts continued to grow slowly, with the steady flow of new recruits adding themselves to the residue of previous recruits who were still addicted.

THE 1970s

Revising the legislation

The 1971 Misuse of Drugs Act, which succeeded the Dangerous Drugs Act, still remains the basis of current legislation. Drugs covered by the Act are grouped into Classes A, B or C (see Table 3.1).

In 1985, the Misuse of Drugs Regulations defined a system of different schedules, cutting across the drug classes, which related to their medical use and prescription (see Table 3.2). Schedule 1 drugs are completely prohibited from medical use and can only be used in the context of specially sanctioned research, with a Home Office research licence for that specific purpose. Schedules 2 and 3 describe different levels of control which are applied to medicines that may be prescribed by doctors, and hence may be dispensed by pharmacists and possessed by members of the general public in receipt of a prescription. There is no direct correspondence between the classes under which drugs are categorised and the schedules.

Table 3.1. Drugs categorised under the Misuse of Drugs Act 1971 and subsequent amendments.

Class A	Class B	Class C
Heroin	Amphetamines	Amphetamine-related drugs
Morphine	Barbiturates	Buprenorphine
Methadone	Cannabis	Most benzodiazepines
Cocaine	Codeine	Anabolic steroids (under certain
LSD		circumstances)
Ecstasy		
Any Class B drug when		
prepared for injection		

The levels of control for Schedule 2 drugs are greater than with Schedule 3, so that the doctor writing the prescription must, for example, complete the entire prescription in his own handwriting and must include a summary of the total amounts of drug on the prescription in both words and figures, and the dispensing pharmacist must keep a separate record of the drugs supplied, recording the details of the patient and the quantities dispensed in a special 'controlled drugs register'.

Schedule 4 applies to certain prescription-only drugs. Schedule 5 covers drugs that are available without prescription, often referred to as 'over-the-counter' products, which may contain small amounts of controlled drugs. Dispensing pharmacists often operate informal systems of scrutiny and monitoring of persons seeking supplies of these drugs. For instance, they may suspect misuse and refuse to sell these preparations to customers asking for them in unusually large quantities.

Barbiturate injectors

A problem distinctive to Britain was the spread of intravenous barbiturate use in the 1970s. Pharmaceutical supplies of barbiturates were occasionally obtained from doctors by patients fabricating medical problems, but often purchased on the black market from chemist break-ins, or sold on by people with legitimate prescriptions. Barbiturate misuse was particularly associated with the danger of overdose so that, through the 1970s, barbiturates were the drugs most commonly involved in overdose deaths among addicts (see Figure 3.4)

Barbiturate addicts who had taken an overdose became frequent unwelcome attendees at the casualty departments of London hospitals, and both the drug

Table 3.2.   Drugs categorised under the Misuse of Drugs Regulations 1985.

Schedule 1	Schedule 2	Schedule 3	Schedule 4	Schedule 5
Cannabis	Heroin	Temazepam	Benzodia-	Preparations
LSD	Methadone	Certain	zepines	containing small
Ecstasy	Cocaine	barbiturates	(other than	amounts of con-
	Dexamphet-		temazepam)	trolled drugs
	amine			e.g. cough medicine
				containing morphine

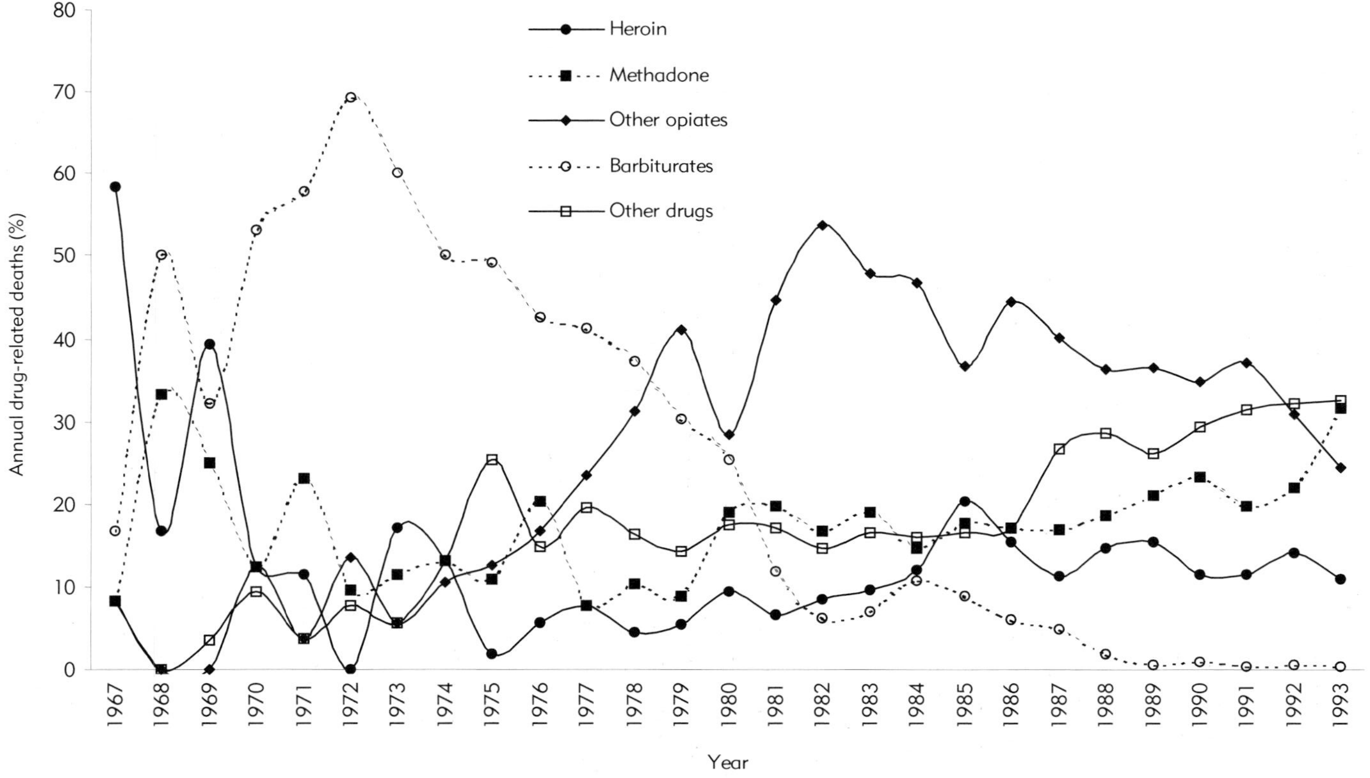

Figure 3.4. Drug-related deaths. Adapted from: Ghodse, H., Oyefeso, A. & Kilpatrick, B. (1998) Mortality of drug addicts in the UK, 1967–1993. *International Journal of Epidemiology*, **27**, 473–478.

field and health authorities mobilised to open up a new emergency in-patient/ residential facility to deal with the needs of these users – the City Roads' residential crisis centre, which remains in operation to this day. Gradually, through the later 70s, the extent of this particular problem began to wane, coinciding with the growth of a new black market heroin problem supplied by large imports of the new type of South-West Asian heroin. On the prescribing side, barbiturates began to relinquish their place to benzodiazepines, the new, safer, and supposedly non-addictive tranquillisers.

The spread of amphetamine powder

The origins of black market amphetamine use within youth culture lay in the pill-popping of teenagers in the 1960s. Then, in 1968 and 69, intravenous amphetamine misuse briefly flourished on the London scene after one of the prescribing doctors (who had already been the subject of attention and concern in the years leading up to the 1967 Dangerous Drugs Act) started prescribing injectable amphetamine in large quantities. However, this avenue was closed off by informal agreements reached between the Ministry of Health, the Home Office and the pharmaceutical suppliers.

Through the 1970s and 80s, the use of illicitly manufactured amphetamine powder silently spread across many parts of the UK (see Figure 3.5) with the main route of use, whether snorting or intravenous injecting, varying from place to place. Although the number of seizures of a drug can be influenced by changes in police and Customs practices, the size of consignments being smuggled, and other factors, the massive increase shown in Figure 3.5, from 1975–1997, gives some idea of the growth of the UK's amphetamine consumption.

Until the mid-1980s amphetamine users did not receive great attention from treatment services as they rarely sought help for their drug use. Then, in the face of HIV/AIDS, their injecting behaviour became a more pressing public health issue for planning services to prevent the spread of the virus.

Over this period surveys repeatedly showed amphetamines to be second only to cannabis as the most widely used drug in the UK, a position it maintains today. In the mid-1990s, a small proportion of these amphetamine users, both injectors and non-injectors, were found to be experiencing significant physical and psychological problems, but very few were in contact with drug treatment services or any medical help. The orientation of services towards opiate users, different patterns of drug use and, because black market amphetamine is not

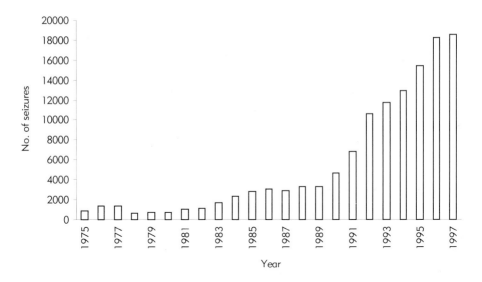

Data collected prior to 1985 is for selected classes of amphetamine and may not represent all amphetamine seized.

Figure 3.5.   UK seizures of amphetamine 1975–1997 (not including Northern Ireland). Data from: Home Office Statistical Bulletins on Drug Seizures.

expensive, the lower likelihood that financial problems will force them to reconsider their drug use, are all possible reasons why amphetamine users rarely seek treatment.

THE 1980s AND 90s

The new heroin epidemic

During the 1980s, heroin use emerged in a large number of communities around the UK, and with a pattern of use that was substantially different from the previous heroin epidemic in the 1960s. This new epidemic chiefly involved adolescents and young adults, and the heroin was now mostly being taken by an altogether new method known as 'chasing the dragon'. This involved heating the brown heroin on tin foil, with the vapours being inhaled through a tube held by the drug user in his mouth. The old heroin injectors and the new young heroin 'chasers' largely ignored each other and, indeed, were often dismissive or critical of one another. 'Chasing the dragon' was certainly a safer method of use as it avoided injecting hazards such as HIV and septicaemia, but many of the new heroin users seem to have believed that it also safeguarded against addiction. This popular myth probably helped to spread heroin use among young people and proved catastrophically mistaken.

Not only were the new heroin users themselves different from the heroin addicts of the 60s, but their heroin was also different in composition and with a different geographical origin. Since the late-70s, initially following the Iranian revolution, Western Europe has been supplied with steadily increasing quantities of black market heroin of various South-West Asian origins – the Golden Crescent, including Iran, Afghanistan and Pakistan.

However, not all of the new heroin users were 'chasers'. Great regional variation was seen with, for example, injecting remaining almost universal in Edinburgh, while 'chasing the dragon' became the favoured method in Glasgow, 45 miles away. Furthermore, many chasers subsequently went on to become injectors, despite widespread awareness, from the mid-80s onwards, of the dangers of HIV transmission from sharing contaminated needles and syringes. Injecting provided a more cost-efficient use of the drug either as their tolerance increased or earning capacity fell. So while some heroin chasers resolutely avoided injecting, approximately 10% a year made the 'transition' to injecting.

A surprising feature of this heroin epidemic has been its capacity to continue to grow (see Figures 3.6 and 3.8). Nearly 20 years on from its onset, it still shows no signs of abating. While the epidemic of the 1960s had seen the numbers of heroin addicts rocket from less than a 100 to 3000 or 4000, the later heroin epidemic of the 1980s and 90s has seen the number of known addicts grow from about 5000 in 1980 to approximately 50 000 by the late 1990s, with the figures still appearing to grow at approximately 20% a year at the time of writing.

Intravenous benzodiazepine misuse

A further specially British drug problem was the intravenous misuse of benzodiazepines, the sleeping tablets and anti-anxiety medication which had become so famous with drugs such as diazepam (Valium). From the first reports of this novel misuse in the mid-1980s, the practice rapidly established itself so that by the end of the decade it was one of the most pressing challenges to drug policy in the UK. Misuse of the benzodiazepine temazepam in capsule form, from which the liquid contents were extracted and injected, was a particularly serious problem.

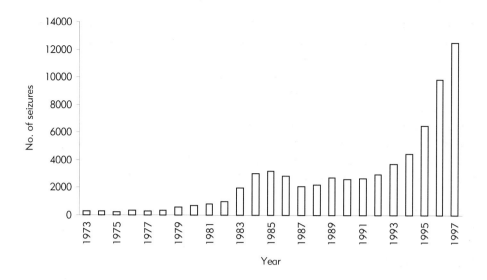

Figure 3.6. UK seizures of heroin 1973–1997 (not including Northern Ireland).
Data from: Home Office Statistical Bulletin and personal communication
(John Corkery, 1999).

In an attempt to prevent misuse, the contents of these capsules were
reformulated into a 'non-injectable' form with a consistency resembling
candle wax, but this led to greater problems for those drug users who resorted
to melting it down to continue injecting. Once injected, the melted capsule
contents cooled and could solidify in the blood vessels with dangerous results,
including ulceration around the injecting site, gangrene and sometimes the
loss of a limb. Consequently, new legislation was passed in the early 1990s
which further restricted temazepam prescribing, reducing the scale of the
problem.

Cocaine and crack

North America experienced a major problem with cocaine misuse during the
1980s. After the relatively quiet spread of cocaine snorting, which was
particularly popular among the wealthy middle classes, catastrophic problems
were encountered when the use of a new form of smokeable cocaine,
'freebase', took hold. Early methods of preparing the freebase involved ether,
and its products were highly flammable, making it a risky drug to smoke.

However, pharmaceutical innovations in the black market created a stable form, sold as 'crack', which could be smoked and would nevertheless deliver a speed of onset of effect similar to intravenous cocaine.

Use of crack cocaine came to be associated with violence and excessive sexual behaviour, simultaneously giving the drug a bad press and an aura of intrigue. It unfairly took the blame for the desperate state of America's impoverished inner cities, whose problems crack had worsened but not created. Predictions were made by American commentators that the tidal wave of crack cocaine would sweep across Europe as Latin American drug suppliers discovered that the North American market was saturated. In fact, while the extent of all cocaine misuse, and consequent problems, did indeed increase considerably during the mid-80s, the speed and extent of penetration of crack cocaine into the UK has been nowhere near as great or as rapid as American commentators had predicted.

Crack cocaine now figures in the domestic polydrug scene as a significant cause of drug problems – but only as one of a number of drugs which operate in this way. Similarly, in other European countries, cocaine has certainly become more firmly established than in previous decades, but Europe has not seen the same catastrophic wave of problems associated with crack in North America during the 1980s and early 90s. Surveys of the general population suggest that snorting cocaine is more common than crack or heroin use and is on the increase, particularly in clubs and on the dance scene. Figure 3.7 shows the steady increase in people coming forward for treatment and being registered on the Home Office Addicts Index, mostly for opiates and cocaine, through the 1970s and 80s. Figure 3.8 shows the trend continuing through the 90s with a steady rise in heroin, methadone and cocaine use. Although the overall upward trends are likely to match changes in the general population, the proportions using each drug probably do not, as a much smaller proportion of cocaine addicts than opiate (heroin and methadone) addicts comes forward for treatment. In contrast, cocaine rapidly overtook heroin as the main drug used by those attending American treatment services, while the numbers using heroin remained stable over this period.

Ecstasy: the British dance drug scene

The late 1980s saw the appearance of another newly available group of stimulant drugs – in particular, the hallucinogenic stimulant ecstasy (MDMA). This development occurred alongside the appearance of a new night club scene and a new form of music which complemented all-night dancing. Like some of the earlier epidemics, such as amphetamine pill-popping in the early

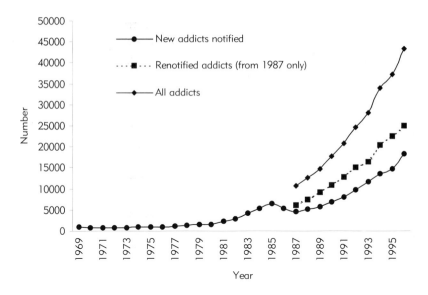

Until April 1997, the Home Office recorded drug users dependent on particular drugs (mostly opiates and cocaine) on a register known as the Addicts Index, from where these figures are taken. The Index was closed down in 1997.

In 1987, the system for notifying addicts previously known to the Home Office was changed. Figures for all addicts before 1987 cannot be calculated on the same basis, so they have been omitted.

NB Until 1968, notification to the Index was voluntary.

Figure 3.7.   Addicts notified to the Home Office, 1969–1996.
Data from: Home Office Statistical Bulletin.

60s, ecstasy use has developed alongside particular types of music which enhance the drug's effects. Although ecstasy has received extensive and sometimes rather hysterical media coverage, and undoubtedly has been culturally influential in the development of the 'rave' scene, surveys consistently show it to be used less frequently than the other dance drugs LSD and amphetamine.

Many of the concerns about young people using ecstasy have similarities to earlier fears about the pervasive use of amphetamines or of LSD. Unlicensed raves and festivals, like many youth phenomena outside the influence and control of older generations, aroused much debate about public order and excited attention from the police and parliament. Later, health concerns

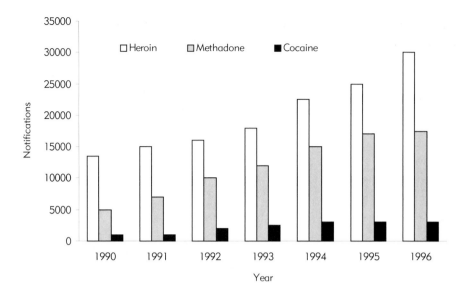

Figure 3.8.   Notifications to the Home Office by drug, UK, 1990–1996. Adapted from: Home Office (1998) The nature and extent of drug use in the UK. In *Drug Misuse and the Environment*, pp. 7–28. London: The Stationery Office.

dominated the debate; these had less to do with addiction and more to do with the dangers of unpredictable adverse reactions (particularly the sudden death of first-time users) or the possibility of long-term brain damage or mental illness. Unfortunately, scientific studies of these consequences cannot keep pace with the speed at which ecstasy use has spread. As a result, the general public and policy-makers must try to piece together the available parts of the scientific jigsaw when attempting to frame a balanced policy response to this recent epidemic.

THE LATE 1990s

Another new heroin epidemic?

In the last two or three years, public and professional concern has again turned from cocaine and ecstasy in particular to the extensive use of heroin by young people, with descriptions of widespread use in Mersey[5] and other large urban areas. Newspaper coverage of these reports has referred to a "new heroin epidemic". It is clear that there has indeed been a significant increase in the use of heroin among young people, and that heroin is more widespread in Britain than during the mid-1980s. However, it is less clear whether this represents a new phenomenon or an extension of the steady increase in heroin use since the 1980s. Perhaps the new heroin epidemic of the late 1990s can best be considered partly as an accurate observation about a substantial increase in youthful use of heroin, with seizures more than doubling between 1994 and 1996 (see Figure 3.6), and partly as a resumption in public concern about heroin which had been somewhat muted during the preceding years.

INTO THE 21ST CENTURY

Other drug 'epidemics' and their unfolding courses

Within the history of drug misuse in the UK, there are other epidemics with their own stories – for example, the misuse of volatile substances by children and teenagers, and anabolic steroids taken by athletes, body-builders and young men attending gyms. The increasing sophistication of alternative and criminal chemists and pharmacologists in developing new 'designer drugs' to evade the drug laws features in this history and further developments in this unwelcome branch of applied science seem likely in the future. The designer drugs of the future may have similar effects to existing prohibited drugs with which society is more familiar, and this may bring new dangers: using mixtures of new drugs may create sought-after interactions for the user but also new hazards, and more such problems may emerge as the number of people trying drugs continues to rise. Indeed, it is already clear that sildenafil (Viagra), a medication with no psychoactive effects recently licensed for the treatment of impotent men, is being increasingly misused in combination with a variety of other drugs, such as amyl nitrite, with which it may have dangerous interactions as a component of experimental 'aphrodisiac cocktails'.

CONCLUSION

The impact of a new drug on a population is extremely variable and finds different expression in different countries, populations and times. While some drug problems, such as heroin addiction, have maintained a tenacious hold on society and, once established, have never significantly receded, other drug epidemics, such as barbiturates, seem to have almost disappeared. Some individual epidemics, like a tide, have approached, washed over us and then receded while others rise unchecked. Although the greater disturbance associated with the appearance of new drug problems may subsequently diminish, the overall level of drug use within society has grown enormously over the last 40 years. It is as if, while individual 'epidemics' might be compared to a tide, first rising and then falling, they occur against a backdrop of a relentless rise in the mean sea level.

Chapter 4. The complex causes of drug use

Summary

Britain's drug users are vastly diverse in their backgrounds and patterns of use and include dependent heroin injectors, occasional cannabis smokers, and the week-end users of dance drugs. What influences their drug choices? Why does one person never try drugs, another take drugs in a controlled way and someone else feel unable to regulate his or her use? Drug use is most common among young people living in prosperous areas, but particularly risky behaviour, such as injecting, smoking crack cocaine or using heroin, is more often linked with growing up or living in a deprived area and other forms of disadvantage. The reasons that ill health and deprivation occur more commonly together may also account for dangerous drug-using behaviour. There are many reasons why drugs may be more freely available in areas with few legitimate prospects and controlled drug taking may be harder for their inhabitants. Nevertheless, these factors only explain some of the differences between those who experience problems with their use, non-users and more moderate users.

While drug choices are shaped by the social and economic environment, a person's biological endowment and psychological development are also of great importance. Recent genetics research has shown that our genes may influence patterns of drug use. Although genetic factors do not 'cause' drug use or dependence in any simple way, they increase those risks in certain individuals if drugs are available.

Family relationships have a big influence on children's development, and experiences such as childhood neglect, homelessness or abuse increase the likelihood that they will develop problems with drugs later on. Risk factors for heavy drug use are much more significant when they occur in combination than alone. Drug use by other family members increases the likelihood that a young person will go on to do the same, partly because of their availability in the household. Drug use in childhood and adolescence is overwhelmingly the best predictor of use later on, but not necessarily an indicator that it will escalate into higher risk use. Despite public interest in the idea of a gateway drug, the evidence is weak. As well as the dangers they may pose to psychological and physical health, it is important not to ignore the fact that drugs can help people relax, experience new sensations, and enjoy social occasions, which is why they are so popular.

Introduction

In this chapter, the following terms are used: *children* – age range 0–13 years; *adolescents* – age range 14–18 years; and *young adults* – age range 19–25 years. The way in which a person's physical development and environment affects their drug use can be best illustrated by a scale. At one end of the scale is Jessica and at the opposite end is Dan and his girlfriend Kerry, fictional characters and purely examples – they are not 'typical' users and only represent small parts of the wide range of drug users' lifestyles and patterns of use.

Jessica's story

Jessica is 32, grows cannabis plants in her flat, and harvests the leaves for herself and her friends to smoke. She's a freelance journalist, has no children, and tends to smoke when she has finished her work. She began using cannabis in the school sixth form, and continued at college, occasionally trying LSD and magic mushrooms as well, but hasn't taken these since she graduated.

Jessica's family inhabited the prosperous, middle-class suburb of Hemplestead. Although her parents struggled somewhat at first, by the age of six she and her younger brother each had a room to themselves in their new semi-detached home, like most of their friends. Her mother and father used to smoke, but both gave up in 1985, joining the majority of their friends who had quit a few years earlier. On sunny days, Jessica and her childhood friends could play in the garden, away from traffic.

Jessica smoked her first cannabis joint at a party when she was 16, when it was passed to her by her friend Matt. In the same situation, it is extremely unlikely that Matt would have offered to inject her with heroin, and had he done so, she undoubtedly would have declined. Heroin, and injecting in particular, were heavily taboo among Jessica's peers.

Dan's story

Dan is 23, a polydrug user and dependent on heroin. He lives with his girlfriend Kerry and their three-year-old son and has smoked cigarettes since he was nine and drunk alcohol since he was 12. His drug use began when he was 14, and has since escalated. Both Dan and Kerry live on social security, but Dan also deals a bit in heroin, and resorts to shoplifting to buy the drugs they use. Kerry used to smoke cannabis and inject amphetamines regularly, and sometimes took LSD, but since she's been living with Dan she too has become dependent on heroin. When times are hard, Kerry might turn to prostitution to fund their drug and living costs. She was found to be HIV-positive a year ago.

Dan's mother was already caring for three children when pregnant with him, and because of their low income had to return to her cleaning job shortly after his birth, giving her little time to develop a relaxed relationship with her new baby. But while Dan's path led into severe drug problems, his brothers and sister, who experienced the same hardships, grew up as moderate drinkers who did no more than experiment with drugs.

Dan started life in East Groxley, one of Britain's poorest districts, 50 miles from Hemplestead. Both of his unemployed parents smoke, and his father's drink problem worsened after he lost his job. With four children, their two-bedroom council flat was one of the more overcrowded on the estate. With few affordable leisure activities nearby, he and his friends hung out in the street, meeting up with other kids and their older brothers and sisters from the neighbourhood.

Like most people who start using drugs, Dan was first offered heroin by a friend, rather than a dealer. Kerry was first injected with heroin by her boyfriend Dan. When Dan first tried cannabis and temazepam at the age of 14, he was already a regular smoker and drinker, with more experience of alcohol and tobacco than Jessica when she was 16.

The decision to try a drug or not, to continue to use it or to stop are influenced by many forces, both internal and external. These include genes, individual psychology, family experiences, availability of drugs, social background, ethnic origins, and the behaviour of close friends. From a wider perspective, cultural attitudes and the economic situation may play a role. Although many of these influences are outside the individual's control, this does not mean that they 'determine' drug-using behaviour – everyone has 'free will' – but these forces may increase the likelihood of making certain choices and limit the ability to make others. First it is helpful to gain an idea of the scale of drug taking in the UK and the ages at which it usually starts.

PATTERNS OF DRUG USE

It is in adolescence that most drug taking begins: the majority of adults who use drugs started in their teens and early twenties. Taking drugs in childhood and adolescence is overwhelmingly the best predictor of drug use in adulthood, far outweighing in importance the numerous other factors that increase or reduce the risk of drug use later in life. Although volatile substance abuse (VSA), including gases and solvents, peaks somewhat earlier, the prevalence of most types of drug use is currently greatest between the ages of 16 and 24.

Surveys of young people's experience with drugs show varying results, with the British Crime Survey suggesting that just under half of 16–19-year-olds (49%) have tried a drug, and a survey of school children in the North of

England finding that by the time they are 18, 64% have taken a drug. Cannabis accounts for most of this drug use; severely problematic drug taking, like Dan's, is still comparatively unusual. However, the number of children, adolescents and young people trying and using drugs has increased greatly since the 1970s, as has their disposable income. Regular use in the mid-teens is relatively rare, although it has increased. The 1998 British Crime Survey (which measures drug use in England and Wales among those aged 16–59) found that, since 1994, the most significant increase has been in cocaine use. It estimates that in 1998, around 105 000 16–29-year-olds had used cocaine in the last month. There has also been a rise in the number of men in this age group using cannabis (from 28% in 1994 to 33% in 1998). However, overall, drug use seems to have been relatively stable across the adult population since 1994.

If a young teenager has ever used a drug, it is likely that this will have occurred in the last year or two, since use before the age of 13 is still uncommon. Data about use in the last year, rather than ever, are likely to give a clearer picture of the distribution of drug use across the age groups (see Table 4.1).

There are relatively minor differences between male and female drug use, boys being slightly greater users than girls with nearly all drugs, but as they get older these differences lessen. Recent findings hint at a widening gender gap in adults over 16, but further data are needed before the extent of this trend is clear. Regional differences are greater, with Scottish teenagers the highest and Northern Irish girls the lowest users of cannabis.

Detailed information about different ethnic groups' drug use is not available, but existing evidence challenges many stereotypes. There are no specific data from the 1998 British Crime Survey, but the 1996 Survey found the use of cannabis, amphetamine, LSD, magic mushrooms, ecstasy, tranquillisers and cocaine powder to be higher among Whites than African–Caribbean, Indian or Pakistani and Bangladeshi ethnic groups. This applied both to those aged 16-30 and to older adults. This indicates that there are no clear grounds for considering drug use in the UK to be higher among any ethnic minority, at any age, than among the White majority. In spite of this, research findings from the Home Office demonstrate that people from ethnic minorities experience disproportionate attention from the police and are stopped and searched far more than their White counterparts. It is therefore not surprising that there is some wariness about giving information on personal drug use; a substantially larger proportion of ethnic minority respondents refused to

Table 4.1. Percentages who had indicated that they had taken particular drugs in the last year, by age group. Data from: Ramsay, M. & Partridge, S. (1999) *Drug Misuse Declared in 1998. Results from the British Crime Survey. Home Office Research Study 197.* London: Home Office.

	Age in years						
	16–19	20–24	25–29	30–34	35–39	40–44	45–59
Cannabis	28	26	16	9	5	3	2
Amphetamines	9	10	5	2	1	<0.5	<0.5
LSD	2	3	1	<0.5	<0.5	<0.5	<0.5
Magic mushrooms	4	3	1	<0.5	<0.5	0	0
Ecstasy	4	6	2	1	<0.5	<0.5	<0.5
Solvents	2	<0.5	0	<0.5	0	0	0
Cocaine	1	5	3	1	<0.5	1	<0.5
Crack	<0.5	<0.5	<0.5	<0.5	<0.5	0	<0.5
Heroin	<0.5	<0.5	<0.5	<0.5	<0.5	0	<0.5
Steroids	1	<0.5	<0.5	<0.5	<0.5	<0.5	<0.5
Any drug	31	28	19	10	7	4	3

answer such questions from the British Crime Survey. This, and the small numbers involved, make it difficult to assess levels of crack cocaine and heroin use across different ethnic groups. Among those seeking help from treatment services, ethnic communities are under-represented, and the question of how all public services respond to the needs of these groups is important, but complex.

Drug dependence measured by a national survey of private households in England (thus excluding those in in-patient treatment) found that 2% of people were dependent on a drug, at some time in the last year. Cannabis contributed significantly to the numbers counted as dependent.

These national figures give a broad but superficial picture of drug-using behaviour. For a more detailed view, studies of particular groups among whom drug use is common are useful. A survey carried out by the drugs advice agency Release into the drug taking and attitudes of club-goers in London revealed that the majority of those surveyed started attending dance

Figure 4.1. In the general population, one in three people has used a drug at least once.

events in their early to mid-teens. More than one in five said they liked attending dance events primarily because of the drug use. Ninety-seven per cent had tried a drug at some point in their lives, up to three times the level of drug use reported in similar age groups by other surveys. Of those who had ever used drugs, four substances chiefly featured on the evening of the survey: 59% had taken or planned to take cannabis, 53% ecstasy, 39% amphetamines, and 16% LSD. The majority were current users and over 60% had also drunk alcohol that evening.

London might be thought to provide a unique set of circumstances. However, other research suggests that the level and frequency of ecstasy use in particular is broadly comparable throughout the UK. Surveys of the number of ecstasy tablets taken per session show that approximately 70% of users had only taken one tablet. Of particular concern is the 3% of ecstasy users taking four or five tablets per session.

The 'gateway effect'

Although experimental drug use in itself is unlikely to lead to significant problems for adolescents or young adults, it has long been argued that using one drug, such as cannabis, can lead to the use of other more dangerous and addictive substances. This is referred to as the 'gateway effect' or 'escalation hypothesis'. What is the evidence for this, and, if there is a progression, which is the 'gateway drug' – cannabis, tobacco, alcohol or even caffeine?

Most of the adolescents and young people who try cannabis do not go on to use any other drug, and although nearly all heroin users have previously used cannabis, only a small proportion of cannabis users ever try opiates. In one study, 96% of opiate users had taken cannabis in the previous year, but only 7% of cannabis users had ever taken heroin. Although 7% is higher than the level of heroin use in the general population (around 1%), this does not necessarily mean that using cannabis is the cause of using heroin later. Furthermore, most heroin and cocaine users have also used alcohol and cigarettes.

One study in south London suggested a strong link between tobacco and other drug use as young dependent smokers were 22 times more likely to have tried a drug than a non-smoker. This could indicate that alcohol or cigarettes, as well as cannabis, could be 'gateway' drugs, but also that, theoretically, caffeine could too, since drinking tea, coffee and cola drinks also precedes drug use, although its role remains unexplored. Trying to establish whether taking one drug is an important reason for the later use of another more dangerous one is therefore very difficult.

The metaphor of a 'gateway' implies that if only the gate could be shut, and the young never experienced alcohol, cigarettes or cannabis, they would not go on to use more dangerous drugs. But to look at this another way, perhaps one or all of these drugs act as a 'buffer', keeping back those who would otherwise use more dangerous drugs, so that their desire to experiment is satisfied with lower risk substances. In other words, so-called 'gateway' drugs could serve precisely the opposite function by preventing people from going on to use more dangerous or less socially acceptable drugs.

It has been argued that taking cannabis introduces people to a criminal subculture where they meet other drug users and dealers who encourage them to experiment with other drugs. However, a first-time cannabis user is much more likely to be offered it by a friend and is only likely to seek out a dealer if his or her use develops into a regular habit, requiring a regular supply.

Research among cannabis users in the late 1960s found that the more often someone had used cannabis, the more likely he or she was to have also tried LSD, but not necessarily other drugs. So if there is a gateway effect, frequency of drug use may be an important factor, but more recent evidence would be needed to confirm this. In fact, many dealers restrict themselves solely to cannabis and do not offer other drugs.

An American study recently found that heavy drug users did not follow the usual sequence of drug use. They were more likely to have used other drugs before cannabis and cannabis before alcohol, suggesting that cannabis is unlikely to be a 'gateway' drug to problem use, at least in that particular setting.[1]

In conclusion, without undertaking experimental research, which is impractical, it is extremely difficult to reach a firm view about whether one event – using alcohol, cigarettes or cannabis – causes other later events, such as the use of heroin or cocaine. In any young person's lifetime there are so many intervening factors – events, circumstances and pre-determined characteristics – that lead people down particular paths, that the 'escalation theory' is difficult to investigate. In so far as there is any 'gateway' drug, the evidence for tobacco is considerably stronger than for cannabis, for it is quite rare, at least in this country, for people who have never smoked to use any drugs.

CULTURAL AND ECONOMIC INFLUENCES

Comparing our case studies, Dan and Jessica's families started them off on very different paths, not only in terms of material conditions, but through their attitudes to health, friendship, education and careers. The environment in which someone grows up and lives may influence his or her likelihood of using drugs through cultural attitudes to drug use, the availability and cost of drugs, and economic circumstances. The British Crime Survey found that use of all drugs is more common among people, particularly under 30, living in neighbourhoods classified as reasonably well-off or prosperous (like Jessica's Hemplestead) than in disadvantaged areas. It is also true that particular professions that have easy access to drugs, such as doctors and dentists, are more likely to develop some drug problems. However, injecting, dependence, polydrug use, heroin and crack cocaine are more commonly found among socially deprived and homeless populations, like Dan living in East Groxley. Volatile substance misuse is also more widespread in socially deprived areas.

DEFINITIONS

The perception of what constitutes problem drug use has changed over time, in terms of both particular drugs and their methods of use, but there is a consistent association between problem drug use, as it is defined at a given time, and deprivation. Cigarette smoking, for instance, has changed from being a widely accepted part of mainstream British culture in the middle of the 20th century to a more marginalised habit at the turn of the millennium. Since the dangers of smoking became widely known in the 1960s, tobacco consumption has fallen among all social groups, but it has become dramatically scarcer among the most prosperous, like Jessica's parents, now ex-smokers. The fall in smoking among the less privileged is more modest. Today, habitual and heavy smoking is likely to be seen as increasingly socially unacceptable, while occasional 'social smoking' is tolerated and even seen as desirable in some settings.

The image and associations or 'social meaning' of other drugs have changed too. In the 1900s heroin was considered an exotic drug used by actors and actresses, criminals and the bohemian 'demi-monde', but utterly foreign to mainstream working-class people. During the late 1950s and early 1960s, heroin injectors were mainly older 'bohemians' within a London-based subculture,[2] and it was not until the mid-1980s that the American phenomenon of deprived inner-city opiate use began to appear in London, Glasgow, Edinburgh and the Midlands. Changes can also occur in the opposite direction. In the 18th century, gin had become associated with poverty and destitution, but today it is entirely socially acceptable, and the consumption of alcohol in general and spirits in particular is higher among the wealthier in Britain than the poor.[3]

Most psychoactive substances, including tobacco and alcohol, have the potential to cause great harm, and it is the interaction between the drug's pharmacology, the individual users and the host society which determines the extent of that harm. The definition of 'problem drug use' changes sometimes, either because of changes in the drugs themselves and how they are taken, or because of the circumstances in which they are used, and society's reactions.

DEPRIVATION AND PROBLEM DRUG USE

What are the processes behind the association between problematic drug use and areas of deprivation? Three explanations have been put forward: first, that poverty and low employment cause problematic drug use; second, that those who function well economically and socially, who are are less likely to encounter difficulties with drugs, migrate away from the affected areas, leaving behind those with greater problems, including those associated with drugs; and third, that individuals and families with these problems, who cannot find housing in more affluent areas, migrate into such neighbourhoods, so that there is a clustering of people with social and economic problems who are more likely to get into trouble with drugs. These explanations are not mutually exclusive.

There is also the possibility that drugs such as crack cocaine acquire the reputation for being particularly dangerous because they are used where problems already exist, by people whose problems are likely to be worsened by drug taking, and who are more likely to come to the notice of health services and fall foul of the criminal justice system.

Some of the same threads linking deprivation with health and social problems may explain the relationship between deprivation and problem drug use, particularly the effects on community ties. Strong social support networks, made up of friends, neighbours or relatives, are thought to contribute to good health, perhaps because during a crisis, or time of stress, there are people willing to help out and 'take the strain'. It may also be that they reinforce norms of behaviour and discourage activities considered to be dangerous, such as injecting drugs, among their members. Deprivation, on the other hand, is thought to weaken the family and social bonds that maintain such networks. As well as lacking the emotional and material support social networks may provide, those living in a deprived environment may see themselves as less answerable to the expectations of mainstream society and more inclined to ignore its norms. Feeling valued and important within a respected group can also affect health and behaviour.

People who are socially deprived are more likely to experience drug problems, particularly dependence, so are they more likely to come into contact with more dangerous drugs such as crack and heroin in the first place? While heroin use has been steadily increasing over the last 20 years, there is the evidence of a new heroin epidemic (both smoking and injecting) within poor areas of Britain. Observers have reported that dealers are setting up in deprived housing estates and selling the drug cheaply, deliberately spreading addiction among young people (14–25-year-olds) in the poorest parts of Britain's towns and cities.[4] In fact, it is still uncertain whether dealers deliberately target such districts. In the 1980s, similar stories were circulated but later discredited of discount heroin being sold to get people hooked. It seems more probable that those who become involved in dealing drugs, like

Dan in the case study, grow up or already live in deprived areas where legitimate employment and recreational opportunities are scarce.

Availability and cost are important factors in whether people use drugs and if so, which ones. But just because a drug is available and cheap does not mean people will use it if, for instance, there are strong social taboos against doing so. A middle-class man in his fifties is unlikely to sniff glue just because he has some in his garage, but he might be more likely to accept a joint passed round at a friend's dinner party. Availability and cost are therefore factors in the selection of drugs, but are unlikely to be the overriding motivation behind such choices.

DEPENDENCE

If there are cultural and economic reasons guiding the initial use of a drug, could these also explain why one user becomes dependent and another does not? Although heroin addiction seems to catch users 'unawares', it is not inevitable. Some evidence suggests that regular, controlled opiate use may be possible without dependence, but requires adherence to strict rules, such as never using the drug on consecutive days. There are likely to be many reasons underlying the development of dependence, including genetic and psychological influences. One explanation that has been put forward is that the motivation to follow such rules may be more likely to exist where there are other commitments, such as a rewarding job, which compete with the attractions and demands of heroin use.[5]

In the working-class culture of heroin use in the 1980s, when unemployment was high, those who had become dependent on heroin appeared to see eventual daily use to be the only pattern imaginable to anyone using the drug. It may be that the daily routine of obtaining money to buy heroin provided a meaningful replacement in the void left by long-term unemployment, as work not only provides an identity, but a structure to the day and week. Among friends who find themselves unemployed, it may be harder for the few individuals with jobs to maintain strict controls on their recreational use when those around them are using drugs daily, and this can then lead to unemployment for them too.

However, unemployment and social deprivation cannot explain all such epidemics and other factors undoubtedly come into play: during the 1960s, the thriving town of Crawley, despite its full employment, succumbed to a sudden epidemic of heroin injecting in its young people. Other epidemics, such as cocaine use in the USA during the 1970s, were clearly associated with affluence. Today, there are signs of heroin penetrating more affluent families and those in work or education. These new users, it is suggested, tend to come from those involved at the more 'serious' end of recreational drug use, heroin being used initially by young adult clubbers to 'bring them down' after using stimulants.

LOCAL FACTORS

The structure of the local drugs economy may influence patterns of friendship among users and the risks which they take or are imposed upon them. A comparison of drug users in the Dutch city of Rotterdam and in the Bronx in New York City found that Rotterdam's stable, high-purity heroin supply allowed users to smoke the drug rather than resort to the more economical, but higher-risk mode of injecting. Maintenance of Rotterdam's supply was assisted by greater neighbourhood and police tolerance of private dealing, and the higher disposable incomes of users than in the Bronx. In the Bronx, dealers were constantly on the move to avoid police scrutiny, and the use of dangerous settings meant that sales were conducted as quickly as possible and quality could not be checked before purchase. This meant that long-term relationships did not develop between groups of users and dealers. In contrast, Rotterdam's patterns of sales fostered the development of friendship networks among drug users, which were characterised by mutual support, and the sharing of resources and information, which tend to contribute to improved health.[6]

The traditions of particular regions may also have an influence on patterns of use. Deaths from volatile substance abuse (VSA) are associated with areas of deprivation, but not consistently. Tyne and Wear is known for its high death rate from VSA, but it is still unclear whether the particular individuals who die are themselves deprived. It could also be that VSA use is no more common in these areas but the patterns of use are particularly risky, for instance, sniffing from plastic bags which can result in asphyxiation, or sniffing alone so that no one is on hand to get help in the event of an accident.

EDUCATION

People's educational experiences have important implications for their future lives, their economic prospects, and consequently their likelihood of getting into difficulties with drugs. Those from more prosperous, middle-class backgrounds usually replicate their economic advantages in their children; and it has been suggested that the reasons for this may not just be that they are able to give their children a higher quality of education, but that the educational system itself favours such children by conforming to current divisions of social class and patterns of material advantage and disadvantage. This means that, right from the outset, middle-class families, such as Jessica's, may rear their children in a way that enables them to gain more from education and achieve greater academic successes than working-class families. These achievements give their offspring greater choice in the employment market and enable them to gain more highly-paid and rewarding jobs, perpetuating their advantages. Middle-class upbringings and the social experience of their education may also enable them to use to their advantage the world around them, including getting the most out of health services and accessing information on health risks.[7] However, these patterns are not necessarily dictated by income or the parents' jobs; there are many instances of impoverished families, particularly migrants, whose high educational ambitions for their children are successfully realised.

HOUSING AND NEIGHBOURHOODS

In deprived areas with their multiple social problems, drug use may be part of a wider picture of delinquency, perhaps involving gang fighting, unemployment, and a black economy where a whole range of commodities are traded and of which drugs are only a part.[8] A ready system of supply is therefore present to respond to demand for drugs.

The housing market is another mechanism that may concentrate social problems in certain neighbourhoods or estates by selecting residents. As an area begins to develop an undesirable reputation, people are unwilling to move in or remain there, and only those with the most urgent housing problems or who are less desirable to other landlords settle, such as the poor, the homeless and discharged psychiatric patients. Difficulties then accumulate, for instance as businesses move out, leading to a downward spiral of higher rates of crime, vandalism and problem drug use.

Housing policies are also responsible for the clustering of social problems on particular estates. Policy changes in the 1980s and 1990s have resulted in seriously unbalanced population mixes on many estates, concentrating together people with high levels of unemployment, lone parent families and the recently homeless. Such estates are very difficult to manage, particularly where, as a result of the high density of lone parents, there is a high ratio of children to adults, making supervision difficult or impossible.

Problem drug users may worsen their chances of obtaining good quality accommodation by their own behaviour, and may find themselves homeless. Dependent and high-risk drug use is dramatically higher among the homeless than the general population, but it can be difficult to disentangle the process by which this comes about. Expenditure on drugs and alcohol could prevent them paying the rent, they may be forced to flee their accommodation because of debts to drug dealers, or there may be complaints from neighbours about their drug use.

DIFFERENT VIEWS OF THE SAME RISKS

Smoking cannabis is less dangerous than injecting heroin, so why do certain behaviours that seem particularly risky become more common among particular groups? What is considered 'risky' in one context may not necessarily be seen the same way in another. For instance, binges of heavy drinking may be seen as normal among young, working-class men in Glasgow, and by their fathers' generation. They may be aware of the 'safe limits' recommended by various health organisations, but the views of their friends, family and community are of far greater significance. What is 'normal', acceptable and familiar may be seen as 'safe' behaviour. At the same time, some people (particularly young men) deliberately choose to act in a way that is perceived as risky for a range of reasons. These may include marking themselves out within their social circle as adventurous or fearless or, as mentioned in Dan and Kerry's case, showing their opposition to and separation from those who would condemn such behaviour.

It may be, too, that people who have less control over their lives develop a system of beliefs that outside forces such as 'fate' or 'luck' are more important than their own actions, and so they take greater risks with their health. The Whitehall studies dating from 1967 took several thousand male British civil servants and related their grade of employment to mortality from a range of diseases. They found that among men who had less control in their jobs, fewer believed that they could reduce the risk of heart disease through lifestyle choices.[9] Conversely, one of several influences on whether individuals behave in a way likely to improve their health seems to be a belief that their health is under their own control. Those in situations where they have few choices or prospects may therefore be more likely to risk their health through dangerous drug-using practices.

How does drug use become so normal and acceptable that it spreads among a network of friends? Such groups are not isolated from the world around them, and are influenced by the youth culture peculiar to their area, which in turn is influenced by national and international fashions, the media, and economics. In some groups, even sharing injecting equipment may be seen in a positive light: a study in Glasgow showed that some drug injectors showed their sense of fellowship and solidarity by this high-risk practice.[10] Conversely, the fact that a person feels excluded from mainstream youth culture may encourage him or her to use drugs in a way that shocks others.

RECOVERING FROM ADDICTION

Social and economic factors play a part in the initiation and continuation of drug use, but do they also influence recovery from addiction? Chapter 8 considers the treatments which can help people to stop using drugs, but very little is known about how those who stop, with or without treatment, succeed in remaining abstinent. In addition to personal motivation, social networks and economic opportunities seem to be important. A recent Scottish study found that recovering addicts employed two main strategies to protect themselves against relapse: the avoidance of former drug-using networks and friends, and involvement in non-drug related activities, including legitimate employment, and relationships with non-users. The success of these strategies depended upon three factors: the strength of ex-users' ties with those still involved in the drugs world (it was particularly difficult if a partner was still using); the ability to develop an alternative drug-free world for themselves; and the extent to which the drugs world could be avoided. Gaining employment was particularly important as it occupied the ex-user's time and gave them a positive self-identity and a stake in the future.[11] These findings are similar to those found by American researchers.

GENETIC INFLUENCES

Our genes play some part, sometimes minor and sometimes very important, in all aspects of our behaviour. What role do they play in drug taking and in problems arising from drugs? In considering this issue, three points need making.

First, the role of genes always depends to some degree on the environmental circumstances in which the individual lives. Some people may be genetically vulnerable to alcohol addiction, but they will not become addicted if, for example, they live in Islamic countries where alcohol is not available. In contrast, if someone is genetically vulnerable to the effects of drugs, like Dan, they will be more likely to be affected if they are living in a neighbourhood where drugs are readily available. Thus, a genetically vulnerable individual, living on a housing estate where there are high levels of unemployment and crime, and where drug dealing is part of the culture, will be at extra risk.

Second, different genes may be involved at different stages of drug taking, for example in drug experimentation and in risk of addiction. The importance of genetic factors in the early stages of drug use is well-illustrated in the case of cigarette smoking. It has been shown that individuals who possess a particular gene involved in the transport of the neurotransmitter dopamine (a chemical substance involved in the transmission of nerve impulses) are less likely to start smoking and find it easier to quit than individuals who lack this gene.

Third, the fact that genes are important in determining whether a particular type of behaviour occurs does not mean it is useless to try to influence the behaviour. This is true both in everyday life and in mental disorders. Musical ability, for example, is partly inherited, but practice and good teaching can make a great deal of difference to a limited talent. The same is true of reading and spelling ability. There is a strong genetic component in the causation of schizophrenia, but both medication and psychological treatments can be effective in treating the illness. The phrase 'genetically determined' is sometimes used about a behavioural problem or a mental disorder. If this is taken to imply a determinist, fatalist view it is seriously misleading. 'Genetically determined' only means that genetic factors play some part in a chain of causation. It does not imply that we are powerless to prevent or to treat.

So what is the evidence for the importance of genetic factors in problem drug use? Drug use tends to run in families. Thus, in one study, problem drug use was found to be between two and three times more common in parents of people with problematic substance use than in parents of those not affected. But this information alone does not tell us to what degree, if at all, the reason for this 'family clustering' is genetic. It could be entirely explained by environmental factors such as the child's experience of drug use in the home.

One approach to this problem involves comparing groups of identical and non-identical twins. An assumption is made that two identical twins have as similar experiences (being brought up in the same family) as do two non-identical twins. Consequently if, for a particular characteristic, identical twins are much more alike than non-identical, it can be assumed that the difference must be due to genetic factors. If, on the other hand, identical and non-identical twins are equally similar, then probably genetic factors play little or no part. Twin studies suggest that about one-third of 'family clustering' in problem alcohol and drug use is explained by genetic and about two-thirds by environmental factors.

Another approach to investigation of genetic influences involves the study of adopted children, their social parents (who brought them up), and their biological parents (whose genes they possess). If, when a particular type of behaviour is studied, children are more like their biological than their social parents, this suggests genetic influences are of greater importance in its development. Adoption studies suggest that there may be a general inherited predisposition to substance problems or dependence and a particular type of personality characterised by disregard of the feelings of others, impulsive behaviour, low tolerance of frustration and lack of guilt.

Some racial differences in susceptibility to alcohol-related problems have been shown to be produced by specific genetic differences. For example, in Chinese and Japanese populations, in contrast to other racial groups, a high proportion of people carry a version of the gene for the enzyme aldehyde dehydrogenase that allows acetaldehyde (a toxic chemical derived from alcohol) to accumulate in the bloodstream shortly after drinking alcohol. As a result, the drinker feels nauseated and develops an unpleasant facial flush. This 'oriental flush' discourages further drinking and so protects the individual against alcoholism. It is likely that similar mechanisms controlled by genes may be involved in explaining differences between individuals in their susceptibility to drugs. For example, genes have been identified in animal studies which influence the secretion of neurotransmitters (dopamine and endorphins) in the brain. These chemicals may influence 'brain reward mechanisms' which regulate the amount of pleasure and excitement an individual experiences when using a psychoactive drug.

To summarise, identification of genes has been shown to explain differences between racial groups in their vulnerability to alcohol problems. Adoption, twin and animal studies have shown that genetic factors have some influence in determining why some individuals are more susceptible than others to all forms of substance use and misuse.

It is highly likely that further scientific advances in genetics will make significant contributions to our understanding of addictive behaviour and underlying biological mechanisms. These new technologies may well make genetic screening for vulnerability to drug and alcohol problems a practical proposition in the not too distant future, a situation that will bring with it major ethical dilemmas. A more distant possibility is the application of genetic knowledge to treatment.

PSYCHOLOGICAL DEVELOPMENT

Psychological development has both intellectual and emotional aspects which are the product of genetic and other biological factors, family relationships, and experiences outside the family. In Western countries, children and adolescents are widely regarded as too psychologically immature to be fully responsible for their actions in relation to risk-taking activities such as the consumption of drugs or other illegal activities. But, in fact, capacity for abstract thinking has reached adult levels by about the age of 13–14 years[12,13] and, by this age, provided they are furnished with adequate information, most adolescents are as capable as young adults of assessing risk and making rational choices. Of course, decisions about behaviour are not necessarily taken by calculated risk assessment at any age, and even rational, mature and fully informed people take different views of the same risks.

Children cannot generally be regarded as adequately capable of making informed decisions, although at the older end of this age group (11–13 years) many will be. Inexperience may be a factor in some risk taking, and 14- and 15-year-olds may therefore take risks with drugs that are considered unwise by most adults, as they may do with other types of behaviour, such as alcohol consumption and sexual activity. However, age and experience do not always match, as some teenage drinkers and drug users will have much more experience than many adults.

Childhood and adolescence are regarded as phases of life during which the young gradually need to develop adult behaviour. From their 16th birthday, adolescents are legally allowed to have sex and get married, and from their 18th, they can buy alcohol in a pub and vote in a general election. There is an expectation that, before the legally permitted age, the young will gradually learn from their parents, teachers and peers how to behave before the birthday in question occurs, and that, after this date, they will continue to receive appropriate advice. Where, as is the case with the consumption of drugs, possession is illegal at all ages, the socialisation of children and adolescents presents special problems. Unless they break the law themselves, parents are unlikely to participate in drug taking with their sons or daughters to provide an example of responsible behaviour. Indeed, they may believe that all patterns and forms of drug taking are irresponsible. Of course, the lack of parental approval and involvement may be part of the allure that drugs hold for some young people.

American research shows that the more emotional problems and distress a person experiences, whether anger, depression, low self-esteem, or serious psychiatric symptoms, the greater the chance of problem drug use at some point in his or her life. In a study tracing adolescents from childhood, those who took drugs were found to be significantly more emotionally distressed than other children when studied at the age of seven. Long before it was known that they would develop drug problems, these children were reported as "not getting along well or forming close relationships with other children, as having bodily symptoms of stress, as afraid of being deprived, [and] as displaying inappropriate emotive behavior".[14]

Like physical health, mental health and illness are greatly influenced by social and economic circumstances, such as unemployment. The interaction between psychological, cultural and economic factors also influences the age at which children begin both to experiment with and to use drugs regularly. Severely socially disadvantaged children, who are more likely to suffer behavioural and emotional disturbances, tend to begin to smoke cigarettes earlier than children from less deprived social backgrounds. At ages 8–12, they are at greater risk of inhaling volatile substances and by ages 13–16 are more commonly found taking other risks also. Indeed, in one well-known study there was more than a five-year difference in average age at first drug or alcohol use between those with no conduct problems (17.5 years), and those with nine or more conduct problems (12.1 years).[15]

While some adolescents develop enduring harmful patterns of consumption, for the majority drug use gradually declines in early adulthood. Research on alcohol consumption suggests that this is likely to occur when they begin to form stable, intimate relationships. This process, known as 'maturing out', is accompanied by giving up other high-risk or delinquent behaviours such as reckless driving and shoplifting.

Even for those who become dependent on drugs for several years, there are many paths out of drug use. A study which traced New York heroin addicts from the 1950s into the 70s found that the peak age of achieving abstinence was 30 years, but it could happen at any age, regardless of the length of the addict's habit or the quantity of drugs he or she had consumed. For some of those who continued to use heroin, chronic addiction acted as a substitute for human relationships. Those who managed to stay abstinent for a year or longer were more likely to have been employed for several years and also to have been married. Other research has shown that family and work colleagues often influence a person to stop their dependent drug taking or to seek help.

FAMILY RELATIONSHIPS

Beyond their genetic input, parents influence their children's development, and perhaps their likelihood of using drugs, by their own patterns of drug or alcohol use and through their approach to child rearing. Family relationships, which are so important in a child's psychological growth, also have a bearing on his or her future drug-using behaviour. American research shows that children of parents who were "high on discipline but low on warmth" or "low on discipline but high on warmth" are more likely to develop problems with drug use. Young people who only experiment with drug use have been found to have the most stable family backgrounds, while those who have never tried any drugs tend, rather surprisingly, to have similar problems to those who become frequent users.[14]

Neglected children are at higher risk of developing drug problems. The lack of early parental support may prevent children from forming close relationships and they do not learn that they are likeable, can solve problems or regulate their impulses. Traumatic experiences when growing up, such as physical or sexual abuse and violence, are also associated with problem drug use. Many drug users in treatment describe how getting intoxicated helps temporarily blank out the memory of such events. Other negative experiences, such as parental divorce or serious hospitalisation, also increase vulnerability to problem drug use. Whether the amount of time families spend together affects drug use has been the subject of speculation, since British parents work the longest hours in the European Union and British teenagers' rates of childbirth (definitely) and drug use (probably) are the highest of all the member states.[16]

Figure 4.2 shows the risk and protective factors that increase or decrease the likelihood of problem drug use during adolescence. Single factors alone are unlikely to be of much significance – it is in combination that their effect is greatest. Most of these findings are based on American studies, and although there are many similarities between the UK and the USA, attitudes to drug use, school systems and many other aspects of life differ considerably.

Table 4.2.   Risk and protective factors for problem drug use in adolescence. Adapted from Bry, B. H. (1996) Psychological approaches to prevention. In *Drug Policy and Human Nature. Psychological Perspectives on the Prevention, Management, and Treatment of Illicit Drug Abuse* (eds W. K. Bickel & R. J. DeGrandpre), pp. 55–76. New York: Plenum Press.

Risk factors	Protective factors
• Genetic predisposition	• Genetic predisposition[i]
• High experience seeking	• Responsibilities e.g. managing a home
• Cigarette use under 12 years old	• Close, enduring, generally harmonious relationships with family and friends who disapprove of drug use
• High psychological distress	
• Psychiatric diagnosis, in particular antisocial personality disorder and schizophrenia	• Parents/consistent surrogate parent who knows how a young person spends his or her time
• High level of use among friends	
• High level of use among family members	• Participating in hobbies/sports
• Physical or sexual abuse	• Effective, age-appropriate discipline by parents
• Homelessness	
• Childhood neglect	
• Delinquency	
• Poor academic achievement	
• Unemployment	
• Separation or divorce of parents during childhood	

i   Genes may act as both risk and protective factors.

Family drug use

Unsurprisingly, growing up in a family with drug users increases the likelihood of drug use in adolescence, but it is unclear what mechanism accounts for this. Most obviously, drugs are more likely to be available, even though they may be taken without permission, and adolescents may learn drug-taking behaviour by example. The implied approval of drug use by parents may also be important: in one American study, adolescents refused available drugs or alcohol 46% of the time when offered by friends and 18%

when offered by relatives, but they never refused drugs or alcohol offered by parents. However, there is too little research evidence to properly assess the impact of controlled or regular parental drug taking on children's development or drug taking.

ATTRACTIONS OF DRUG USE

The positive aspects of drug use by young people are rarely considered by those adults who write about the 'teenage drug issue', but from the point of view of young people themselves they exist and are vital to the drug debate. Very little work has been published on the benefits of drugs, and given the political fear of being seen to condone drug use, funding for research may be harder to obtain than for the negative aspects. Even when research funding has been obtained, the bias in favour of drug problems may also extend into publishing. A literature review of research into the effects of prenatal cocaine exposure found that studies which reported adverse consequences were more likely to be published in the scientific press than those which showed no negative effects, regardless of the validity of the research.

It is well-known that people suffering from certain medical conditions sometimes use recreational drugs, including cannabis, to 'self-medicate'. Drugs that are prescribed for pain relief, such as opiates, may also be used illicitly by drug users with chronic painful conditions. Of course, some users may claim that they have medical needs to justify what is purely hedonistic use. It has been proposed that problem drug users are, in fact, self-medicating in their use of drugs: they have particular difficulties in regulating their emotions, self-esteem, and relationships, and use drugs to relieve or change a range of painful emotional states. This theory suggests that their drug use is a form of 'self-regulation' that helps them to cope.

For young people lacking confidence, or prone to anxiety in social settings, taking drugs such as amphetamine or ecstasy in moderation may help them to relax and join in, in much the same way that alcohol acts as a social lubricant. Others enjoy drugs for their pleasurable effects and the altered perceptions they offer. A survey of young people attending 'raves' and night clubs carried out by the drugs advice agency Release found that, for every drug used, fewer claimed to have suffered psychological or physical problems than to have experienced beneficial effects. Over three-quarters said they had experienced positive effects of cannabis whereas only one-third reported any problems associated with its use. More frequent negative effects were experienced with ecstasy, amphetamines and LSD but, as the researchers noted, this could have been because of higher levels of usage compared with other drugs. However, it is quite probable that those who enjoyed their drug use were more likely to continue to attend such events, while those with more negative experiences dropped out of the scene. Interestingly, these dance-drug users rated ecstasy both the most problematic, in terms of unpleasant effects, and the most enjoyable.

Problem users, even those who are dependent, may still gain enjoyment from their use, and a noted characteristic of many drug users seeking treatment is their ambivalence to changing their behaviour. Although they may want to give up or reduce their consumption, they still feel that they benefit from taking drugs.

For those who see adolescence as a time of inevitable rebellion, occasional use of the less dangerous drugs is perhaps one of the least harmful ways of achieving non-conformity to adult rules. Long-term tobacco use and excessive drinking can easily be more damaging, and the risks involved in violent forms of antisocial behaviour are higher still.

CONCLUSION

When growing up, children like Dan and Jessica are subject to widely different conditions and influences. Their psychological development will be affected by their genes, family relationships and early experiences. These factors can all influence whether an individual goes on to use drugs, and the patterns of use he or she might adopt.

The likelihood of encountering heroin may be greater when living on an urban council estate than in the suburbs, and when unemployed with few job prospects it may become more appealing. The alienation felt by those with an apparently bleak future from people thriving in the legitimate job market may reduce their desire to conform to mainstream society's norms of behaviour. Consequently, when offered heroin for the first time, the incentives not to try it and then use it again are weaker than for those with more to lose and a greater number of activities competing for their time.

Areas of high unemployment and deprivation are usually associated with poor health and a higher chance of using drugs problematically, and it is these very districts that are least well-equipped to cope with the consequences. The congregation of people with social and economic difficulties who may have little support from friends or family, and the lack of legitimate leisure and employment prospects, may mean that there are fewer encouragements for users to control their drug use.

Crime rates in deprived areas are likely to be higher as people seek alternative activities to busy themselves and acquire status. An underground economy supplied by criminal activity, where prohibited and stolen goods are traded, may provide a ready supply of drugs and a system of exchange in the absence of legitimately earned cash. There may therefore be a 'fit' between the consumption and sale of drugs and other features of the economy in poor areas.

Less is known about factors protecting against problem drug use. The benefits of a stable background, a good education and good career prospects may enhance the likelihood of drug use forming only a small and mainly harmless part of an individual's life. But this is not always enough: there is evidence that heroin use is becoming more common among affluent families both in the UK and the USA.

Negative early experiences and family problems are likely to have a detrimental effect on a young person's development, which in turn may increase his or her chances of using drugs harmfully. Childhood depression, physical or sexual abuse, pre-existing mental illness and neglect during childhood are all implicated. Genes play a part in drug-using behaviour and influence an individual's vulnerability to dependence; the importance of any genetic predisposition to problem drug use will depend on environmental factors such as the availability of drugs and life experiences. This knowledge has yet to be successfully applied to preventing or treating drug use.

Bearing in mind the risk factors outlined in this chapter, a broad, indirect approach to prevention may be successful. We are deeply impressed by the present government's determination to combat social exclusion. Alleviating poverty, improving housing, reducing social inequality, improving educational standards for the deprived sections of the population and providing effective support for families with children in their early years ought to reduce the number of vulnerable children, and thus the number of children at risk of running into problems with drugs. Initiatives designed to promote the well-being of infants and young children in areas of deprivation through developing parenting skills should form a cornerstone of tackling some of the underlying causes of drug problems.

Chapter 5. Consequences of drug use – for the individual and society

SUMMARY

How do different patterns of drug taking affect users, their friends, family, neighbourhood and the wider society? For many people who use drugs, there are no adverse consequences, but a pregnant mother's drug taking can affect her developing baby, and parental drug use may have an impact on their child's development and welfare. If a young person's own use becomes problematic in the context of other delinquent behaviour, such as truanting, he or she may miss educational opportunities important for his or her future prospects. Accidents and absenteeism from work undoubtedly result from drug use, as they do from alcohol, but their prevalence is hard to estimate with any accuracy.

If someone shares a friend's injecting equipment and develops hepatitis, the cause and consequence are quite clear, but the relationship is usually more complex. Drugs can play a part in crime, violence and mental illness: drug use that becomes expensive can lead users to commit crimes to meet these costs, but a lucrative criminal career can also facilitate costly drug use. No drug consistently produces violence but users may become violent under a drug's influence. Violence may be used by those involved in the drugs trade to enforce deals and to gain advantage over rivals. Psychiatric illness is often found among heavy drug users, but it can be difficult to distinguish whether their drug use has led to the mental disorder or the other way around. Adverse effects on health, probably the most significant drug consequence after crime, can result from the toxic effects of the drug itself, the method of administration or dependence. Hundreds, or even thousands, of deaths occur every year as a result of drug use, but accurate figures are not available.

INTRODUCTION

Jessica's story (continued from page 60)

Jessica's drug use could affect her health, and perhaps her work efficiency, but if she doesn't finish an article on time, as a freelance, she wouldn't be paid by the newspaper, so she alone loses money. She doesn't buy drugs, so plays no part in the illegal market, and being single and without children she has relatively few responsibilities. Jessica's mother smoked cigarettes during her pregnancy at a time when little was known of the adverse effects. Aside from her smoking, Jessica's mother's chances of having a healthy baby were increased by her relatively stress-free pregnancy, good nutrition, and regular prenatal health care. Both parents are moderate drinkers.

Dan's story

Dan's drug taking has enormous repercussions for himself, his family, and his local area. Kerry and Dan spend up to £600 a week on drugs, and because they have few formal skills or qualifications it would be hard for them to support themselves and their child through legitimate employment. Holding down any kind of regular job is particularly difficult for Dan because a lot of the time he is either trying to obtain drugs, using them, or recovering from their effects. Because heroin was so often around, Dan's drug use and dealing made it easier for Kerry to start using heroin – although you could argue that the choice was hers – and it is from sharing a syringe with a friend that she contracted HIV. Dan's behaviour affects many other lives, but most drug users are closer to Jessica's end of the scale, with effects that have limited impact on other people. Most do not inject, are not dependent and are not involved in acquisitive crime, but a small number of problem and dependent users cause a disproportionate amount of trouble. Dan's mother also smoked during her pregnancy and was already caring for three children when he was born. She does not drink but Dan's father's heavy alcohol intake was a constant source of tension in the household.

Taking drugs can have a number of adverse effects for the user, for other members of their family, for other members of society, and the economy at large. These include health problems, crime (other than possessing or supplying the drugs themselves), relationship problems which can lead to family breakdown, neglect or abuse of children, accidents, transmissible diseases, lost productivity and lost government revenue from black market transactions. It is worth remembering, however, that a large proportion of drug use, such as weekly dance drug use and occasional cannabis smoking, is relatively controlled and affordable. Adverse effects, if they occur, are likely to be primarily on the health of the user rather than directly on others. Indirect consequences, however, result from the proceeds passing into criminal hands.

DRUG USE DURING PREGNANCY

The ill effects of smoking on developing babies have been clearly established. Such babies are more likely to be born prematurely and to be underweight. They are also more likely to have problems after birth, such as an increased risk of developing infections, poor weight gain and a higher risk of dying in the first month of life. Several other drugs are likely to be associated with similar or greater risks but their effects are not as clear-cut as it first may seem. To what extent these effects are the direct consequences of taking any drug or the result of other associated factors is not known.

Women who use drugs during pregnancy, such as Kerry, Dan's girlfriend, tend to lead less healthy lives than other women. In particular, they are more likely to have poor diets, infections (often chronic and untreated), tend to smoke cigarettes and generally have poor access to basic health care. When pregnant, for all sorts of reasons but predominantly because they fear being judged and having their children taken out of their care, they may not attend antenatal care until late in the pregnancy, and so complications remain undetected. A small proportion do not seek medical care until they are actually in labour and this obviously markedly increases their risks of complications during and following the birth.

Opiates such as heroin appear to cause babies to be underweight, although this effect is reduced if the woman receives health care. Cocaine taken in pregnancy can cause narrowing of placental blood vessels which provide nutrients and oxygen to the developing baby, causing growth retardation and stillbirth. However, apart from smoking, there is little 'hard' evidence of the direct effects of drugs taken in pregnancy.

PHYSICAL DEVELOPMENT

Until they have reached maturity, the bodies of children and adolescents do not deal with drugs as efficiently as those of adults. Little is known about the way in which the body's capacity to deal with drugs changes with age. However, the activity of the enzyme responsible for breaking down alcohol in the body is known to increase during adolescence. When drunk, the young experience a fall in their blood sugar and body temperature, and develop seizures and coma at lower levels of alcohol in the blood than mature adults.[1] Drug use at a very young age is therefore not only worrying in terms of a child's psychological development but also because they are at greater risk of physical harm. From what is known of the development of the liver and other relevant organs, it is probably reasonable to assume that from about the age of 14 years, the efficiency with which the body deals with drugs has reached adult levels.

CHILD REARING AND DRUG USE

As a child grows up, the impact of drug taking by parents may have both positive and negative effects. At least some parents find using some drugs such as cannabis pleasurable, relaxing and without significant side-effects. In that it is easier to cope with the stresses of bringing up children in a relaxed frame of mind, it is quite possible that, for some children, parental drug use brings with it some advantages. Research findings suggest that some parents who are regular users of cannabis do find the drug makes them more relaxed with their children. Parental consumption of moderate amounts of alcohol not causing drunkenness or violence is rarely thought of as harmful to children, and controlled, recreational drug use like Jessica's – aside from the fact that possession of drugs is illegal – may be no more of a threat. However, problematic use of either drugs or alcohol, like Dan's father's, is likely to have a damaging effect on family life and child rearing.

As with the effects of drug use during pregnancy, the impact of parental drug use on the child and adolescent is difficult to separate from other adverse influences with which drug taking can be associated, such as poverty and poor social support. To complicate the picture, many studies measuring the effects of drug dependence in parents have failed to take account of exposure of the foetus during pregnancy. Moreover, the best evidence comes from American studies, and these may not be readily generalisable to the UK.

Compared to parents in the general population, parents taking cocaine and heroin were found to be more likely to be arrested for drug-related offences, and for prostitution and theft. They were also more likely to have personality disorders and to suffer from depression and anxiety, all of which are likely to have an adverse effect on child rearing. Mother–child relationships were often characterised by insecurity, anxiety and confusion. Evidence of a link with poor school progress both in learning and behaviour has also been found. Many opiate- and cocaine-dependent parents appear to have experienced troubles in their families of origin, as well as with their own partners, and in particular to have experienced abuse both as children and adults. This may explain the inappropriate child-rearing techniques of some addicted parents.

In an English study of children who died as a result of maltreatment between January 1993 and December 1994, it was found that alcohol and/or drug misuse was a factor in 4 out of 35 (12%). A study of families known to social service departments found a history of substance misuse in 20% of parents in a non-fatal sample. Overall, studies indicate that children of opiate- and cocaine-dependent parents are at risk for abuse and/or neglect, but when compared with children from similar (impoverished) neighbourhoods, levels are equally high.[2] Children whose parents are hospitalised for their drug dependence or imprisoned for drug offences will also suffer breaks in care and separations that may be profoundly damaging to their development.

Drug use and adolescent development

Problem drug use is often seen as a trigger for young people 'dropping out' of mainstream society. Those who truant or are involved in other delinquent behaviour not only fail to fulfil their own potential, but may harm others through becoming persistent offenders, or later in life, be like Dan, depending on state benefits for lack of employment skills. But such situations rarely have a single cause.

Drug use, and problems with drugs later on, are much more common among delinquent young people. Young people who truant or are delinquent tend to have suffered from many early disadvantages, including poor parental supervision, coming from a low income family, and separation from their parents at some point during childhood,[3] so that adverse effects due to drugs are difficult to disentangle from other disadvantages.[4]

Challenging behaviour at school can lead to a breakdown in relationships between pupils and teachers, leading to further truancy. For some children, this situation may lead to temporary or permanent exclusion from school, but drug use in itself rarely seems to be a cause of exclusion. Once excluded from school, however, there may be more opportunity to obtain and use drugs, as well as committing other offences.

Drug use and work

As well as all the complications which arise from contact with the illegal trade in drugs, there are some which result from irresponsible use of drugs. The specific problems that may affect work or education may be dependence, where time is spent in the search for drugs, the after-effects of bingeing or excessive use, or intoxication during work. These may lead to mistakes, lost productivity, and accidents.

Dependence on any drug may mean that the need to obtain supplies takes precedence over all other priorities, including work. If the problem of availability is removed, either by the prescription of the drug itself, or a substitute such as methadone, or if the addict has easy access to the drug, the degree to which his or her work will be affected by intoxication or withdrawal will depend on several factors: his or her degree of tolerance; his or her motivation to use only enough to assuage withdrawal rather than 'get high'; and the route of administration. Injected drug use tends to bring about cycles of intoxication and withdrawal whereas the slower onset of oral use reduces these peaks and troughs. These factors will influence whether an addict can function satisfactorily and undetected.

Where the problem involves bingeing (which both Dan and Jessica might indulge in), the effects on work or studying may be more severe, for a weekend of heavy drug use, like heavy drinking, may require several days for recovery. For stimulant drugs such as amphetamine, this may include symptoms of depression, as well as exhaustion, impaired attention and vigilance, and as people age it takes longer to recover from such excesses.

It is extremely difficult to estimate the impact of drug use on work. In most working environments people are unlikely to willingly admit that an absence from work is self-induced, especially if the cause involves an illegal activity. There are very few good studies of such behaviour, but one or two surveys have been carried out by employment organisations, including the Confederation of British Industry, which found drink and drug-related problems to be one of the seven most common causes of sickness absence. Unfortunately, the survey did not distinguish between the effects of drink and drugs. Fifteen per cent of large companies have reported drug use as a problem at work, although what was meant by a 'problem' was not defined. Although less common than in the USA, a study by the Institute of Personnel and Development found that 1 in 10 organisations in Britain carried out pre-employment testing for drug use, and 1 in 20 randomly tested their employees.

For alcohol, it has been estimated that 14.8 million working days are lost each year in Britain as a consequence of 'inappropriate drinking', and sickness absence owing to problem drinking was estimated to cost employers over £1 billion in 1992. By comparison, problem drug use is much less common so the drug figure is likely to be considerably lower. Most of those seeking treatment for their drug taking are not in regular employment. Although this means that they do not cause difficulties at work, they are likely to take up considerable resources through social security payments, or if they are involved in criminal activities. Little is known about the impact of occasional or recreational drug use, like Jessica's, on work performance.

CRIME

Drug-related crime is a source of great concern in Britain and much of the rest of the world, and consequently it has been widely studied. Apart from breaking the laws governing the possession, distribution and production of drugs themselves, it is acquisitive crime that is most frequently attributed to drug users (usually heroin addicts in Britain and cocaine addicts in the USA), perpetrated with the intention of raising cash to buy drugs. This might involve property crime against cars, homes, or businesses, theft, or defrauding social security. The organised crime involved in drug manufacture and supply and the associated activities such as money laundering are considered in the next chapter.

Most recreational or experimental drug use, certainly of the popular drugs cannabis, amphetamines and LSD, is no more costly than drinking alcohol, so one wouldn't expect it to push users into criminality to acquire extra funds. But heavy use of heroin or cocaine is much more expensive, with heroin costing £60–£100 per gram (an average user would take three quarters of a gram a day) and cocaine £40–£60 per gram (enough for one day's use). It is often suggested that dependent users are powerless to make rational choices because they are controlled by their addiction, but this overstates the importance of chemical dependence and ignores the fact that they could seek treatment. Furthermore, some heavy users are involved in crime before they begin using drugs. Indeed, their ready supply of cash from robberies and theft may have enabled them to develop an expensive habit in the first place.[5]

Even users who are also criminals may rely on a number of income sources to buy drugs and support themselves, including social security, casual employment, and loans. Levels of use are also likely to be important. A study of Scottish prisoners found that, as one might expect, heavy opiate users committed crimes significantly more often than moderate opiate users and other drug users, but interestingly, moderate opiate users did not commit crimes any more often than the other drug users.

Estimates of what proportion of crime is drug-related vary enormously. An analysis of acquisitive crime by heroin addicts concluded that they were responsible for anywhere between 1% and 21% of recorded acquisitive crime in England and Wales during the 1990s.[6] However, this study used a fairly conservative estimate of the amount of heroin consumed, so the proportion of crimes committed to pay for the drug is likely to be more modest than in other estimates. By its broadest definition, when including the offences of drug possession and supply, several police forces have suggested that around half of all recorded crime could include a drug-related element (although this does not imply drugs are a cause of the crime). Local studies in Bristol suggest a figure of around 60–70%. Among problem drug users, imprisonment is common, and roughly half to three quarters of injecting drug users have been in prison at some time, but this includes imprisonment for offences under the

Misuse of Drugs Act, such as possession or dealing, as well as for acquisitive crime. Although not yet part of legislation, the UK Government recently announced plans to test every arrestee for drugs, their bail being conditional on the results.

A recent British study found that from an intake of 1075 drug users entering treatment, 52% (562) reported taking part in 31 575 separate crimes, excluding offences of selling drugs, in the three months prior to their entry into treatment. The costs of the whole intake's contact with the criminal justice system, some of the costs of crime to its victims and costs of contact with health care and addiction services were estimated at £12 million for one year (at 1995/96 prices). Because there was so much variation between individuals, calculating an average cost per user would be misleading: 10% of the sample accounted for 80% of the costs to victims. The individuals studied are fairly representative of those in contact with treatment services but not of the general drug-using population.[7,8]

Similar links can be found between prostitution and drugs as with acquisitive crime and drug use. While prostitution may be resorted to in order to pay for otherwise unaffordable drugs, some prostitutes only start using drugs after they have become involved in the sex industry. Those already working as prostitutes may find themselves working longer hours or taking greater risks, such as being less selective about clients, to meet their drug costs. As with other forms of criminal activity, prostitution may contribute only a part of their income. The strongest links between drug use and prostitution have been found with heroin, particularly severely dependent use, like Kerry's (Dan's girlfriend). More recently, crack cocaine has been implicated, especially among polydrug users. Some women fund their partner's drug use through sex work. Drugs are also used by prostitutes to help them cope with the stresses of their work.

Whether a drug user, particularly someone severely dependent, is likely to turn to prostitution to fund their use seems to depend on how normal or acceptable it is among their circle. One London study showed that 90% of drug-using prostitutes already knew other prostitutes before their involvement and most were introduced to the work by a close friend.

The variety of connections and the strength of the links between crime and drug use are shown in Table 5.1. The most frequently discussed link (row E in the table) is where people become involved in a lifestyle dominated by acquisitive crime, drug dealing or prostitution to meet the costs of dependence on expensive drugs, but they are the minority. Most offenders either do

Table 5.1. The crime/drugs–drugs/crime matrix. Adapted from: Parker, H. & Bottomley, T. (1996) *Crack Cocaine and Drugs-Crime Careers*. London: Home Office.

	Type of user/offender	Drugs–crime/ crime–drugs connections
A	Offenders who never/occasionally take drugs. Drug users (recreational and dependent) who rarely/never break the law (other than the Misuse of Drugs Act)	None or very little
B	Offenders, mainly young adults, whose crime is about sustaining a lifestyle which includes drug use	Unclear; evidence strengthening
C	Offenders who supply drugs for illegal financial gain. Drug dealers/suppliers who are primarily involved for financial/illegal gain	Strong
D	Offenders, not regular drug users, who under the influence of a psychoactive drug commit 'out of character' offences. Drug users who under the influence of a psychoactive drug commit 'out of character' offences	Occasional
E	Offenders prior to heavy drug use which creates or amplifies a drugs-crime career. Drug users whose dependency moved them beyond legitimate financing into crime and often complex drugs-crime careers	Strong

not take drugs or only use them recreationally and the majority of drug users are not significantly involved in breaking laws other than the Misuse of Drugs Act (row A). Row C shows dealers or suppliers who sell drugs with the primary aim of making a profit, rather than supplying themselves or friends with drugs. They are most likely to have started out as career criminals. Row D shows the occasional link between drug use and an 'out of character' criminal act committed when under the influence of a drug. Finally, drug users may also be the victims of crime when buying drugs: they are easy targets for stealing money or being 'ripped off' since they are unlikely to wish to explain the circumstances to the police.

Violence

There are many forms of violence, not all of which constitute criminal activity. Violence may be directed against objects, other people, animals, or against the self, as with suicide or self-harm. Drugs and violence are linked for three main reasons. First, drug users may act violently because of the direct effects of the drug, or drug withdrawal. Second, violence is an element in some sectors of drug distribution as a means of enforcing the rules of business and deterring the police and other enforcement agencies.[9] And third, acquisitive crime committed by users and dealers may involve violence. There are no British data on the proportion of violent crimes in each of these categories and there is also some overlap. For instance, before committing a violent crime a drug user or dealer might take amphetamine or alcohol to bolster his or her courage.

Violence resulting from the drug's direct effects

Although alcohol and the stimulants cocaine and amphetamine have been particularly associated with violence in Western societies, no drug consistently produces a violent response among those who use it. Some people, for instance, become aggressive when drunk while others become sleepy. If a drug user becomes violent while taking a drug, it is the culmination of many factors, including: cultural expectations of the drug experience; the perpetrator's personality and their state of mind prior to the effects of the drug; opportunity; what is to be gained by violence; provocation by the victim; frustrating circumstances; and sometimes the presence of mental disorder in the user. Violence may result from a range of drug effects: the sought-after effects of intoxication that encourage violence; non-sought after effects of intoxication; withdrawal symptoms when the central nervous system has adapted to the presence of the drug; and personality changes associated with regular, prolonged use.

Less commonly, the effect of a drug may be intentionally sought by those wanting to fight or attack others. Drugs such as barbiturates help lower inhibitions and also dull pain, and were taken for those purposes by punks and skinheads during the 1970s and early 1980s. Teds and Mods used amphetamines similarly in the 1960s.[10]

Some interesting patterns emerge when the relationships between alcohol and violent crime are investigated. A study of Scottish prisoners, all of whom were heavy drinkers, found that in the week preceding their crimes, those who had committed violent crimes had drunk more than usual and those committing non-violent crimes had drunk less than usual. There may be a number of explanations for this, including that the non-violent criminals cut down their drinking to prepare for their 'job'. It is not known why the violent criminals were drinking more heavily, but the crimes could not be put down simply to intoxication, as they had not drunk much more than the non-violent criminals just before or during the offence. The research does, however, support a strong association between heavy drinking and both violent and non-violent crime. This is confirmed by numerous police reports, which show alcohol to be a factor in many cases of disorder and assault, most of which occur at weekends around closing time near licensed premises.

A person's drug and alcohol intake may also contribute to the likelihood of their falling victim to violence. Studies of murder victims have consistently shown that a large proportion have recently used drugs and/or alcohol, particularly in America. In one study of homicides in Los Angeles, 20% of murder victims were intoxicated with cocaine at the time of the killing, and half had also drunk alcohol. Anecdotal accounts of drugs used to intoxicate and disorientate victims, such as the benzodiazepine flunitrazepam (Rohypnol) in rape cases, are common.

The prevalence of suicide among regular drug users and heavy drinkers is far higher than in the general population, regardless of their socio-economic status, but so is pre-existing mental illness, which is another risk factor for taking one's life. Associations between alcohol and cannabis use and violent death (mainly accidents, suicide and homicide), may be a product of general high-risk behaviour rather than a result of the drugs themselves, although the clouded judgement of intoxication undoubtedly increases these risks.

Violence among dealers and users

Because the drugs market operates outside the law, agreements between different parties need somehow to be enforceable. If a contract is broken, one drug dealer cannot sue another in the courts, and violence is used both as a deterrent and a punishment for broken promises. Moreover, because dealers are not working within the law, they are able to act more ruthlessly than is normal in legitimate business.[11] The murder rate in the USA rises and falls with the markets for illegal goods, whether alcohol in the late-1920s and 1930s or heroin and cocaine in the late-1960s or early-1970s.

Disputes that erupt into violence may involve arguments over territory between rival drug dealers, assaults and murders of members of dealing gangs who step out of line, punishment for failing to pay debts, and punishment of informers. The greater the competition between dealers, the more likely that violence will be the norm. It has been argued that the levels of violence associated with the heroin trade are directly proportional to the drug's availability. Shortages create frustration, where fraud and theft by and from dealers can be an important cause of violence.[12] Perversely, this can result from a successful police crack-down in a drug-dealing area. Violence associated with drug distribution and use has been the subject of great concern in the USA, and there are many more American studies than British ones. Compared with Britain, guns are much more widely available, and crack dealing, notorious for its violent culture, is also more widespread.

The immediate effects of crack cocaine on the brain and its addictive qualities have been blamed for much of the violence seen in American inner cities, but the relationship between the drug and the behaviour with which it is associated is complex. Neighbourhood overcrowding in itself is known to strain relationships and lead to violence, particularly where many of the inhabitants are poor and have few prospects, and these problems were already worsening prior to crack cocaine's appearance in the mid-1980s. Crack offered the prospect of instant fortunes to dealers, many of whom were very young and immature, and from different and rival ethnic minority groups between whom tension already existed. As it is a drug that tends to be con-sumed in large amounts at a single sitting, the employment of user dealers can leave little to sell, so non-user dealers dominated the market and were more likely to be motivated only by profit. All these factors together, along with the high stakes involved, in contrast to less profitable drugs such as cannabis, created the now familiar violence-ridden 'crack neighbourhoods' of America.[13]

Acquisitive violent crime

Where drug users and dealers take part in acquisitive crime, the aim is often to obtain money to pay for drugs. In many cases, robbery with threatened or actual violence is the means used to obtain money or property. Violence is not always premeditated or deliberate, but may result from the victim's reaction to a theft or robbery, the perpetrator's own nervousness, or bystanders intervening. American research suggests that the most common victims of such crimes are those living in the same neighbourhood as the perpetrator, who may be involved in criminal activities themselves. However, it is thought that most crimes committed by drug users are not violent, being largely restricted to shoplifting, prostitution, and drug dealing, but much of what is known relies on their own accounts. Because violent crimes are more socially stigmatised than so-called 'victimless' crimes such as shoplifting and benefit fraud, their perpetrators may be less ready to admit to them.

A rise in violence associated with the British drugs trade has been attributed partly to the interaction between law enforcement agencies, such as the police and the courts, and drug distribution networks. Certain enforcement strategies pursued in the 1970s and '80s, involving the cultivation of police informants and the raising of legal penalties, have made the drugs trade more concerned to protect its security and more prepared to use violence to deter informants and enforcement agents. Such a working environment has then attracted high risk takers, perpetuating its brutal reputation, in turn prompting calls for heavier law enforcement, in an upward spiral of violence.[14] The law enforcement strategy, rather than simply the level of police activity, is therefore crucial to how criminals organise themselves.

PHYSICAL HEALTH EFFECTS FOR THE USER

As well as presenting risks to other people, drug users can suffer physical health problems as a result of their drug use. Aside from crime, the health risks from drugs, and particularly fatalities, concern the public most. Specific hazards have been discussed in detail in Chapter 1.

As with alcohol and tobacco, occasional use of cannabis is unlikely to present a significant danger. The more often a drug is used, the greater the likelihood of harm resulting, whether in terms of developing dependence, cumulative damage to health, or just from greater exposure to the risks. Overdose is likely to be a particular risk for inexperienced users.

Despite the fact that most young people who try drugs remain relatively unscathed by their experiences, a minority experience severe health problems, and a number of deaths occur each year. The question of how many people die from drug use can only be estimated because accurate figures for the UK are not available (see Table 1.1, Chapter 1). Figures are collected separately on deaths from VSA; 1 in 50 of all deaths of young people aged 15–19 was due to sniffing volatile substances in 1997 – a total of 73 deaths. Total drug deaths are, however, far fewer than for either tobacco or alcohol. Tobacco tends to cause death from lung cancer and heart disease in middle or old age, and alcohol is implicated in deaths at both ends of the age range, with young people involved in car crashes and other accidents, and older people also dying from cirrhosis and circulatory diseases. Those dying from the results of drug use are usually young.

MENTAL HEALTH EFFECTS

Psychological problems can make a person more vulnerable to problem drug use, but drugs may also cause such difficulties, or worsen existing conditions. Depression and anxiety states can set in when the euphoriant or relaxing effects of drugs have worn off, and psychotic reactions can also occur. The possible links between individual drugs and prolonged psychotic illness is discussed in Chapter 1. What is not in dispute is that heavy drug users in both the adolescent and adult population show high rates of associated mental disorders, especially conduct disorders, but also mood disorders, anxiety states and personality disorders.

It is often extremely difficult to determine the reason why mental health problems and drug misuse so frequently occur together – and especially whether the drug usage has led to the psychiatric disorder or the other way round – but where there is a prolonged serious mental disorder, it is more likely that it preceded the drug use. One study which followed young people aged between 6 and 17 over a four-year period found that those who already had conduct disorder or bipolar disorder (manic depression) were more likely to develop problem drug use during adolescence.[15]

ACCIDENTS

With the exception of mild stimulants such as nicotine and caffeine, all psychoactive substances can impair a whole range of skills needed for driving, operating machinery or tools, crossing roads, and so on. Judgement, coordination, reaction time and the sense of time passing can be affected by stimulants, central nervous system depressants and hallucinogens. Drug users are therefore likely to be at particular risk of accidental injury and even death and there is particular concern that they may be putting others at risk. Clear rules are in place regarding the use of alcohol by those responsible for public safety, such as train drivers and airline pilots, based on the widespread use of accurate testing methods, and there is a large body of evidence showing at what blood or breath levels alcohol adversely affects performance. Such information is not available for drugs.

The effects of several drugs together, often accompanied by alcohol, are more unpredictable, and depend on the dose of each drug, previous experience and the state of mind of the user at that time. In a population of long-term cannabis users in New South Wales, accidental injuries were more common than in the general population. This might have been a result of their cannabis use, but because some of the users also drank alcohol in a potentially hazardous way, it is impossible to attribute the accident rate to cannabis alone. Laboratory evidence suggests alcohol and cannabis together have an 'additive' effect (equal to the sum of its parts) on coordination.[16] Because of its slow elimination from the body, cannabis affects performance for more than 24 hours after use, but this may vary depending on the dose taken.

Accidents are also associated with a range of other drugs including injected temazepam and opiates, probably due to their sedating effects, and LSD. Inhaling highly flammable vapours, for instance, of butane cigarette lighter fluid, particularly in an enclosed space, carries the added risk of causing a fire.

ROAD TRAFFIC ACCIDENTS

Over 300 000 people are killed or injured every year in road accidents in Britain, and it is thought that drug use plays a part in a significant number of these. A recent survey by the Department of Environment, Transport and the Regions, found that of 619 road-user fatalities (drivers, pedal and motor cyclists, passengers and pedestrians), 16% tested positive for drugs, half of which were cannabis. However, cannabis remains detectable up to 30 days after its use, long after any significant effects on driving are likely. The level at which cannabis and the chemicals into which it is broken down in the body is associated with raised accident levels is currently unknown and for those who tested positive for cannabis, it is impossible to tell whether or not it was a factor contributing to their accidents. Although it is an offence under the 1988 Road Traffic Offenders Act to drive a motor vehicle when unfit through drugs, developing controls to address this problem is difficult. From the same sample of road fatalities, 23% were found to be over the legal limit for alcohol.

In an American study of reckless drivers stopped and tested by the police for speeding, driving on the wrong side of the road, driving through red lights, and other offences, both urine and behavioural tests were used. Over half of those who were not drunk were found to be intoxicated with drugs. Interestingly, two of the drivers who tested positive for cocaine performed normally on the behaviour test, despite being stopped for driving directly into oncoming traffic.

Diseases spread through shared injecting equipment are medical problems, but they also have an impact beyond those infected, in costs to the health service and the loss of skills and labour from the economy, as well as in human distress. AIDS and hepatitis B and C can debilitate people over a long period, so that long-term care from relatives or friends might also be needed, removing further skills from the economy.

Although there is still no cure for HIV/AIDS, the prognosis for people who are HIV-positive is now brighter, at least in wealthy countries like the UK, than a decade ago, as new drugs have been developed that help to control the virus. However, their cost is very high and the good personal organisation needed to keep to their complex prescribing regimes may be impossible for chaotic drug users, like Kerry, Dan's girlfriend. HIV is generally rarer in the UK among injecting drug users than hepatitis B and C.

Only a small proportion of those infected with hepatitis B will become carriers, and of these only a minority will develop chronic active hepatitis or liver cancer. Hepatitis C, which has only recently been identified as a major public health problem, can be transmitted through contact with much smaller quantities of blood than with HIV. The outlook is uncertain for those infected; most will only experience a mild initial illness, but may develop cirrhosis of the liver and liver cancer 20–30 years later – the exact proportion who will experience these consequences being still uncertain.

Treatments for hepatitis B and C are costly and effective only in a minority of cases. An effective vaccine which protects against hepatitis B exists, and is used around the world, but many injecting drug users and their sexual partners have not been immunised, and about 22% are infected, although this varies by age, gender and region. Like HIV, there is at present no vaccine for hepatitis C.

Hepatitis C, of which there is still little public awareness, may have particularly worrying implications for the future: the virus is much more easily transmitted than HIV, and the majority of injectors tested are positive for hepatitis C, not only in Britain but worldwide. The prevalence of hepatitis C among injectors varies across different groups studied – for instance, in Glagow it was found to be 77%, in London 85% and in East Anglia 59%. This may well mean that large numbers of injecting drug users will eventually place a heavy burden on health and social services later in life.

HIV and hepatitis B can be transmitted sexually, also infecting non-injectors. The intoxicating effects of drugs can assist the transmission of viruses during sex in terms of loosening inhibitions, so that people are less wary about having unprotected sex.[17]

Positive effects of drug use

Although drug use may be a source of widespread harm, it can also play a positive role which partly explains its popularity. Work on the social role of alcohol shows how different styles of drinking and settings help individuals to bond in groups and define them apart from others. The choice of whether to use drugs or not, which ones to use, and by what method, can also play a part in the development of personal identity and self-expression. These choices may serve to include or exclude the person from a particular group or activity, just as fashion, music and other patterns of consumption do. Perhaps as people's identities are defined less and less by fixed characteristics such as family origins, gender and class, individual lifestyle choices, including those associated with drug use, become increasingly important.

Alcohol and food can act both as a form of payment for favours and as a shared social activity,[18] and, in some groups, drugs may play a similar role. More controversially, the search for drugs and the money to pay for them as an activity in itself have also been described in positive terms, bringing users into meaningful contact with others, and providing a 'career' that is exciting and rewarding, while demanding considerable skills for survival, in the absence of legitimate alternatives. The life of the drug dealer has been similarly portrayed, for instance in the USA, where the cocaine and crack economy and subculture provides standards of behaviour, values and money for inner-city youths who have few other options.

Conclusion

A polydrug user's lifestyle, like Dan's, has effects which extend, like the ripples in a pond, from himself to his family and those he steals from or sells drugs to. Closer to home, performance in a range of activities can be affected by drug use, both when users are intoxicated and afterwards, affecting themselves and others. Like alcohol, some types of heavy drug use can affect the quality of work people carry out, or result in absenteeism, causing problems for employers who pay sick leave to their staff. Some drugs increase the likelihood of having an accident, but until the safe and unsafe levels of drugs are known and can be conveniently tested for, it will not be possible to tell what proportion of traffic or other accidents can be attributed to intoxication.

The health risks that arise from drug use span a similarly wide spectrum. Occasional use of a drug may have no noticeable impact, while heavy use is often severely damaging. Over the course of 20 or 30 years, most heroin addicts either enter methadone maintenance programmes, become abstinent, or die. Individual vulnerability is important too: the same amount of cannabis which harms one person no more than a packet of cigarettes may cause the condition of someone with schizophrenia to worsen dramatically. Another quite different set of risks to health arises from sharing drug injecting equipment. Chronic blood borne diseases, such as HIV and hepatitis B and C, have potentially huge consequences not only for those infected, but also for their family and friends and for health services.

Like Jessica, most drug users are not involved in breaking the law, other than the Misuse of Drugs Act; but others, like Dan and Kerry, who become dependent on expensive drugs such as heroin and cocaine often commit crimes to meet these costs. Even then, their criminal activities may predate, or even facilitate, their initial use of expensive drugs. In other words, they may be criminals who have started using drugs rather than drug users who have turned to crime.

The links between violence and drug use are a major cause for concern. Increased competition between dealers can have dangerous results and police strategies need to take into account the risk of escalating violence when seeking to suppress drug markets. Although no drug consistently causes a violent reaction, aggression may be more predictable with stimulants such as cocaine and amphetamine which can cause psychotic episodes. The user's expectations of a drug's effects also play a significant part.

The assumption that without drugs the most severely problematic users would be gainfully and legitimately employed, perhaps helping to support healthy families, is probably mistaken. Many of the apparent consequences of problem drug use are part of a wider picture of social deprivation, family difficulties, genetic susceptibility and poor economic prospects. These factors tend to interact, and addressing one, such as problem drug use, will only provide a partial solution.

Chapter 6. The international drugs trade

SUMMARY

Political and technological developments in the last 20 years have unintentionally facilitated drug smuggling, and along the route from factory or farm, bribes and intimidation are frequently used to smooth the path. This lucrative trade has been used to finance wars and to support or undermine governments, although it has also averted complete economic collapse in certain Latin–American countries. Social and economic upheaval, at its most extreme in war, feed both the supply and demand for drugs. Changes in travel and transport in the last 30 years have eased the process of smuggling drugs between countries, and the globalisation of banking systems and other technologies has facilitated the laundering of proceeds from the drugs trade, helping criminals dissociate themselves from their involvement. The massive profits from the drugs trade passing into criminal hands and the consequences of this probably represent the strongest arguments in favour of widescale legalisation.

INTRODUCTION

When buying drugs such as heroin and cocaine, Dan (see Chapters 4 and 5) is at the end of a long line of supply that originates in the countries where opium and coca leaves are grown, are then processed into refined drugs, and smuggled across the world to the consumer. Although the cost of growing and processing these drugs is small, the risks involved in transporting them to the user undetected raise the price at every stage of their journey (see Table 6.1), costs that may include bribing politicians, police and customs officials to smooth their path. Synthetic drugs consumed in the UK, such as amphetamines, LSD and ecstasy, are often manufactured here or in mainland Europe.

Britain's involvement in drug trafficking is not new. In the 19th century, British merchants, with their government's support, defied the Chinese emperor's edicts against opium smuggling into his country. This trade, which yielded significant revenues to the British Government, was helping to undermine Chinese attempts to stop its population smoking opium and played a part in starting two rather ignoble 'Opium Wars' fought between 1839 and 1860.

Successful drug trafficking is hugely lucrative, and the world drugs trade has repercussions across many areas of life. The inhabitants of any area through which drugs are being transported frequently start consuming the drugs themselves. This 'spillage' is not inevitable but has been observed in many countries, including parts of Latin America. The simple proximity of drugs may, in itself, not be enough, but if social and economic conditions change so that a demand develops, the ready availability of drugs along the trafficking route will allow a problem to develop rapidly.

Money gained from the drugs trade may remain part of an underground economy, being used to buy other illegal commodities such as weapons and stolen vehicles, or to finance terrorist activities, or it may be 'laundered' and invested or spent in the legitimate economy across the globe.

In countries that produce drug crops, such as Bolivia and Colombia, most of the profits are retained by those at senior levels of the drug organisations and those colluding with the trade, with little redistribution of this wealth. There are, however, some exceptions, such as Pablo Escobar Gavira, leader of Colombia's notorious Medellin cartel, responsible for the production and

Table 6.1.   Prices from farm gate to retail market. Adapted from: United Nations International Drug Control Programme (1997) *World Drug Report*. Oxford: Oxford University Press.

Process	Price
Opium (farm gate Pakistan) (refined in laboratories near production sites)	$90/kg
⇩	
Impure morphine base, refined in more sophisticated laboratories into morphine and/or heroin	
⇩	
Wholesale export to country of consumption	
⇩	$2 870/kg
Wholesale in domestic market	$80 000/kg
⇩	
Retail sale 'on the street' ('purity' about 40%)	$290 000/kg

distribution of huge amounts of cocaine, who spent some of his revenues on building low-cost housing and a hospital for the poor. Indeed, his popularity led to his election to the Colombian Congress. Neither should it be overlooked that the drugs trade has helped cushion the effects of recent Latin–American economic crises by providing large-scale employment for hundreds of thousands of people.[1] Bolivia's tin-mining industry, source of the country's main export for over a century, contracted by 30% in the early 1980s, unemployment tripled to 20% and personal income, already low, declined to desperate levels. Coca production provided the employment and foreign exchange that averted total economic collapse, and 20 000 Bolivian miners who had lost their jobs found employment in the coca fields.[1] Parts of the former Soviet Union and the Balkans currently appear to be experiencing a similar process.[2]

The changes in the drugs economy that followed the corruption and final collapse of the Soviet regime exemplify many of the stages through which transitional societies pass to the benefit of the drugs trade. Organised crime existed throughout the lifetime of the USSR, but the effects of the immense economic changes that followed the collapse of the communist regime greatly favoured its expansion and increased influence. Large sectors of the population had become impoverished and the welfare system had collapsed. Crime offered employment and, in the absence of effective, legitimate law and order institutions, the use or threat of armed force abounded. Between 1991 and 1993, the murder rate rose by 40% and it is estimated that over one-third of the money currently circulating in Russia has been generated by illegal activity.

In this context, drug production and distribution became big business, with Russian-based criminal groups developing contacts in existing areas of drug cultivation and establishing the laboratory facilities to produce supplies for Western Europe. The number of dependent Russian drug users has also increased, fuelling the rise in acquisitive crime. Such users also provide labour as dealers at the bottom of the drug distribution pyramid.

Prior to the fall of the Soviet regime and the opening of its borders, there was considerable drug production for domestic consumption, mostly of hashish and crude, home-made, opium-based products. With new opportunities for export, Moscow-based criminal gangs intensified their commercial contacts in the less economically developed Kazakhstan and Tajikistan, the traditional drug producing areas where unemployment was high. These Russian criminals paid poorly for these products, while carrying out the refining and distribution themselves, and laundering the much greater proceeds.

As occurred in Latin America and other producer countries, those involved in the cultivation and sale of unrefined drugs slowly began to appreciate the enormous exchange value of the crops they were handling and saw that, by refining the crops themselves, they could keep part of this added value. Consequently, as with the effects of 'spillage', the availability of refined drugs in the producer region enabled their use to spread among young people, who slowly shifted away from traditional drugs such as opium to heroin (or in Latin America, from coca leaves to cocaine).[3] The demand for refined drugs at home, and the supply channels needed to meet consumption styles like those in Europe and North America in turn encouraged the emergence of similar criminal organisations.

It is clear that times of economic upheaval help black markets to flourish and demand for drugs may rise because of the stressful conditions and the interruption of drug treatment and prevention services. This is particularly the case during wars and revolutions where civilian populations are widely affected. The controls on people's behaviour that are part of 'normal' life may be weakened as families and friends are separated and daily routines changed beyond recognition. Wars can also spread drugs and different methods of use, as people move and new trade routes are established, taking with them new fashions and habits.[4] As Iran demonstrated after the Islamic Revolution, large numbers of people deprived of their livelihoods make willing drug dealers, which further stimulates the market for drugs.[2] The experience of Afghanistan shows how war and drug production can go together to produce major changes in the global drug market and, in turn, in patterns of use nearer home.

FROM WARFARE TO HEROIN ADDICTION: THE CASE OF AFGHANISTAN

Eighty per cent of Europe's heroin originates in Afghanistan and its surge in heroin production coincided with the civil war against the Soviet-backed Government in 1979. The Mujahedin's victory depended on backing from Western governments and arms bought with money from opium cultivation. Clearly, for the liberal democracies of the West, the 'War on Drugs' took second-place to the Cold War against the then Soviet Union.

The dominant Taliban militia (religious students of Islam) now controls two-thirds of the country and, although theoretically opposed to heroin, levies a 25% tax on its revenue. During two decades of continuing civil war, heroin production has become the mainstay of the Afghan economy and there is no imminent prospect of change. The USA has little influence in the region and is, compared to Europe, relatively unaffected by Afghan heroin. The Taliban are not recognised as the legal government by any Western country, nor by the United Nations. Nevertheless, the Taliban have promised to eradicate opium cultivation in exchange for UN aid. The UN therefore faces the dilemmas of whether to believe Taliban promises (which have previously been dishonoured) and whether to provide aid to a regime whose infringements of human rights include confining women to their homes. Moreover, an interruption in the supply of brown, smokeable heroin, so that only injectable white heroin from South-East Asia would be available, could lead heroin smokers to become injectors,[5] or those trying it for the first time to inject.

The rise in heroin addiction occurring in Britain and Western Europe during the late 1970s and early 1980s coincided with the emergence of the 'Golden Crescent' (parts of Pakistan, Afghanistan and Iran) as a major producer of heroin. The overall increase in heroin production and shorter transportation routes from the Golden Crescent than from the Golden Triangle (the border areas of Myanmar (formerly Burma), Laos and Thailand), made heroin widely available in Europe at low cost to the potential user. Unlike 'white' heroin from the Golden Triangle, 'brown' heroin from the Golden Crescent is easy to smoke. The combination of low street prices, an alternative to injecting heroin, and a myth that smoking heroin did not lead to addiction brought widespread use of the drug.

GLOBAL OPIUM TRENDS

The three main areas of the globe illicitly cultivating the opium poppy are Latin America, South-East Asia and South-West Asia (see Figure 6.1). Worldwide opium cultivation doubled between 1986 and 1989, but since 1990 it has remained relatively stable. The area under cultivation in 1998 is estimated at approximately 240 000 hectares yielding about 3800 tons of opium per year (see Figure 6.2).

The large North American market now obtains a substantial part of its heroin from poppy fields in Latin America rather than Asia (Figure 6.6). From within the Golden Crescent, Afghanistan has emerged as the major producer of heroin for Europe. Myanmar and Afghanistan together now produce 90% of the world's heroin.

Figure 6.1. Global illicit cultivation of opium poppy and production of opium, 1998 (breakdown by subregion). Source for Figures 6.1–6.4: United Nations Office for Drug Control and Crime Prevention (1999) *Global Illicit Drug Trends 1998*. New York: UNODCCP.

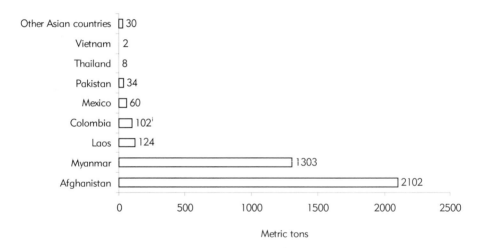

i According to the Ministry of Foreign Affairs of Colombia, production of opium amounted to 61 metric tons in 1998.

Figure 6.2. Global illicit production of opium, 1998.

Global coca trends

Illicit cultivation of coca, which was sharply rising in the 1970s and 80s, seems to have decreased since 1990/91, with most originating from Bolivia,

Colombia and Peru (see Figures 6.3 and 6.4). In these three countries, the total area estimated to be under cultivation was 180 000 hectares in 1998, a decline of 7% compared with 1995, although this varied between countries – Peru seems to be reducing its cultivation while Colombia's is increasing. Global coca production was estimated at almost 340 000 tonnes in 1998 (see Figure 6.4).

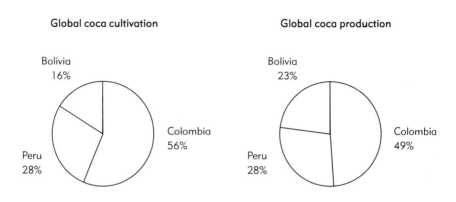

Figure 6.3.   Global illicit cultivation of coca bush and production of coca leaf, 1998 (breakdown by countries).

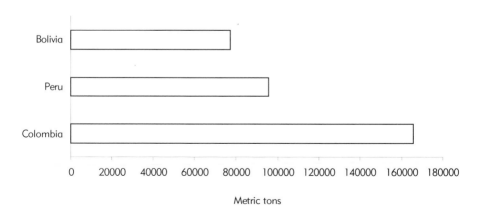

Figure 6.4.   Global illicit production of coca leaf, 1998.

Synthetic drugs

Without the environmental requirements of coca or opium, synthetic drugs can be produced close to their consumer markets, resulting in fewer chances to intercept them and, in consequence, fewer seizures and substantially lower transportation costs. Production costs are so low that it has been estimated that the profit from the retail sale of one ecstasy pill is between 2300% and 4600%. Europe is one of the world's major production regions of amphetamine and ecstasy, with illicit laboratories in most EU member states. Since 1997, Eastern Europe, particularly the Czech Republic, Poland, Bulgaria and the Baltic States, has also become a major supplier of amphetamine type drugs destined for northern European countries. There is also manufacture and trade flowing between Europe and Asia in these drugs, and local production in the Golden Triangle for the South-East Asian market.

Transport and distribution

Britain's drugs trade has seen major changes in the last two decades, with suppliers forming more tightly structured groups and the involvement of other 'career criminals', particularly former armed robbers, in drug wholesaling. Their attraction to the drugs trade has been attributed to a number of causes: increased sentences for armed robbery, greater use of firearms by the police, and the lack of a 'victim' reporting to the police. It has also been suggested that these professional criminals were brought into contact with drug distributors through the criminal justice system and learnt in prison of the big profits to be made at a lower risk than their usual activities. The 1980s saw a generally more ruthless approach emerging in the drugs trade across the world, with the involvement of more individuals motivated by profit, greater use of violence and guns, and fewer 'ideological' traffickers and dealers who had become involved through principled opposition to the drug laws.

More recent developments have greatly increased the ease with which drugs can be transported and distributed. A new influx of low-cost heroin has been apparent in Britain since the mid-1990s, most of which is believed to be moved through the Balkans to western Europe. The break-up of the Soviet Union,[6] wars in the Balkans, and the relaxation of some of the restrictions on movement within the EU have all made smuggling easier. The huge increase in world trade since the 1980s, and containerisation in particular, has allowed easy transfer of goods from ship to rail and road, assisting the trafficking of drugs as well as legitimate cargo businesses.[7] The parallel growth in international tourism and large scale migration from the Middle East, South-East Asia and the Caribbean to Western Europe and America have also created greater opportunities for smuggling drugs across frontiers. In the UK visits abroad have more than doubled between 1981 and 1997 (see Figure 6.7).

Because communications across the world and particularly Europe are so much more fluid, heroin distributors and manufacturers can respond quickly to demand.[7] Telecommunications can help organised crime syndicates avoid detection or prosecution as they can direct their business without having to be present in person, from a location of greater safety. Proliferating technologies such as mobile phones also make local distribution on the ground more efficient, with a dealer being able to respond immediately and deliver drugs where and when they are required.

THE STRUCTURE OF UK DRUG DISTRIBUTION

Despite these technological changes, the environment in which traffickers and distributors operate remains a hazardous one and research shows how drug distribution in the UK has been structured to take this into account. These organisations face three main sources of risk: betrayal by colleagues; being 'ripped off' by other organisations; and unknowingly dealing with undercover law enforcement agents. Some traffickers seem to enjoy the risks involved in their trade, or lack the resources to minimise the dangers, but others go to great lengths to protect themselves. If a courier, for instance, is caught by Customs carrying a drug consignment, it will be important to his or her colleagues that he or she cannot provide evidence against them. This requires tasks to be separated between individuals and all information to be strictly controlled. This can involve the employment of trusted middle men who act as 'buffers' between the 'Mr Big' who has raised the finance and planned operations and those with 'hands on' contact with the drugs. Such arrangements also help protect organisation chiefs from contact with unknown individuals who could be undercover agents.[8]

MONEY LAUNDERING

Money laundering has been defined as "the process by which one conceals the existence, illegal source, or illegal application of income and then disguises or converts that income to make it appear legitimate".[9] The cash involved in drugs transactions, particularly higher up the distribution network, is likely to need laundering if there are laws governing the provenance of capital in that country.

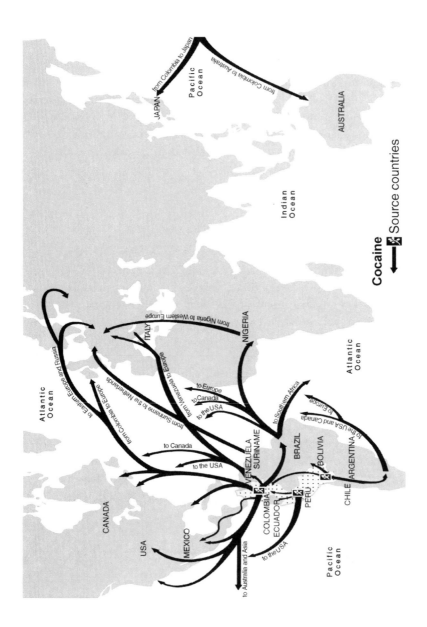

Figure 6.5. International cocaine trafficking flows. Figures 6.5 and 6.6 adapted from: Office of National Drug Control Policy (1999) *National Drug Control Strategy.* Washington DC: ONDCP.

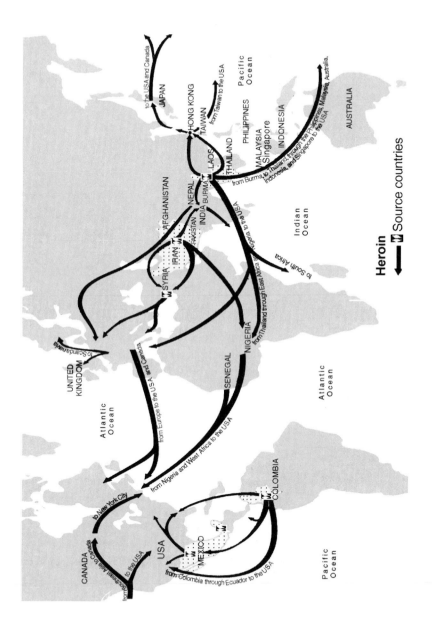

Heroin
➤ 🌱 Source countries

Figure 6.6. International heroin trafficking flows.

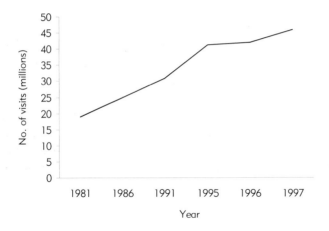

Figure 6.7. Number of visits abroad by UK residents in millions. Source: Office for National Statistics (1999) Personal communication.

In the last 30 years, the trade in drugs has become a multi-billion pound industry and, in 1997, the United Nations Drug Control Programme estimated that its turnover represented about 8% of total international trade, a staggering sum for a single industry. The vast profits that accrue from this go to a wide variety of people across the world and are used for many different purposes, but it is estimated that at least $120 billion (£73 billion) is laundered through the international banking system every year.

Large quantities of cash are also inconvenient, being at risk from theft or loss, and are very bulky: $200 000 in $10 bills weighs 18 kg and £1 million in £5 notes weighs 182 kg. Currency restrictions can also hamper traffickers wishing to take cash across borders. There are many methods of money laundering, including investing capital in businesses where disguising its origins takes priority over profitability, producing an unrealistic picture of an economy's health. Alternatively, illicit capital can cushion the blow of economic hardship as investments are made in companies on the verge of bankruptcy, which in a time of crisis are willing to accept less respectable sources of credit. The monetary policies and budgetary forecasts of governments that aim to control the money supply can therefore be undermined by the influx or loss of large amounts of unaccounted for illicit capital. Large scale investment in businesses can also enable these companies to undercut legitimate businesses who have to borrow to finance their activities.

Trends in money laundering

The increasing integration of the world's economy and financial markets has made it easier for money launderers to move funds around from one 'offshore' bank to another and exploit the variations in countries' regulatory control systems (or lack of them). The future of cashless technology will also have an impact on money laundering. While credit and debit cards have removed the anonymity of cash, making life harder for money launderers, if cards were introduced that could be charged up using cash and both debited and credited, tracing the movement of money would become even more difficult.

CORRUPTION

In 1993, at an international conference Senator Gomez Hurtado, Colombian Ambassador to France and high court judge, said:

> "Forget about drug deaths and acquisitive crime, about addiction and AIDS; all this pales into insignificance before the prospect facing the liberal democracies of the West, like a rabbit in the headlights of an oncoming car. The income of the drug barons is an annual $254 thousand million, greater than the American defence budget. With this financial power they can suborn all the institutions of the State and, if the State resists, with this fortune they can purchase the firepower to outgun it. We are threatened with a return to the Dark Ages of rule by the gang".[10]

The Western liberal democracies may not yet have reached a stage of being held to ransom by drug barons, but in view of their potential financial muscle, the problem of corruption, and its extent, needs to be considered very carefully.

Politicians and public servants such as the police, judiciary and local government officials are open to many influences, and if they are persuaded, even intermittently, to abandon expected standards of conduct for the sake of unsanctioned personal advantage, this could be defined as corruption. It may be achieved by intimidation (such as blackmail) or by incentive in the form of a bribe. In practice, it is sometimes hard to draw the line between authorised and unauthorised benefits, as what is acceptable varies between cultures and generations. What may be seen as a bribe in one country may be legitimate practice in another. In countries where there is rapid political development and social change, these boundaries can be particularly hard to distinguish.

Some governments in Latin America and their armed forces are known to have been heavily influenced by drug interests. In 1980, the leaders of Bolivia's armed forces were involved in the cocaine trade and their *coup d'état* was supported by major drug traffickers.[11] Despite the advent of democratic government in 1982, corruption was reportedly still widespread in 1988. It has been suggested that the same reasons lie behind persisting corruption in the Andean countries. The cocaine industry provides one of the few major sources of wealth; poverty is widespread; economic opportunities are limited; and the salaries of public servants are often barely above subsistence level.[12]

In other countries where corruption is less overt, it is hard to measure the extent to which the state has been subverted by fear of, or bribery by, drug barons. There are, however, circumstances which make this more likely. Countries where there is a diversity of values and traditions between regions regarding what is considered socially acceptable (or perhaps excusable) are particularly vulnerable to corruption. Where business arrangements cannot be enforced by legitimate means (either because the legal framework is inadequate or through under-resourced enforcement), criminals may step in and settle things to their own advantage outside the law.[13] In some cultures, what Westerners would consider corrupt, with decisions being made on the basis of favours and allegiances, is merely part of the normal way things are run.

One of the most convincing arguments in favour of the legalisation of drugs is its potential for lessening the powers of criminals to corrupt governments and public servants. However, as in the USA at the repeal of Prohibition, the growers, manufacturers and large-scale traffickers might legitimise their businesses and form strong commercial lobby groups to promote their wares, or turn to other forms of crime to replace their lost trade. Tackling the problem from a different angle, there is also a range of ways to reduce corruption in government bureaucracies: the greater use of outside inspectors, such as auditors, to increase the chances of detection; removing discretion from bureaucrats; making government activities more visible and open to public scrutiny; and employing individuals with high standards of honesty and/or who subscribe to professional codes of conduct.[14] Laws governing the connections between business and politics which are persistently and evenly enforced, and which reflect existing codes of behaviour, may also help to prevent corrupt practices.

While the drugs trade has the potential to corrupt those who could stand in its way, regimes that are already corrupt often become involved in drug production and trafficking. Governments whose power relies on business favours, although not necessarily considered corrupt within their own culture, may tolerate or even encourage drug producers and traders. Western democracies may even hold such regimes in place, as in the case of General Manuel Noriega, the "strong man" of Panama from 1983–89. Noriega was involved in drug trafficking, prostitution, gambling rackets and arms smuggling in the full knowledge of the Central Intelligence Agency and the US Defense Department, to whom he was providing intelligence. His usefulness in this regard, and his role in keeping his democratic left-wing opponents out of power, apparently outweighed these offences until they became too public an embarrassment and, in a dramatic US military invasion of Panama, he was arrested on charges of drug trafficking, money laundering and racketeering.

Conclusion

Across the world, the drugs trade shows no sign of diminishing, and many of the economic and technological changes of the last 20 years have aided criminals' ability to evade conviction. However, technological advances should also have the potential to assist in the collection of evidence. As with many legitimate forms of trade, the spread of technology has altered the sequence from cultivation to manufacture to consumption. Developing countries previously saw their crops exported for refining into more valuable commodities, but seizing the opportunity to set up laboratories of their own enabled them to retain more of the proceeds. Unfortunately, the farmers growing the crops still see little of this profit as it is retained by those higher up the producing organisation. Greater potential for producers to profit seems to lie in synthetic drugs, of which the EU is one of the world's largest producers. The relatively simple equipment required to manufacture large quantities of ecstasy, amphetamines and LSD close to where they are retailed results in lower prices for the consumer and fewer seizures by enforcement authorities.

Like legitimate businesses, the drugs economy is constantly changing in response to altered circumstances. Drug fashions fluctuate as demand for new or old substances varies, and demands can be stimulated by lower prices or novel products. Different approaches to enforcement, such as undercover operations, stimulate traffickers and dealers to shape their organisations to protect themselves and deter the efforts of the authorities. Changes in government in producer or transit countries may require different sources or routes to be found, but so far the drugs trade has proved itself remarkably successful in surviving to meet an ever-growing demand.

Chapter 7. Policies for prevention and control

SUMMARY

Prevention refers to those diverse activities, ranging from regulation to education, that are aimed at controlling the supply of drugs and reducing the demand for them. Borrowed from economics, the concept of supply and demand appears to make a sharp distinction between those two aspects of the drug problem, but they are in fact closely intertwined. Supply – the availability of drugs – can drive demand; laws directed at controlling supply affect demand because most people tend to obey reasonable laws. Policy-makers recognise that various subgroups within a society will respond differently to drug control and prevention efforts depending on their exposure to and experience with various drugs, and also that they experience the benefits and burdens of various policy options differently.

Demand reduction programmes are categorised in terms of the techniques used (education, mass media, mandatory drug testing, and so on); the target populations (young people, experimenters or the general population); and where they are based (in schools, in the community or in the workplace). They differ widely in cost and presumably in efficacy. Although each type of programme has its advocates and believers only limited data exist to permit rational prioritization and allocation of resources.

The notion that drugs must be either legal or illegal is simply inaccurate. Societies have a surprisingly wide range of control and regulatory options ranging from total and absolute prohibition (the substance is not available even for medical use), to acceptance with no constraints (substances with psychoactive properties available even to young people, such as caffeine in cola drinks, tea, and coffee). Often, a substance that is readily available to adults is prohibited to young people, as is the case for both alcohol and tobacco. No matter what the drug, regulatory policy represents a balancing of competing values. Any policy will have its supporters, beneficiaries, critics, and sometimes its victims; policy revision rarely occurs rapidly or without controversy. When contemplating change, three generally valid principles should be considered:

1   Drugs that give pleasure will be used by some people if they can afford them; if they are prohibited an illicit market will emerge.

2   Greater availability of drugs will lead to more use, and, except where the drugs are relatively innocuous, more health problems will occur.

3   It is almost impossible to keep drugs that are available to adults out of the hands of children and adolescents.

INTRODUCTION

The history of how certain psychoactive drugs, such as cocaine, amphetamines, opiates and cannabis, out of the thousands of natural and synthetic
substances known to mankind, have been singled out for special regulation
has been recounted in Chapters 2 and 3. This chapter considers the various
ways a society tries to prevent the problems that can arise as a result of the
use of this relatively small group of substances.

Society is also faced with the task of deciding where to make its investments
in prevention – which drugs, among which sections of the population, and at
which levels of involvement in that drug use. Decisions-makers will partly
rely on evidence of what action is effective but society must also make
political choices about where the greater importance lies. These priorities
change as scientific study and public opinion contribute to the debate about
different drugs, such as alcohol, heroin, ecstasy or tobacco, and the significance of the consequences of their use, such as HIV/AIDS, or violence
and crime.

PREVENTING DRUG PROBLEMS

It is self-evident that it is better to prevent damage than to try to repair it
once it has occurred. This is as true for drug problems as for all other ills. As
applied to drug problems, the concept of prevention refers to numerous,
often diverse, activities that range from regulation to education. Prevention
activities are based in varying degrees on five major findings that have
emerged from research over the past 30 years:

- the importance of availability and access to drugs;

- the role of the drug user's, or potential user's, perception of social context
  (support or opposition to use);

- beliefs about the risks associated with use;

- the observation that the factors influencing initial use are not identical to
  those influencing continued use and dependence; and

- the observation that, of those who use drugs, some are clearly more
  vulnerable than others to becoming dependent on them. (Current
  understanding of the basis for this vulnerability is discussed in Chapter 4.)

The goals of policy: controlling access, reducing demand and minimising harm

A society's preventive efforts can be directed at the entire population, as with laws and mass media campaigns that apply to all its citizens. However, it is more likely that prevention programmes will be targeted at specific groups, such as young people, believed to be at higher risk, and will typically focus on particular drugs, such as tobacco, alcohol or heroin, or on particular behaviours, such as needle sharing and drug use during pregnancy. Even laws dealing with drug possession or sale may be more or less targeted, for example by specifying more severe penalties for selling to young people than to adults.

Preventive activity aims to prevent:

- the initial use of a drug – primary prevention;

- the adverse effects of occasional use – secondary prevention;

- current use from progressing to heavy use and dependence – secondary prevention; and

- those who have become dependent from doing harm to themselves and others – tertiary prevention.

More recently, these distinctions have been supplemented by the following categories:

- *universal*: delivered in a non-focused manner to the general population;

- *selective*: targeted at sections of the population who are presumed to be 'at risk', with the aim of reducing risk factors and enhancing protective factors; and

- *indicated*: preventive interventions that are targeted at individuals who are already involved in drug use but who are not yet experiencing major medical problems, e.g. preventing the progression to dependence or the development of associated problems such as overdose or HIV infection.

Although the distinction is not quite as clear as it might seem at first, preventive efforts may be divided into two broad categories with terms borrowed from the world of economics: those aimed at eliminating or controlling the supply of drugs, and those aimed at reducing the demand for them. Measures on both sides of the supply/demand equation are diverse, and the diversity continually raises the issue of how a society should allocate its resources to achieve the best balance.

In the UK, expenditure on tackling the drug problem is spread across a range of different areas, which makes it very difficult to calculate the financial burden. However, in preparing its new drugs strategy and following the appointment of the first ever UK Anti-Drugs Coordinator (popularly known as the 'Drug Czar'), the UK Government published data on the amounts spent in different areas in tackling the drug problem – these are shown in the pie chart in Figure 7.1. As can be seen, out of a total annual expenditure of £1.4 billion devoted to tackling drug misuse in the UK, law enforcement and customs/interdiction efforts accounted for 75% of expenditure, with education and prevention comprising 12%, and treatment and rehabilitation 13%. By comparison, Figure 7.2 shows the USA's proportionate expenditure. Total law enforcement, interdiction and crime intervention adds up to a smaller 69% of the budget, prevention is the same as in the UK, but treatment receives half as much again with 19%. This is federal expenditure. It does not include substantial State expenditure on their own prisons or State and private expenditure on health care. One of the important decisions that politicians must make on behalf of the society they represent is the optimal distribution of this expenditure for maximum benefit for the years ahead.

It can be argued that laws and regulations aimed at controlling access to drugs and at raising their price serve the goals of both primary and secondary

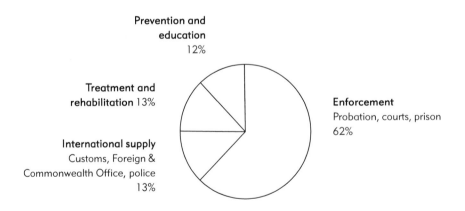

Figure 7.1. Estimated total expenditure on drug misuse in the UK 1997–98.
Adapted from: *Comprehensive Spending Review*, UK Government, quoted in *Tackling Drugs to Build a Better Britain – The Government's 10-Year Strategy for Tackling Drug Misuse – Guidance Notes*, April 1998.

prevention. But it has also been pointed out that this gain may be at a price: by raising the price of drugs and driving supply into illicit channels, efforts at controlling drug supplies may increase the complications of any drug use that nevertheless persists. Despite these possibilities, it must be recognized that, in both theory and practice, laws and law enforcement have effects on demand as well as supply. For a variety of reasons, most people tend to obey the law.

The impact of laws dealing with what are currently illicit substances therefore goes considerably beyond merely reducing their availability or raising their price. To some indeterminable degree, laws against drug use serve to reduce both consumption and demand. Certainly, even at the highest points in epidemics of drug use, the levels of consumption were far below those of the currently legal, albeit regulated, alcohol and tobacco products. And there is evidence of enormous variability in this behaviour. The most detailed data on the general public's drug-taking behaviour is from the USA, where we can look at changing trends in use of any drug over the last month in different age groups of American citizens. Whatever the factors that have caused the changes, the reduced levels of 'last month' drug use shown in Figure 7.3 are a telling demonstration of the extent to which this behaviour changes over time, and this is one of the reasons why there is particular worth in identifying the factors which contribute to such startling changes.

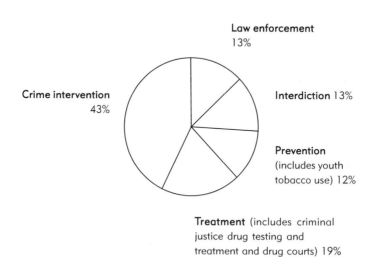

Law enforcement
13%

Crime intervention
43%

Interdiction 13%

Prevention
(includes youth
tobacco use) 12%

Treatment (includes criminal
justice drug testing and
treatment and drug courts) 19%

Figure 7.2.   Expenditure on drug misuse in the USA, 1999. Adapted from Office of National Drug Control Policy (1999) *National Drug Control Strategy*. Washington, DC: ONDCP.

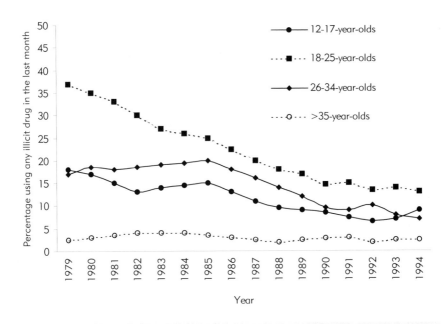

Figure 7.3.   Trends in monthly prevalence of any drug use by age in the USA. Adapted from: Substance Abuse and Mental Health Services Administration (SAMHSA) (1995) *National Household Survey on Drug Abuse: Population Estimates 1994*. Rockville, MD: SAMHSA.

Different types of target population

People differ, and not all people will respond to drug control strategies and prevention efforts in the same way. The impact of increased public disapproval of a behaviour may dissuade uninvolved individuals from engaging in the behaviour, but at the same time driving some of those already involved in that behaviour to more desperate methods to continue their practice while concealing it from public gaze. Six different types of target population can be identified, and it may be useful in debate to consider the following:

The never-exposed

Many of the general public will never previously have been offered some of the drugs being considered, and are unlikely ever to be offered these drugs. They may, nevertheless, be caught up in the broad general public information programmes in a society making choices about its drug control options.

The exposed never-used

Another large section of the general public may, on a small number of occasions, have been presented with the opportunity to use drugs, but chose not to do so. If it is presumed that these individuals may, at some future date, again be in a situation where there is the opportunity to use, then the decisions a society makes about its drug control and prevention strategies may have an impact on the future decisions of current non-users.

The experimental user

Around the time of initial use of a drug, individuals may go through a stage of experimental use at which they are exploring both the drug effect and the place of this drug use within their own lives. At this stage it is likely that their future significant engagement with, or disengagement from, further drug use has not yet been firmly determined.

The non-dependent regular user

Among the population of users of any particular drug, there will be some for whom this drug use has not (at least not yet) resulted in dependence or any discernible problems. For such users, it is likely that primary prevention messages may have little impact, and secondary prevention messages may be more suitable. Furthermore, their perceptions of the adverse consequences of detection/arrest may influence the extent to which they become more heavily involved in their drug use. Paradoxically, actual detection/arrest may lead them into a more firmly established relationship with this pattern of drug use, accompanied by a move to more disadvantaged social, economic and employment circumstances.

The addicted user

For users whose drug use has come to be perhaps the most important aspect of their life, the impact of public opinion and of drug control policies may be different. The extent to which they are influenced by these public opinions and policies is likely to be determined in part by the extent to which they consider themselves to be part of the society that has chosen these values and policies.

The vulnerable ex-user

Former drug users who have now become drug-free are likely to have a greater vulnerability to unexpected opportunity to use their previous drug, and hence may be particularly susceptible to changes in drug control policy and its implementation.

Any selected drug control policy or drug prevention initiative can consequently be seen to exert different influences on individuals in these different target populations, and the selection of one or other control or preventive option must be preceded by a consideration of the sum total of these different impacts.

Targeting prevention efforts

Prevention policies that are implemented by controlling drug supplies are generally aimed at the total population – that is, universally. But even laws can be targeted; laws that prohibit the sale of alcohol and tobacco to minors are two examples. Other types of prevention efforts such as mass media or school educational programmes are aimed at different audiences. Several examples of more narrowly targeted mass media and youth press prevention programmes have been employed in the UK in recent years. These have include warnings about the insidious onset of heroin dependence, such as the poster from the UK Government's anti-heroin campaign "Heroin screws you up" in the early 1980s, and specific warnings about HIV transmission from sharing needles and syringes – for example, one of the first HIV awareness posters, printed on billboards and in the national and youth press by the UK Government in the mid to late-1980s, was a poster with a deliberate *double-entendre* warning that "It only takes one prick to give you AIDS".

Over the past few years, there has been considerable debate about how much emphasis should be given to primary prevention, aimed at preventing any use whatsoever, and how much to secondary and tertiary prevention – keeping drug use from progressing to dependence and minimising the damage drug use does to the individual and to society. Emphasis on the latter goals is sometimes called 'harm reduction' or 'harm minimisation' and includes activities such as encouraging drug injectors to avoid sharing injection equipment so as to reduce the spread of the viruses that cause AIDS and hepatitis. Indeed, in the guidelines issued by the UK health departments to all British doctors in 1991, a diagram showed how injecting drug misusers might clean potentially contaminated needles and syringes. This was deliberately included so that it might be copied and given to potential injectors who were identified by GPs and hospital doctors (see Figure 7.4).

Chapter 4 discussed what is known about the particular individuals and groups at increased risk of developing drug problems. If a better

Cleaning used works

Draw cold water into the syringe and then flush it out (sterile or cooled boiled water is best).

Do this twice.

Draw some household bleach or diluted washing-up liquid into the syringe and flush it out.

Do this twice as well.

Finally flush it out twice with fresh water.

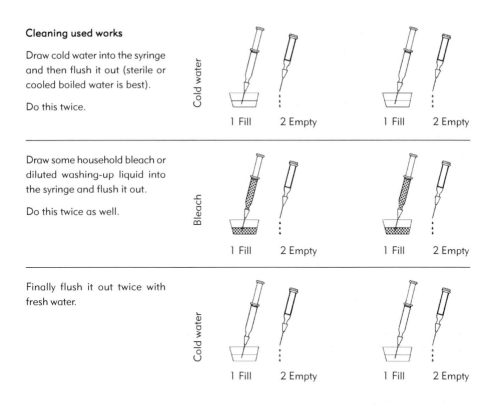

Figure 7.4. An early HIV/AIDS information leaflet. Based on: UK Health Departments (1999) *Drug Misuse and Dependence – Guidelines on Clinical Management.* London: HMSO.

WARNING: THIS DOES NOT DESTROY HEPATITIS C VIRUS

understanding could be achieved of the features indicating increased individual risk, it should point the way to the development of more effective primary and secondary prevention strategies. Improved methods of targeting prevention are particularly important since an intervention that seems appropriate for the young person who has already started experimenting with drugs may have an entirely different effect on the young person who has not yet done so, and vice versa. Although the available evidence suggests that merely providing information rarely changes drug-taking behaviour, it nevertheless seems appropriate for young people to have access to accurate, objective information about drugs. Groups at particularly high risk, such as school children truanting, may be especially poorly informed and hence may need to be the target of specific initiatives.

Most of the time, there is no fundamental contradiction between public policies aimed at controlling and reducing drug supplies, which are generally but not exclusively in the hands of law enforcement agencies, and public health policies aimed at persuading or enabling potential users to avoid or minimise drug use. The interaction of these approaches can be seen with drugs that are not prohibited, such as alcohol and tobacco. Access to these substances is limited by law to adults, prices are raised through taxes, and the criminal law is used to prevent excessive use in certain situations, such as driving under the influence of alcohol. At the same time, public health messages are aimed at discouraging excessive use of alcohol and any use of alcohol while pregnant or when driving, and encouraging smokers to quit. At the end of the day, there are no simple single solutions, and it is usually a mix of policies and responses that is best.

Demand reduction programmes

Prevention programmes directed at demand for drugs can be categorised not only on the basis of the groups or behaviours targeted, but also on the settings in which they take place, for instance mass media efforts, school or family programmes, workplace or community approaches. Arguments have been made for each of these activities as essential elements in a comprehensive prevention programme, but the evidence for efficacy varies widely. In some instances, there are no data available – the approaches have simply not been evaluated using valid methodologies; in others, the data that exist show little or no impact on the behaviours of concern.

Under the auspices of the National Institute of Drug Abuse (NIDA), an impressive amount of preventive work has been carried out in the USA. As a result of the experience gained, NIDA has developed a number of principles that underlie successful preventive work. These are that preventive programmes should:

- be designed to enhance protective factors and move towards reducing known risk factors;
- target all forms of drug misuse, including tobacco, alcohol, cannabis and solvents/inhalants;
- include interactive methods;
- include a parents' or care-givers' component;
- be long-term e.g. over the school career;
- be family-focused;

- be combined with media campaigns and policy changes;

- include community programmes that strengthen norms against drug use;

- be adapted to address the specific nature of the drug problem in the community to be targeted; and

- be age-specific and culture-sensitive.

A number of studies have now been published supporting the claim that comprehensive approaches with multiple components can be modestly successful in reducing rates of drug use, and therefore, probably, problem drug use. For example, one study[1] which focused on predominantly White 7th grade (14-year-old) students reported 44% fewer drug users and 66% fewer polydrug users in the intervention group compared with a control group when both were followed up six years later. The intervention involved 15 class periods directed at the provision of information and skills for resisting social influences to use drugs, together with generic personal and social skills to increase social competence. Booster sessions were held in the 8th and 9th grades. Positive, but less striking, results have also been obtained with ethnic minority groups[2] and a massive community study has reported partially successful findings.[3]

In the UK, in contrast, although a great deal of money and rhetoric are directed at programmes for reducing demand for drugs, it is difficult to point to any evaluated work of significance. Even when evaluations have been undertaken, as in the case of the Home Office-funded 'Project Charlie',[4,5] a life skills drugs prevention programme targeted at primary school children, the small sample sizes used have not produced conclusive findings. The follow-up evaluation of Project Charlie was, for example, based on two main comparisons. The first was a sample of just 44 pupils who were randomly assigned to receive Project Charlie or to be in the control condition (i.e. not receiving specific drugs education at primary school), of whom only twenty of the Project Charlie and 14 of the controls were contacted at follow-up; the second comparison looked at 24 pupils who received Project Charlie compared with 24 pupils matched at that time who did not receive the programme, of whom 21 in each group were compared at follow-up. In considering what actually works in prevention initiatives, we therefore have to look to North American and other international research.

It is also important not to confuse the enthusiasm with which a prevention programme may be delivered with evidence of its effectiveness. The international evidence on their success is sobering. Indeed, many of the UK's drug prevention initiatives, when reviewed, have been shown to be ineffective in preventing drug use.[6] This is clearly an area in which careful attention must be paid to those features of the content and delivery that have been found to be associated with beneficial impact. It is also important to remember that one 'success' of these programmes can be increasing knowledge to which young people are fully entitled. There is no evidence to suggest that such knowledge *increases* their likelihood of using drugs.

It must also be remembered that the physical and social circumstances in which young people grow up influence their subsequent attitudes and behaviour regarding drug use. These matters are considered in Chapter 4.

School-based programmes

It had been repeatedly observed that most drug experimentation begins in adolescence. In the UK, several different research approaches have all found evidence of substantial increases in drug use in recent decades, and particularly during the 1990s. Several recent studies have found that between 40–50% of 15- and 16-year-olds have used a drug on at least one occasion, with similar proportions among males and females, although with significant regional variation (for example, much lower levels in Northern Ireland). The proportion of young people who have had some involvement with illicit substances rises dramatically from the beginning of this age band with around 10% of 12- and 13-year-olds and 30% of 14- and 15-year-olds reporting that they have used a drug.

Because of such findings, school-based prevention programmes have frequently been launched. Such programmes have been extensively evaluated in the USA (though not in the UK) over the past 25 years. Over that period, five types of programme have been implemented and evaluated there:

- *information dissemination*: involves providing facts about drugs, presented through teaching, discussion, audio-visual presentation, display, posters, pamphlets or group programmes;

- *affective education*: deliberately promotes individuals' personal and social development with a focus on improving self-knowledge and relationships with other people, and helping them to find fulfillment without drugs;

- *providing alternatives to drug use*: typically involves alternative activities in non-drug surroundings as a means of reducing the likelihood of drug use, and includes active involvement in sports, hobbies and community service;

- *psychosocial approaches*: in which specific skills are taught for resisting influences that might encourage or support drug use, while also teaching generic skills for coping with life (e.g. problem-solving and decision-making); and

- *comprehensive approaches with multiple components*: involve several social institutions including schools and family and community organisations over an extended period of time; recommended by America's National Institute of Drug Abuse (see page 126).

Despite their popularity, all the evidence to date indicates that providing information and affective education and providing alternative after-school activities have little or no effect on preventing the use of alcohol, tobacco, or drugs. Worse still, any effects on knowledge or attitudes about drug use are short-term, and no longer detectable after a year or two. In the past, most school-based programmes have targeted young adolescents, because they are entering the period when drug experimentation most commonly begins. More recently, there have been school-based interventions aimed at children in the very early school years. Some data suggest that classroom-based interventions in the 1st or 2nd grades (6–8-year-olds) aimed primarily at reducing conduct disorder can modulate a downward cycle of misbehaviour that is a strong sign of later use of alcohol, tobacco and drugs. However, it is with the last two types of programme that the most promising results have been demonstrated, with reductions in levels of drug use and associated problem behaviour.

The *psychosocial approach* typically involves increasing the awareness of youngsters of the social influences that promote drug use, modifying their views on acceptable behaviour, while also teaching general problem-solving skills alongside specific skills for resisting drug use pressures. The *comprehensive approach*, with its wider lifestyle focus and greater involvement of family and local community, was described above and badly needs to be replicated in the UK to find out whether it would be effective here.

Mass media

Few mass media efforts aimed at drug use have been thoroughly evaluated. There is evidence that television advertisements aimed at informing the public of the dangers of smoking, shown in the USA in the early 1970s, corresponded to a period when the steadily increasing percentage of smokers in the general population levelled off as more of them tried to quit. A similar mass media campaign in California in 1990, combined with a tax increase, appeared to have an effect in reducing sales of cigarettes. Mass media efforts specifically targeted at adolescents, particularly when combined with school-based interventions, were more effective in reducing the number of teenage smokers than were school-based programmes alone.

The attractiveness of using television, radio and print media is that they represent a relatively efficient way to get a message to large populations. There is a belief among those skilled in advertising that if it is possible to create a desire for products, then it should also be possible to 'unsell' them. However, it must also be borne in mind that media coverage of drugs issues often glamorises drug use, and, hence, preventive drugs education needs to be designed so as to be influential in the context of such glamorisation. The data suggest that knowledge of ill effects of drugs and attitudes about use can be shifted, but it has been harder to show that actual use patterns are substantially altered by these shifts. Nevertheless, changes in the attitudes of young people to lesser acceptance of drug use have closely tracked the reductions in the levels of drug use seen among adolescents in the USA in the 1980s (see Figures 7.5–7.7)

One study in Australia targeted its media efforts at amphetamine users and attempted to convey the dangers involved. Evaluations showed that the campaign successfully reached the target audience, who as a result were more aware of the dangers of amphetamine. However, there was little or no change in patterns of amphetamine use.

Community-based programmes

Different types of community-based programme have been described in a recent major report from the UK's Advisory Council on the Misuse of Drugs (1998). As this points out, although there are many descriptions of projects planned and delivered, evidence of their impact is extremely thin. Nevertheless, one substantial analysis of more than 100 American drug prevention programmes found peer-based interventions to be the most effective.[7,8] Additionally, the provision of opportunities to improve employment prospects has been found to increase the likelihood of acquiring skills and reducing drug use. It is therefore important, also, to consider wider initiatives that address the nature of the community – initiatives such as the Safer Cities Initiative or City Challenge of the 1990s in the UK. For the last decade, the Drug Prevention Initiative at the Home Office has supported a substantial number of local drug prevention teams, identifying new opportunities for local, community and neighbourhood-based approaches to drug prevention. The impact of these projects is, however, still being evaluated.

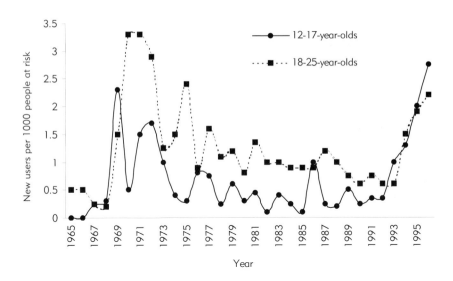

Figure 7.5. Age-specific rate of first time use of heroin in the USA, 1965–1996. Source for Figures 7.5–7.7: Substance Abuse and Mental Health Services Administration (1998) *Preliminary Results from the 1997 National Household Survey on Drug Abuse.* Rockville, ND: SAMSA.

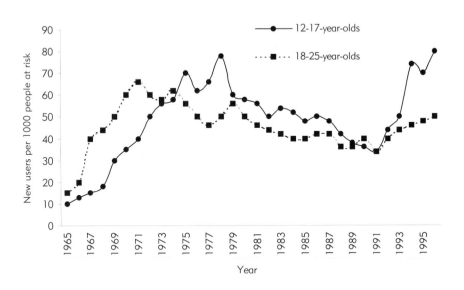

Figure 7.6. Age-specific rate of first cannabis use in the USA, 1965–1996.

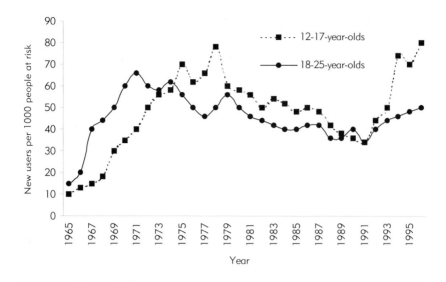

Figure 7.7. Age-specific rate of first time use of cocaine in the USA, 1965–1996.

The risk of involvement in drug use by young people raised in circumstances of major disadvantage has led to a study of young people in social exclusion programmes, among whom particularly high levels of delinquent or criminal behaviour and drug use have been found. So far, in this particular study, the published results relate to the characteristics of this group of disadvantaged young people at their point of entry into the study. Information on their changing behaviour over time will be published by the researchers at a later date when follow-up data have been collected. The importance of looking at the influences on this vulnerable population is considered in greater depth in Chapter 4.

Workplace-based programmes

Three different types can be identified within workplace prevention initiatives. First, there are straightforward educational approaches in which the dangers of tobacco, alcohol or drug use are addressed, especially when these may have an impact on competence to operate machinery or vehicles. A second type of approach involves early identification and intervention for employees with emerging drug or alcohol problems. Specific employee assistance programmes have now been established in many companies, both large and small, and provide a means of addressing the alcohol or drug problem within the context of continued employment at a stage prior to the development of major problems or accidents at work. The most recent development has been the introduction by some companies of policies of drug testing of prospective employees and continued testing, usually random, of the current workforce. This approach has been more widely applied in the USA during recent years, and is now being introduced in a number of companies in the UK. Evidence from the USA is mixed, with some studies suggesting that the introduction of such programmes in the workplace leads to reduced levels of self-reported drug use and lower accident rates[9,10] and others showing no beneficial changes.

Mandatory drug testing in prisons

A recent policy initiative with some relationship to workplace testing is the introduction of random, mandatory urine testing as an attempt to reduce the extent of drug use by current inmates on remand or serving sentences in British prisons. The politically-driven nature of the intervention resulted in implementation of the policy before the implications could properly be thought through, and the scheme has consequently attracted criticism, as well as expressions of concern that the whole approach may be ill-founded.

Early findings suggested that the new policy might inadvertently have led to an increase in heroin use, with some inmates switching their drug use from cannabis to heroin, because the latter is detectable for a much shorter period of time in urine, and hence more likely to elude a system of random drug testing (see Table 7.1). However, a more recent analysis of the data has shown reductions in cannabis use, with no sustained increase in the proportion positive for heroin and no good evidence of a substantial shift from cannabis to opiate use.[11]

THE RANGE OF OPTIONS FOR DRUG CONTROL POLICY

It is important to recognise the wide range of policy options available to deal with any specific substance. The notion that drugs are either legal or illegal is simply not in keeping with the way things work in the real world. There are several different sets of legal and regulatory stances that can be implemented for any given substance, with *total and absolute prohibition*, and *total acceptance with no constraints, either moral or legal* at the two extremes. Under a regime of total prohibition, the substance in question is deemed to have no legitimate use, even for the treatment of disease under medical

Table 7.1. Duration of detectability of drugs in urine samples.

Substance	Duration of detectability
Amphetamines	48 hours
Barbiturates	24 hours–7 days depending on whether the compound is short- or long-acting (e.g. phenobarbitone)
Benzodiazepines	12 hours–7 days depending on whether the compound is short- or long-acting (e.g. diazepam)
Cocaine metabolites	2–3 days
Methadone	
Single dose	4 days
Maintenance dosing	7–9 days
Codeine/heroin/morphine	48 hours
Cannabinoids (marijuana)	
Single use	3 days
Heavy use (daily)	10 days
Chronic heavy use	Up to 4 weeks

supervision, although exceptions may sometimes be made for medical research. Generally, there are civil and/or criminal penalties for violating the laws. Such penalties are typically more severe for trafficking the substance than for possession of it for personal use. In some countries, such as Malaysia, sellers of drugs such as heroin may be sentenced to death.

Variations of prohibition

Even within a general policy of *total and absolute prohibition*, there is room for variation. In some countries, the sale of heroin is punishable by long periods of imprisonment, but using the drug or possessing small amounts for personal use may not be a criminal offence. Although it is not generally recognised, America's 'noble experiment' – prohibition of alcohol – never involved criminal penalties for possession or use; the laws merely prohibited the manufacture, sale and distribution of alcoholic beverages. There were wealthy families who continued to enjoy the contents of their wine cellars and liquor cabinets throughout the entire period of Prohibition.

Other policy variations within a total prohibition regime involve the level of resources a country is willing to invest in enforcing the law. These resources are not measured only in terms of the money devoted to enforcement and customs personnel, courts and prisons, but may extend even to the willingness to make relationships with other countries subservient to the goals of the regulatory scheme. At one point in its efforts to reduce the availability of cannabis coming into the country from Mexico, the USA so carefully inspected cargo and people crossing its borders that commerce and tourism between Mexico and the US Customs were severely affected. The policy had a transient effect on reducing the availability of cannabis from Mexico, but it also stimulated the expansion of cannabis cultivation within the USA. There is no evidence that this approach had any lasting impact either on the drug's supply or price.

Similarly, the USA put pressure on Turkey in the early 1970s to cease the centuries-old practice of harvesting opium from the opium poppy. At that time, Turkish opium was used mainly as a source of morphine and codeine for medicinal purposes. While only part of this opium found its way into the illicit market, the bulk of heroin entering the USA at the time originated in Turkey. In this case, the elimination of Turkish opium as the raw material for the production of heroin led to a period of a year or more in which the purity of heroin in the USA went down and the price went up. Not long thereafter, however, the production of opium expanded in South-East Asia (the Golden Triangle) and Mexico, and these new sources of heroin more than filled the void. A few years later, Turkey began to produce morphine and codeine for medical purposes from poppy straw (the entire poppy plant), a new method that was less vulnerable to diversion.

The USA and other developed countries have also used a variety of strategies to motivate producer countries in Latin America to eliminate the coca plants that supply the raw material for the production of cocaine. But despite the investment of billions of dollars annually and the expenditure of much international good will, each time a coca field has been destroyed other areas are brought into production, more than filling the void. Indeed, it has proved exceedingly difficult to determine whether the resources expended on source country control produce any substantial benefits at all in terms of decreased access to the drug in consumer countries. There have been only limited efforts to compare the effects on actual consumption levels achieved from different interventions: source country efforts, control at the borders, law enforcement within the consumer country, and treatment of the drug-dependent population. One notable exception was a study by the RAND Corporation on consumption of cocaine in the USA. Making the most conservative of assumptions about the impact of treatment on cocaine dependence (i.e. only considering effectiveness from a societal point of view, rather than the benefits to individual dependent patients), this study concluded that to produce a 1% reduction in the amount of cocaine consumed, each dollar spent on treatment was seven times as effective as a dollar spent on local law enforcement, 10 times as effective as a dollar spent on defending the country's borders, and more than 20 times as effective as a dollar spent on source country supply control (see Figure 7.8).[12]

Efforts to prevent drugs entering the consumer country or their manufacture within its borders not only aim to reduce the availability on the street, but also to raise the price to discourage users. Increases in the price of alcohol and cigarettes have a significant effect on consumption, resulting in people drinking and smoking less. The same is probably true for drugs, and young people, who are the largest consumers of drugs, are particularly price-sensitive. However, efforts to increase the price of drugs and reduce their availability in consumer nations, either by persuading or pressuring another country to stop producing it or by border and internal enforcement activities, have not generally been successful. In the UK, for example, the price of heroin fell from around £90 per gram in 1986 to around £60 per gram in 1996 without any reduction in 'purity' (see Figure 7.9). This shows that, for all the

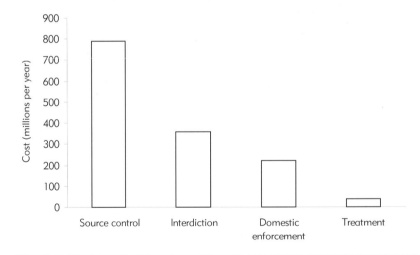

Figure 7.8. Relative effectiveness of cocaine control strategies in achieving a 1% reduction in annual consumption. Based on: Institute of Medicine (1996) *Pathways of Addiction. Opportunities in Drug Abuse Research.* Washington, DC: National Academy Press.

highly publicised drug seizures, so much heroin is getting through that dealers can afford to sell the same product for less despite the fact that demand has increased. In the USA, there is similarly discouraging evidence: heroin's average purity has risen from just under 20% in 1981 to over 50% in 1998 while the price has fallen in real terms.

Total prohibition policies vary in a number of other ways that may influence their efficacy and cost-effectiveness. These include which specific elements in the chain of illicit trafficking are targeted by enforcement agencies – such as the large importers, the mid-level distributors, or the street-level sellers – and the severity of the penalties. There are further variations available within the judicial system, which may mete out more or less severe penalties depending on the offender's role in the illicit trafficking chain. The financial and economic consequences of these policies are readily measured in terms of the costs of police and prosecutors, judges and juries, as well as in the costs of maintaining a large population of drug offenders in prison. To the degree that those so imprisoned might have engaged in predatory behaviour entirely apart from their involvement with drugs, there may be some benefit to society as a

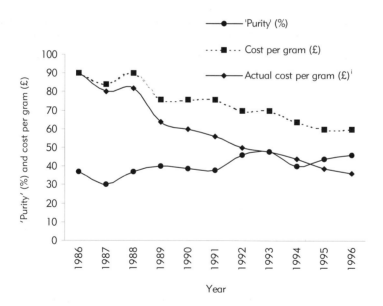

i Prices corrected for changes in Retail Price Index.

Figure 7.9. 'Purity' and price of black market heroin, 1986–1996, UK. Adapted from: Strang, J., Griffiths, P. & Gossop, M. (1997) Heroin in the United Kingdom: different forms, different origins, and the relationship to different routes of administration. *Drug and Alcohol Review*, 16, 329–337.

whole. But the costs of the lost productivity of those who might have been law abiding citizens must also be weighed up, along with the impact of their imprisonment on their families.

Given the limited impact of the vigorous efforts to totally prohibit a number of drugs, even at great cost, it is no surprise that several observers have suggested greater emphasis on reducing demand for drugs and, in the process, alternatives to the total prohibition policies just described.

The other extreme

Before moving down the scale of severity of regulatory control, let us consider the other extreme that a substance may occupy in society's perception of potential problems: *complete acceptance without social or legal constraints*. In such a framework, the substance is available to all who can afford to buy it. Producers are permitted to advertise it in order to increase consumption. If there are any government regulations, they are similar to those applied to other products intended for human consumption and are for the purpose of ensuring safety and purity; if there are sales or excise taxes, they are comparable to other goods. There are no official constraints on individual use and, generally, there are no moral impediments to use regardless of age or health status. Even the recognition of occasional health problems associated with use does not result in anything more than an occasional article in a health magazine. In developed countries, there are very few psychoactive drugs that have such widespread acceptance. The active ingredients in tea, coffee and cocoa (caffeine and theobromine) are the only common examples. While most parents might be concerned about children under the age of seven or eight drinking tea or coffee regularly, Coca-Cola or coffee ice-cream are considered acceptable even for toddlers.

There was a time not so long ago when tobacco came close to having such a status. It was used openly by virtually all segments of society and while one might have been distressed to see a 10-year-old smoking, the same behaviour in a 14- or 16-year-old might not have elicited surprise. Of course, attitudes toward tobacco have changed dramatically in the past 30 years.

It is unlikely that any of the substances currently considered illicit will ever be viewed with the insouciance with which we now regard tea and coffee. However, as Chapter 2 showed, both knowledge and attitudes can change. It might, therefore, be useful to consider the various regulatory schemes that lie between the extremes of total prohibition and total acceptance and how they might affect both the user and society as a whole.

Moving from total to relative prohibition and other regulatory schemes

What policy options might exist that are neither at the extreme of complete prohibition nor the opposite extreme of a completely free market? Between these two extremes might exist any one of the following – and most of the examples subsequently listed can actually be found somewhere at the current time.

Just a notch below a policy of total and absolute prohibition is one that allows a drug to be used under careful medical supervision for the treatment of disease, but maintains severe penalties for its use outside these circumstances. In such a scheme, medical treatment might, or in other circumstances might not, include providing the drug to addicts who have become dependent on it. A good example of such a regulatory framework is the controls on morphine and cocaine in the USA. Physicians may prescribe large amounts of morphine for long periods to patients in pain, but they are not permitted to prescribe it at all to heroin addicts to prevent withdrawal symptoms. Doing so would risk criminal prosecution and severe penalties. Surgeons may use cocaine for local anesthesia, but there are severe criminal penalties for any other use. In the UK, a similar policy covers the medical prescription of heroin. With the exception of about 100 physicians who have received special Home Office licences to prescribe it to addicts, doctors can prescribe it for pain but not for the treatment of addiction. Any manufacture, sale, or distribution of opiate drugs or cocaine, except by those licensed to do so, is subject to severe criminal penalties.

A regulatory policy just slightly more tolerant of drug use than that just described is one in which a drug is not only available for use in the treatment of disease; but under carefully defined circumstances, those addicted to it or to other drugs in the same pharmacological class can obtain it under medical supervision. Several examples come to mind. In many countries, individuals who have become addicted to heroin can be provided with synthetic opiates such as methadone. In most of those countries (Switzerland and the UK are notable exceptions), these addicts cannot obtain heroin itself, even under medical supervision. Further, there are severe penalties attached to selling or possessing the drugs when they are not obtained through proper medical channels.

The decision of the Swiss Government to allow special clinics to provide heroin to addicts has generated considerable controversy and was opposed by several other countries which wanted to maintain an absolute prohibition against any medical use of the drug. The argument in defence of the scheme was that no less radical policy was likely to bring the hard core of injecting heroin users voluntarily into treatment, or curb their criminal behaviour. The arguments against the scheme included concerns about diversion of prescribed heroin onto the black market and the condoning of the very 'disease' that the heroin 'treatment' purported to correct. Added to this was concern that attitudes among the general public, especially the young, might change as dependent heroin use was apparently looked upon as normal behaviour, thereby increasing use. At the time of writing, the Swiss clinicians and investigators have established the feasibility of operating a tightly con-trolled treatment programme of heroin substitution, and have avoided the establishment of a black market by requiring all prescribed heroin to be consumed under supervision on drug clinic premises (unlike the UK where supplies are provided on a take-home basis, mostly from a community pharmacy). However, the wider impact and implications of this experiment still remain unclear and are bound to be the subject of further study and heated debate. In fact, the 'Swiss experiment' has generated far less controversy in the UK than elsewhere because heroin was never totally prohibited here.

In many developed countries, a wide variety of drugs are regulated under the *general prohibition scheme: available for use in medicines but not for non-medical use*, for example to relax, obtain more energy, or 'get high'. Use of these drugs outside medical channels is subject to penalties. However, the penalties as well as the likelihood of arrest and prosecution vary widely, not only from one drug group to another, but also from country to country and even within the same country over a period of years. Thus, the patient who sells some morphine obtained from a physician to a heroin addict might face severe criminal penalties if arrested. The same patient selling a few Valium tablets to the same addict might not be arrested; if arrested, the likelihood of prosecution would be low, and, if convicted of unlawful sale, the penalty would be far less severe than for the sale of an opiate. And if the drug concerned was an antibiotic, the sale would probably attract no more attention than a raised eyebrow.

To summarise, if prohibition and legalisation are considered as the A and Z of the spectrum, then we might consider possible intermediate options, such as a grudging acceptance of the behaviour by a small minority, or the imposition of extensive safety controls in the wider public interest, as being located in the alphabetic spectrum in between – perhaps C or D, and V or W respectively, for example.

A special concern – cannabis

Cannabis occupies an odd and unique place in the spectrum of psychoactive agents. In most developed countries, the cultivation, production, sale or importation of cannabis leaves or its refined ingredients is illegal, and the crude material has no approved medical uses. Its main active ingredient, tetrahydrocannabinol, is approved in a number of countries for the treatment of nausea and may be prescribed as dronabinol or Marinol. From a regulatory perspective, cannabis in its many crude forms (cannabis leaves and stems, hashish and oil) is much like heroin in the USA – totally forbidden, not available even from medical channels. However, it differs from heroin in a number of important respects. Its use has become so widespread that most countries have adjusted their criminal justice statutes so that penalties for possession of small amounts are not likely to result in severe punishment. Thus, in the UK, there has been a considerable degree of de facto decriminalisation of the offence of cannabis possession over the last quarter of a century. As illustration of the change in police practice in recent years, during which there has been no change whatsoever in the law regarding cannabis, there has been a major increase in the extent to which police deal with the offence of possession of cannabis by confiscation. Indeed, cautioning is now the most frequent course of action and accounts for more than 50% of cases of possession (see Figure 7.10). HM Customs mirrored this change in 1982 when it introduced 'compounding', a fine in lieu of prosecution for offences of bringing into the UK small quantities of drugs for personal use. Even so, there are many who argue that even under conditions of reduced criminal penalties the control policies inflict more damage than the use of cannabis.

Cannabis policy

Perhaps more than any other drug, cannabis is a good example to illustrate the wide range of policy options available. While zealots to the left and right might call for one or other extreme of absolute prohibition or a free market (the A and Z of the spectrum), it is probable that the best policy options with the least public harm lie in the in-between zone. If total prohibition were embraced and vigorously applied, considerable harm would be done to those individuals caught up with cannabis use, for whom the penalties would undoubtedly exceed the potential harms of the drug, on top of which society would bear the considerable costs of enforcement, detection and imprisonment.

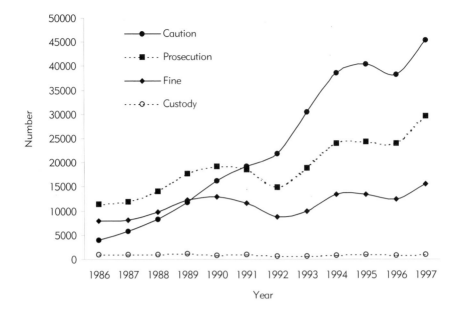

Figure 7.10.   The changing consequences of cannabis possession in the UK.
Source for 1986–1995: John Corkery, Home Office Research and Statistics Directorate, Crime
and Criminal Justice Unit. Published in Hansard, February 1998. Source for 1996–1997,
from which figures for Northern Ireland were not available: Drugs Research
and Statistics Section, Home Office.

At the other end of the spectrum, in the free market, levels of use of cannabis would increase with the removal of deterrents and would presumably also become subject to active promotion by all the new legitimate producers and distributors, with a consequent substantial increase in the health, public safety and wider social ill effects, imposing an additional major burden on various public services. It may therefore be more profitable to explore the intermediate territory where the optimal degree of control significantly dissuades people from use while not requiring disproportionate expenditure, or harm to the minority who nevertheless continue to use cannabis.

Values and ethics

For each drug, a society's regulatory policy represents a balancing of competing interests and values. Presumably the objective is to minimise health and social problems at the least cost, both financially and in terms of personal freedom and enforcement, while in some cases allowing availability of the drug for treatment. Since the health impact and the difficulties of drug control are not always known, policies are instituted that sometimes misjudge the health impact or the likely costs of implementation. However, revisions of policy typically occur only slowly. Whatever policy is in place will have its supporters and beneficiaries as well as its critics and sometimes its victims. This is so even in the case of a readily available drug that has been commercialised, tobacco, for instance, or a drug such as cannabis that is used widely despite total prohibition.

Three principles that seem to have general validity have been summarised by Mark Kleiman, an American researcher. First, drugs that give pleasure or satisfaction will be used if people want and can afford them; and if they are prohibited, an illicit market will emerge. Second, the more available a drug is the more it will be used and, unless it is relatively innocuous, such as the caffeine in tea or coffee, the more health problems there will be. Third, it is difficult to keep drugs that are available to adults out of the hands of children. The crucial choice is not between specific means of regulating demand or supply, but whether a society wishes to have low crime and high health costs, as with tobacco and alcohol, or high crime and relatively low health costs, as with heroin. Once that decision has been made, selecting the optimal regulatory policy becomes easier, but still requires many value judgements.

A conflict can sometimes exist between a policy which, although bringing overall public good, nevertheless results in an increase in the level of harm for some of those deeply involved in that drug use. Thus, a policy which ostracises the opiate addict, the drink-driver or the addicted physician may successfully reduce the extent of the offending behaviour, but it may also bring profound disadvantages to the smaller number who transgress. Conversely, a policy that seeks to accommodate and adapt to these behaviours may inadvertently remove the taboo against the practice and thereby increase the extent to which people engage in the behaviour. One practical demonstration of this ebb and flow of what is regarded as acceptable behaviour can be seen in the changing last-month prevalence rates from household surveys in the USA, shown earlier in Figure 7.3. As drug use has become increasingly condemned in America, the number of people taking drugs has fallen. Another example is the enormous differences in the male predominance of drug use in different societies in which there are differing views on the role and position of women in society – from something in excess of a 40:1 male predominance in studies from the Indian sub-continent through to a 2:1 ratio across the general population in the UK and closer to parity among British teenage drug users.

The benefits and burdens of various policy options will be experienced quite differently by various groups within the population. The extent of drug use and associated health problems in the population as a whole tend to be lowest under conditions where use is totally prohibited and the penalties for sale, use and possession are harshest. One result of such a policy for heroin and cocaine, in addition to heavy law enforcement costs, is that the drug users as well as the drugs are stigmatised and marginalised. They typically suffer a range of serious medical disorders and have very high mortality rates. Frequent encounters with the law result in periods spent in jail, at additional expense to the public, and because of these interruptions in employment and the association with chronic criminals, there is a diminished likelihood that the user will ever become a law-abiding and tax-paying citizen. For the poor and unemployed or under-employed, trafficking in drugs is a constant temptation. The net effect is that the neighbourhoods where drug users live become areas where trafficking occurs, thereby increasing ease of access for young people living in those areas. The work of the drug trafficker may seem, to young people, an easy, even glamorous, occupation with ample monetary rewards, leading many into early delinquency and a loss of interest in more remote vocational goals requiring schooling and discipline.

To this list of the adverse effects of total and absolute prohibition must be added at least two others. The best recognised is that some drug users and most addicts engage in a variety of crimes to obtain money to buy drugs (see also Chapter 5). While the impact of this crime falls most heavily on the cities and neighborhoods where the users live, the costs are in fact redistributed to the whole of society in the form of higher insurance rates and higher costs for security services and devices. More recently recognised is the burden placed on health services when addicts contract, and pass on, viral diseases such as hepatitis and HIV. The latter disease must be seen as the gravest threat posed by users of drugs within a total prohibition model, because HIV, once acquired, is almost invariably fatal, and can be sexually transmitted to others. Heroin and cocaine addicts are also more likely than people in the general population to have multiple sex partners. Some of these multiple contacts are part of a general lifestyle, but some represent exchange of sex for money or drugs and are directly driven by the pursuit of drugs. Many people who have contracted HIV from injecting drug misusers have in turn passed on this disease to unsuspecting spouses and partners, and in several countries the prevalence of HIV among injecting drug misusers now exceeds 50%. Furthermore, even in countries with a relatively low HIV prevalence, such as the UK and Australia, clinicians and researchers have recently identified an alarmingly high prevalence of infection with another virus, hepatitis C – often

50% and sometimes as high as 80% of injecting drug users. It is already clear that chronic hepatitis C infection, after up to twenty or thirty years of apparently good health, will lead to premature death for some former injectors who have long since given up the practice.

In the UK, the rates vary widely from region to region and reflect in part the rapidity with which different communities modified total prohibition policies to focus on prevention of HIV transmission, rather than on completely suppressing the use of heroin, cocaine and amphetamines. The extent to which these HIV prevention measures will also protect against infection with hepatitis C remains unclear, but the available data are not reassuring and suggest that, even among injectors whose initiation into drug use post-dated HIV awareness, hepatitis C infection has spread widely.

Enumeration of these consequences of a total prohibition policy should not necessarily be taken as an argument that these drugs should be made more widely available to the general public. However, focusing on controlling the drug supply, while giving too little attention to ways of reducing the pursuit of drugs by those who have become dependent on them, raises the cost of the control policy far more than would a more balanced approach that invested more in treatment and in reduction of adverse health consequences.

The adverse effects of a policy of almost total acceptance of moderate use can also fall disproportionately on different sectors of the population. Here we see major differences according to age, gender and social class. The chief reductions in prevalence of smoking, for example, and the consequent health benefits, have been largely restricted to the more affluent socio-economic groups and have contributed little to the well-being of the working classes and unemployed. Youth is, disturbingly, now associated with high prevalence of cigarette smoking and, as with drug use, the traditional male predominance of the behaviour has now completely disappeared. We should also note that, although acute fatalities as a direct result of drinking alcohol and smoking tobacco are low, the overall burden on society in terms of alcohol-related accidents, crimes, lost productivity, diseases and deaths dwarfs that associated with all the other drugs combined.

Conclusion

There are two important conclusions from this chapter. First, the choice of drug policy for a society is not a simple choice between prohibition and legalisation. Not only are there several different legislative options to be considered (with probably different optimal choices for different drugs), but it is also important to consider the manner in which these laws are applied. As a drug policy researcher commented many years ago in a corrupt quotation from Charles Dickens' Mr Bumble, "The law may be an ass, but it is sometimes an extremely subtle and sensitive ass". The second important conclusion is that drug-taking behaviours are extremely malleable, and hence our choice of prevention strategies and policies is likely to matter greatly. If the history of drug use showed that prevalence remained constant regardless of policy choices, it would matter little which policy we chose. But with such major changes over time in the prevalence of different drug-taking behaviours, we would do well to adopt a disciplined approach of scientific study to identify the beneficial and harmful influences, to conduct the appropriate individual and societal cost benefit analyses, and to adjust our public policies accordingly.

Chapter 8. Treatment of drug misuse

SUMMARY

The aim of treatment is to prevent or reduce harm resulting from the use of drugs. Treatment benefits not only the individual drug user but, through reducing drug-related crime and the spread of blood-borne diseases, the wider community. At least for some forms of drug use, the cost of treatment is recouped several-fold by the benefits accrued.

The UK has a long and influential history of treating drug misuse. Most notably, the adoption of harm reduction measures, such as needle exchange schemes, has successfully contained the spread of HIV. The relative freedom of the 'British system' encourages practitioners to develop new treatments, but this has not been properly exploited. The UK also has a lamentable record in evaluating treatment and in adopting treatments shown to be effective elsewhere. While recent national drug strategies have recognised the impact treatment can have on the nation's drug problem, there is a need for considerably greater funding for the potential to be realised.

INTRODUCTION

Does treatment work? And, if so, what treatments should be used to manage which problems being experienced by which types of drug users? In golf clubs, launderettes and pubs throughout the country, everyone has something to say about how drug misuse should be managed. "Put them in prison and throw away the key", "legalise all drugs" and "let doctors give them drugs on prescription" are opinions that are not only common but have existed for longer than their protagonists probably realise.

Treatment, along with law enforcement, education and prevention, is the means by which the government intends to achieve the objectives of reducing drug-related crime, the prevalence of drug use, and the health risks both to drug users and to the general population. Means and objectives are inter-related. Law enforcement aims to reduce the manufacture, importation and distribution of drugs, and reduce drug-related crime. Education and prevention are aimed at stopping individuals using drugs and reducing the dangers to those who use drugs.

Unlike that of most medical conditions, treatment for drug problems aims to address both the needs of the individual and other broader goals, and these can conflict. For instance, taken to an extreme, an effective measure to reduce drug-related acquisitive crime would be for doctors to prescribe drug users unlimited quantities of their drug of choice, but this would be detrimental to the health of the user, and could result in the sale of surplus prescribed drugs on the illicit market.

For individual patients, conditions for which they seek treatment might include dependence, side-effects such as psychosis, or physical complications such as blood-borne diseases. While much drug use can have adverse effects on health, like alcohol, it may not always require treatment. On the other hand, a drug user may have a clear need but no effective treatment may exist. With some types of drug problem, specific types of treatment have been shown to be extremely effective, while other therapies have been found to be weak or ineffectual. Furthermore, the potential contribution of treatment is greatly dependent on the type of problem being experienced by the individual.

If a doctor is asked to advise on the treatment that could be offered to a heroin addict with withdrawal symptoms, or who is trying to break the drug–crime link that is driven by his dependence, there are clear answers. On the other hand, if the concerns about drug use are being expressed by third parties such as family and friends, or the courts, and not by the individuals them-selves, and if the pattern of drug use is, for example, non-dependent use of amphetamines or cocaine, then the confidence with which a doctor can prescribe a specific course of treatment is much lower. Indeed the doctor might eventually conclude that, in the absence of a condition to be 'treated', his or her intervention should be restricted to preventive efforts designed to draw the individual's attention to the potential dangers that lie ahead (in much the same way as doctors might give important advice on the health implications of excessive drinking or smoking).

The evidence of the effectiveness of treatment summarised in this chapter would be of greatest value to the treatment and policy communities and the reader if it could draw extensively on evidence from carefully designed research studies. In some areas, such studies have been undertaken and provide valuable information on the strengths and weaknesses of the different treatments studied. However, in many of the areas described in this chapter, treatment has evolved in a rather arbitrary manner, swayed greatly by one or other fashion of the day, by reliance on clinical impressions rather than scientific study design, and hence with great variation between different countries, different cities and even different practitioners within the same practice. The move of modern medicine towards a more rigorous base for treatment, and controlled trials of these treatments if the research evidence base is lacking, is therefore to be welcomed as it should lead to a much greater professional consensus once there is a sufficient body of evidence. For the time being, however, it is necessary to move forward with scrutiny of the available research evidence, mixed with a description of the gradual evolution of clinical practice.

THE ROLLESTON REPORT: THE BIRTH OF THE 'BRITISH SYSTEM'

At the beginning of the 20th century, addicts were largely middle-class professionals who had become dependent on opiates used for medical purposes. Asked to advise the Government, Sir Humphrey Rolleston's committee responded to the situation in 1926 by endorsing the prescription to addicts of regular supplies of the drug to which they were addicted, if attempts to reduce the dose left them incapable of leading a productive life. This was the cornerstone to what has since become known as the 'British system'. Essentially, this was a pragmatic approach and the precursor to 'harm minimisation'. While abstinence remains the ultimate goal, for those who are currently unable to stop using drugs, other treatment measures which reduce the harm from drug use are also employed. The recommendations of the Rolleston Report contrasted markedly with the approach in the USA where, following the 1914 Harrison Act, government officials pressurised doctors not to prescribe opiates to addicts, preferring the goal of a 'drug-free America'.

DRUG DEPENDENCE RECEIVES SPECIALIST TREATMENT

Between 1958 and 1964, the number of known heroin addicts rose from 62 to 342, and it was clear that a drug culture of young people taking opiates for pleasure had emerged from the excessive prescribing of a small number of London doctors. In 1964, John Owens, a psychiatrist working in Birmingham, established the first specialist health service clinic. Working closely with three local pharmacists, the police and the judiciary, Owens prescribed heroin for Birmingham addicts whose prescriptions were dispensed by pharmacists on a daily basis. During the 1960s and 70s, there was also a significant development of services for people dependent on drugs by voluntary and non-governmental bodies. The late 1960s saw the setting up of specialist drug and therapeutic residential communities, particularly in London and the home counties. The period also saw the beginnings of so-called 'street' services and day centres providing counselling and other forms of social care, particularly in London but also in some other cities. Interestingly, some of these initiatives were supported, and in some cases initiated, by NHS specialists.

From 1968 until 1972, on the recommendation of a government committee under the chairmanship of Sir Russell Brain, President of the Royal College of Physicians, Drug Dependency Units (DDUs) were established in the major cities where drugs were prevalent (see Chapter 3). These were run by psychiatrists with a special interest in the problem and limited the prescribing of heroin or cocaine as a treatment for addiction to doctors who had obtained a special licence from the Home Office.

How these units operated was largely determined by the psychiatrist in charge. Most had access to in-patient beds. Treatment regimens varied from those that were entirely abstinence-based to those that continued prescribing heroin in non-reducing, 'maintenance' doses. Overall, though, there was a definite trend for DDUs to prescribe oral rather than injectable drugs, and methadone in preference to heroin.

Throughout the 1970s, heroin addiction escalated and amphetamine and barbiturates were also widely misused. Some DDUs established treatment programmes for amphetamine users, prescribing oral or injectable amphetamine, but they could not always meet the demands of the emerging and changing drug culture. The voluntary and non-governmental bodies developed their range of services to meet needs for community and residential treatment and to work with different disciplines. Following from the work of church-based individuals carried out mainly on the street or in cafés, drop-in centres were established which, in some instances, provided sterile needles and syringes and facilities for addicts to inject. Therapeutic communities also offered rehabilitation for addicts in residential programmes usually lasting 12 months.

EXPANSION OF SERVICES IN THE 1980S

The demand for treatment continued to escalate and the spread of drug use from major cities into every provincial town revealed even further the limitations of DDUs. In the 1980s, Community Drug Teams (CDTs) were therefore established, initially in the North West of England but later throughout the country. They were based in easily accessible sites and provided many of the treatment services previously only available at DDUs.

In 1982, the Government's Advisory Council on the Misuse of Drugs published a report, *Treatment and Rehabilitation*. It recommended a framework of services with CDTs based in each health authority. CDTs were expected to absorb most of the demand for treatment and have access to

Regional Drug Problem Teams for expert advice to help them manage particularly difficult cases. Further, the report acknowledged that specialist services would not be able to treat all drug users, and that the continuing increase in numbers necessitated general practitioners (GPs) becoming involved in treatment, albeit with support from specialist services.

A network of advisory committees was established to monitor the extent of problem drug misuse, improve services and develop future strategies. Each district health authority would have a District Drugs Advisory Committee (DDAC) and each regional health authority a Regional Drugs Advisory Committee (RDAC). These advisory committees included representatives from CDTs, voluntary organisations, social services, probation, police, pharmacies, general practice and specialist treatment services.

The importance of the nature and sources of funding to the development of drug treatment services, especially during the 1980s but also subsequently, cannot be over-estimated. In 1983, the Central Funding Initiative, which funded both NHS and voluntary services, resulted in the proliferation of many small voluntary organisations providing care for drug users, particularly residential centres. Unlike funding through health authorities, this method of providing initial grants led not only to a fragmented treatment service, but also problems of continuity after the grants finished.

During the latter half of the 1980s, funding was made available to both NHS and non-governmental organisations to respond to concerns about HIV. Also, up until 1993 residential services were primarily funded through the social security system. This changed with the introduction of community care, whereby local authorities became responsible for the social care of drug and alcohol misusers for the first time. The next few years will see the rapid development of drug treatment services funded through the criminal justice system, notably prisons and probation. Many of these are and will be provided by the voluntary sector.

A Medical Working Group on Drug Dependence was convened in 1984 by the Department of Health in England. It produced *Guidelines on Good Clinical Practice in the Treatment of Drug Misuse*, and this influential document was distributed to all doctors later the same year. A revised and more detailed version of the guidelines in 1991[1] stated that "Every doctor should address the general health needs of his patients who misuse drugs, including straightforward treatments for drug dependence such as methadone withdrawal from opioids". "Longer-term prescribing" within "a broader programme of social and psychological support" was acknowledged to be of value in some cases but was "a specialised form of treatment best provided by, or in consultation with, a specialist drug misuse service".

HIV AND THE PUBLIC HEALTH RESPONSE

The last decade has seen a panoply of interventions developed to counter the worldwide escalation of injecting drug misuse. The catalyst for these developments was HIV infection, and it is impossible to exaggerate the effect of HIV and AIDS on the management of drug misuse in the UK.

Underpinning the further development of drug services was a fundamental change of emphasis in treatment – from the health of the individual to the health of the general public. If an HIV epidemic was to be avoided, spread of the virus had to be contained. The Government initiated a mass public education programme but, while gay men were likely to be a receptive group, achieving fundamental behavioural change in injecting drug users was always going to be more difficult. Most injecting drug users were unable or unwilling to stop injecting. Advice on how to clean needles and syringes was confusing and unlikely to be heeded by addicts who were desperate for an injection to relieve their craving and withdrawal symptoms. Clean injecting equipment was also difficult to obtain: most chemists would not sell needles and syringes to addicts. In Edinburgh, the inevitable consequences of this state of affairs were all too apparent. Within a few years of the first known case of HIV infection, almost two-thirds of the city's injecting drug users were infected with the virus.

Clearly a radical response was required. Pioneering voluntary and health service agencies led the way, but soon even the most conservative drug services were reacting. Needle exchange schemes (NESs), providing sterile injecting equipment, were established throughout the country.

This dramatic change of emphasis was bolstered by a further report of the Advisory Council on the Misuse of Drugs in 1988.[2] *AIDS and Drug Misuse Part I* stated "The spread of HIV is a greater threat to individual and public health than drug misuse. Accordingly, we believe that services which aim to minimise HIV risk behaviour by all available means should take precedence in development plans". The report advocated a hierarchy of goals: stopping sharing injecting equipment; moving from injectable to oral drug use; decreasing drug use; and abstinence. Harm minimisation was reborn, with the active support of the Government.

In 1995, *Tackling Drugs Together: a Strategy for England 1995–1998*[3] was published and the equivalent strategies for Scotland and Wales soon followed.[4,5] *Tackling Drugs Together* committed the Government:

> "to take effective action by vigorous law enforcement, accessible treatment and a new emphasis on education and prevention to:
>
> - increase the safety of communities from drug related crime;
> - reduce the acceptability and availability of drugs to young people; and
> - reduce the health risks and other damage related to drug misuse".

The strategy did not specify what treatments should be available, nor how they should be given, but promised specific advice to health purchasers through the report of a task force into the effectiveness of drug treatment early in 1996.

Tackling Drugs Together fundamentally reconstructed local advisory bodies, abandoning RDACs and DDACs, replacing them with Drug Action Teams (DATs) and Drug Reference Groups (DRGs). Although there is scope to adapt the structure of these new groups to fit local circumstances, the principle is that the DAT is a small group of budget holders, which ideally comprises the heads of key local services: local authority, health authority, social services, education, police, probation and prisons. Each DAT is advised by a Drug Reference Group made up of local people with expertise in the various services represented.

The terms of reference of the Task Force to Review Services for Drug Misusers, set up in 1994, were:

> "to conduct a comprehensive survey of clinical, operational and cost effectiveness of existing services for drug misusers; to review current policy in relation to the principal objective of assisting drug misusers to achieve and maintain a drug free state, and the secondary objective of reducing harm caused to themselves and others by those who continue to use drugs; to make recommendations where appropriate to Ministers".[6]

The Task Force examined evidence from three sources: from visits to and written evidence submitted by services, from reviews commissioned from leading international authorities and from specially commissioned new research. By far the largest new research commissioned by the Task Force was the National Treatment Outcome Research Study (NTORS). NTORS recruited a total of 1000 drug users in four types of treatment (methadone reduction, methadone maintenance, residential rehabilitation programmes and specialist in-patient drug dependence units) with a planned follow up of five years.[7]

In January 1998, the former Chief Constable of West Yorkshire, Keith Hellawell, was appointed to the newly created post of 'Drug Czar' or UK Anti-Drugs Coordinator. Three months later, a further drug strategy was published.[8] *Tackling Drugs Together to Build a Better Britain: the Government's Ten-Year Strategy for Tackling Drug Misuse* reiterated the main themes of its predecessor:

- to help young people resist drug misuse in order to achieve their full potential in society;

- to protect our communities from drug-related antisocial and criminal behaviour;

- to enable people with drug problems to overcome them and live healthy and crime-free lives; and

- to stifle the availability of illegal drugs on our streets.

In 1999, a more detailed revision of the guidelines on the clinical management of drug misuse brought advice to doctors in line with the National Strategy.[9] Acknowledging a continuum of expertise ranging from that expected from all doctors (generalists) through those non-specialists who had substantial experience in treating drug users (specialised generalists) to specialists in drug dependence, the guidelines outlined the types of treatment that each level should be expected to provide.

A few months later, Keith Hellawell published an annual report with performance targets for the next decade. These included the ambitious aims of reducing the number of young people under 25 using heroin and crack cocaine by 25% within five years and by 50% within 10 years, and increasing the numbers in treatment by 66% by 2005 and by 100% by 2008. Financial resources to realise these targets were also promised: over three years, an extra £20.5 million for social services and £50 million for health authorities, which was expected to increase the numbers in treatment by about one-third by 2002.

There is little point in setting performance targets unless this performance can be and is measured. Yet it is far from clear how progress towards some of these targets will be gauged. Indeed, since the Addicts' Index was suddenly abandoned by the Home Office in mid-1997, presumably partly to save money, there is now no equivalent way of tracking the number of addicts seen by doctors or in treatment with drug services. Suggestions that an existing voluntary anonymised database system could properly replace the Addicts Index seem ill-founded. Competent monitoring of progress towards the performance targets will only be achieved if a new version of the Addicts Index is re-introduced. In our opinion, this new incarnation of the Index should have a more explicit responsibility for tracking, at an individual as well as a population level, the extent and nature of the prescription of controlled drugs like methadone and heroin, as part of the treatment being provided.

AIMS OF TREATMENT

The aim of treatment is to prevent or reduce harm resulting from the use of drugs. Since there is no such thing as a totally safe drug, to prevent all harm from drug use necessitates stopping people using drugs. To restrict treatment to those who are willing or able to stop using would, however, exclude the vast majority of drug users and so ignore most of the harm to individuals and society that results from drug use.

The remit of treatment is extensive, including addressing harm that may be social, psychological or physical, that affects the individual drug user or the general public, and includes that which may occur in the future as well as that which is already manifest. Treatment may involve medical, social and educational interventions, and medical interventions may involve treating harms caused by the drug, the method of using the drug or the lifestyle of the drug user.

Treating drug users therefore requires many different agencies – statutory, voluntary or charitable, specialist and generalist – to work together to address various aspects of the drug user's life and behaviour. Crucially, treatment also aims to prevent or reduce harm to the general public as well as to the drug user.

Harm reduction

For many services and practitioners, the essence of treatment today is 'harm reduction' or 'harm minimisation', and it is important to recognise that this pragmatic response is widely applied in the management of many chronic, relapsing disorders. Although the origins of harm reduction as applied to drug use can be traced back to the beginning of the century, the concept has only gained widespread acceptance since the advent of HIV.

In working towards an eventual 'cure' in the form of sustained abstinence, harm reduction addresses a series of intermediate goals that include drug-related and broader goals (see Table 8.1).

Influencing those who do not come forward for treatment

The advent of HIV made it imperative to influence the behaviour of those injecting drug users who were not in contact with treatment services. A range of methods have been successfully used to educate and inform this group. Similar principles have been adopted towards those whose drug use is less harmful and who may view it as unproblematic.

An imaginative array of materials has been used to reach drug users, including: 'lifestyle' postcards and magazines distributed at clubs and specialist record shops informing dance drug users of the dangers of heat stroke from using ecstasy; explicit comics that advise injecting drug users on safer injecting; and CD-ROMs with an array of drug facts for teenagers presented in the form of a game. Advice over the telephone is also available 24-hours-a-day through a National Drugs Helpline.

Table 8.1. Drug-related and broader goals involved in harm reduction.

Drug-related goals	Broader goals
Stop or reduce:	*Increase, improve or maintain:*
• sharing of injecting equipment	• practice of 'safe sex'
• injecting	• health consciousness
• illicit drug use	• stable lifestyle
• prescribed drug use	• employment
• offending behaviour	• non-offending behaviour

'Outreach' is a means of establishing contact with drug users not in contact with services, influencing their behaviour and, where appropriate, attracting them into treatment. Outreach workers may work in the community (for instance on the streets, in pubs and clubs), or specifically target those seeking help from other agencies such as youth clubs, police stations and courts.

Youth workers and others who may come into contact with drug users but are not themselves drug specialists have a key role in educating and influencing drug users. Those most likely to be in contact with drug users are GPs, social workers, probation officers and the police.

GENERAL TREATMENT MEASURES

Although drugs that cause dependence may require specific treatment techniques, there are broad approaches that are universally applicable to all drug users.

The therapeutic relationship and confidentiality

The relationship between the drug user and the treatment service is of crucial importance. Most drug users are involved in criminal activities, if only because the drug they are using is illegal. They will inevitably have had reservations about seeking help and anxieties about confidentiality. Although for the most part confidentiality will be honoured, there are circumstances when it will not. This is most likely to occur if there are concerns about the safety of children. It is likely, too, that the drug user will benefit from having other agencies involved such as their GP or social worker.

Those working with drug users also have concerns: the overwhelming majority of drug users cause no significant difficulty, but threatening behaviour and, rarely, violence may occur, particularly if the professional is inexperienced and the drug user is seeking prescribed drugs. However, conflict may be minimised by staff anticipating and openly discussing any untoward behaviour early in a consultation, and by fostering a non-judgemental, open and supportive relationship.

Counselling

Counselling is a fundamental component of treatment, but what is meant by 'counselling' can vary. At its most rudimentary level, it involves discussing the drug user's problems, exploring possible solutions, giving advice on practical difficulties, monitoring progress and planning the future.

Counselling may be applied to specific problems that are relevant to why an individual takes drugs or has difficulty stopping, such as bereavement counselling, anger management, relaxation techniques or assertiveness training. Counselling is also used to tackle offending behaviour. Often, tasks are set to be completed by the next session. More drug-focused counselling includes motivational interviewing which works from a basis of assessing drug users' ambivalence to change, by examining the advantages and disadvantages of both stopping and continuing to use drugs. After this, the user is encouraged to examine and address the pros and cons so that the balance shifts to make change appear more advantageous, hence increasing motivation. Increasingly, more structured treatment programmes are being developed, such as residential rehabilitation, day programme care services and new programmes for offenders, both in prison and the community. Sometimes, these may be managed in conjunction with pharmaceutical treatments.

Returning to drug use after giving it up – 'relapse' – is a constant risk during treatment as well as after abstinence has been achieved. Preventing this is therefore an important aim of counselling and involves examining factors implicated in previous relapses, anticipating 'high-risk' situations when users will be vulnerable to drug use, devising strategies to deal with these situations, and putting them into practice.

Although counselling would seem to be an essential component of any treatment intervention, there has been very little research into its effectiveness. American research suggests that focused counselling, provided in a structured manner by trained therapists, produces significant benefits in reducing illicit drug use amongst those on methadone maintenance programmes and enhancing continued abstinence amongst those who have become drug-free. There is a lack of evidence from the UK, where counselling is mainly limited to imparting information and advice, and therapists are rarely trained as counsellors.

Pharmacological treatments

The use of prescribed pharmaceutical drugs is an important part of treating drug dependence and, in particular, heroin dependence. Drugs are prescribed to drug users for two main reasons: as substitutes for the drug(s) they are dependent upon and to provide relief from withdrawal symptoms.

Treatment with substitute drugs is used for either 'maintenance' or detoxification. Maintenance, where the drug user remains dependent on a prescribed drug, has been a controversial treatment for the last two decades, yet its origins date back to the beginning of the century. The Rolleston Committee effectively condoned maintenance treatment with opiates in 1926 in circumstances where "the patient, while capable of leading a useful and fairly normal life so long as he took a certain non-progressive quantity, usually small, of the drug of addiction, ceased to be able to do so when the regular allowance is withdrawn".

Maintenance treatment involves prescribing a drug for an indefinite period because an individual is unable or unwilling to become abstinent. It is usually designed as a positive step towards eventual abstinence rather than as a treatment of last resort. Those who are dependent on drugs and come forward for treatment will usually have multiple problems. To expect every dependent drug user to detoxify and remain abstinent is unrealistic when many have been ostracised by their family, have multiple debts and nowhere to live except with other drug users. Maintenance treatments 'buy time' for drug users to address these issues. Usually there are better alternatives to the drug of dependence which can be prescribed. Thus methadone is widely used as a substitute for injecting heroin dependence because it is taken by mouth, produces less variation in mood, and need only be taken once daily.

An interesting difference between different countries and cultures is the philosophy underlying such methadone maintenance treatment. In some countries, such as the USA, the approach to methadone maintenance has been considered to be largely a 'medical model' (in which the methadone is considered in some way to be correcting something close to a metabolic disorder or a deficiency state). In other countries, such as the UK, methadone maintenance is seen as part of a 'substitution model' in which it forms part of a contract between the patient and the doctor, with the methadone being an appropriate compromise alternative medication that satisfies enough of the drug craving while also being more compatible with a stable, productive life.[10]

Substitute drug prescribing is also a common method of detoxification. Gradually reducing the dose of the substitute can lead to abstinence without significant withdrawal symptoms. However, detoxification courses often progress so slowly that they become de facto maintenance.

Most of the physical withdrawal symptoms of drugs of dependence can be ameliorated by administering an appropriate pharmacological remedy. Unfortunately the anxiety, sleep disturbance and depression that are common withdrawal symptoms respond less well to pharmacological treatment and those drugs, like benzodiazepines, that provide the best relief carry the danger of dependence themselves.

Alternative therapies

Alternative or complementary therapies are becoming increasingly available at drug services. They include acupuncture, hypnosis, aromatherapy, reflexology and shiatsu. There is no substantial evidence that any of these treatments are effective. Nevertheless, they are popular, may attract users to services and help retain them in treatment,[6] allowing other proven interventions and advice to be given.

Monitoring progress

Drug users' own accounts of their drug taking are generally found to be reliable when investigated by researchers. However, in everyday clinical practice, the picture may be complicated by other pressures. Whether out of embarrassment, a desire to please, fear of censure or fear of having their treatment terminated, drug users cannot always be relied upon to give accurate reports of their drug use. Analysis of urine samples for the presence of drugs allows progress to be monitored and improves the chances of patients following treatment correctly. Instant urine tests can be used or samples may be sent to biochemistry laboratories for detailed analysis. Not surprisingly, biochemical analysis produces more detailed and accurate results than instant tests.

Research studies from the USA have explored the different ways in which urine testing can be used within treatment programmes. Development of approaches of 'contingency contracting' involved the deliberate reward and reinforcement of sought-after progress (e.g. regular attendance and correct following of treatment programmes, 'clean' urines in which there is no evidence of continued heroin use, and the securing of regular employment), with the provision of privileges such as less frequent attendance and take-home supplies of the daily methadone dose being linked to this progress against agreed therapeutic objectives.[11,12] However, in the UK, urine testing and the provision of privileges are only rarely linked in this explicit contingent manner. This approach is not without its difficulties, which include staff dissatisfaction, concern about patients who may fail to comply with such contingency management systems[13] and the higher drop-out rates from these structured programmes.[11]

Disadvantages of urine testing include only detecting recent drug use and ease of falsification unless the sample is produced under direct observation. Hair analysis is increasingly available and provides a record of drug use over time. Its high cost discourages its routine use, but in some circumstances it is an invaluable aid.

TREATMENT SETTINGS

Treatment is provided by staff with a range of skills and expertise working from a variety of settings. There are now over 500 agencies providing treatment and rehabilitation for drug users in England and Wales, over half of which are in the voluntary sector.

Needle exchange schemes and associated counselling

The main purpose of needle exchange schemes (NESs) is to prevent transmission of blood-borne diseases (HIV, hepatitis B, hepatitis C). They issue injecting equipment and condoms and take back used needles and syringes. Although returning needles and syringes is encouraged so that used ones are taken out of circulation, those who do not are still provided with new supplies.

Many NESs offer additional services including advice on safer injecting, health clinics, and HIV and hepatitis counselling and testing. They operate from a variety of settings, including drug treatment services (DDUs and CDTs), non-statutory street agencies and community pharmacies, and may be provided by outreach workers. Each setting has its own merits and disadvantages. Pharmacies are more widely accessible than drug treatment services, but the latter are better placed to offer advice and encouragement for drug users to enter treatment. Outreach workers may provide basic NESs.

NESs and their associated counselling have proved effective in reducing sharing of injecting equipment, thereby containing the spread of blood-borne infections. They have also encouraged injectors to seek help from other health, drug treatment and welfare services. They do not appear to have caused an increase in injecting.

Community drug teams

CDTs are one of the major providers of treatment for drug users, with nearly 200 in England and Wales. Their staff complement varies, but usually comprises community psychiatric nurses, social workers, and others. All provide counselling to some degree and many offer needle exchange facilities and pharmacological treatments. Medical treatment is through part-time clinical assistants (usually GPs) and should be supervised by a consultant with expertise in drug dependence. Most CDTs also provide support to GPs who treat drug users themselves.

In-patient units

Most in-patient treatment of drug users probably occurs on general psychiatric wards. When the predominant need is psychiatric treatment, as, for instance, in the case of treating amphetamine psychosis or a suicidal drug user, this is appropriate. However, specialist expertise is usually minimal in this setting, and, whenever possible, drug users needing in-patient admission should be treated in specialist units.

Specialist in-patient units usually provide services to several health authorities. Their size varies from between 10 and 20 beds. Some are dedicated drug dependence units, although most also treat alcoholism. Most are staffed by psychiatrists and psychiatric nurses. Maximum lengths of stay vary from 2–8 weeks.

Most admissions to specialist in-patient units are for detoxification from opiates. Other reasons why admission to a specialist unit may be required include stabilisation on prescribed medication, detoxification from stimulants, benzodiazepines or alcohol, assessment and treatment of physical or psychiatric conditions, and crisis intervention.

Inpatient units offer a combination of group and individual therapy with a structured programme that incorporates health education, financial advice, anxiety management, assertiveness training, and recreational activities, in addition to more direct drug-related work like relapse prevention.

Residential rehabilitation centres

'Rehabs' aim to prepare drug users for returning to as normal a life as possible in the community without misusing drugs. The first ones were introduced from the USA in the late-1960s and followed the principles of the therapeutic community. There are now over 100 centres providing residential rehabilitation in the UK. The majority are run by the voluntary sector with an increasing number of private centres. Most have retained the ethos of communal living, group meetings and shared domestic responsibilities.

Insistence on residents being drug-free at intake is now less rigidly applied, with some centres offering detoxification. Funding and referral have recently been through social rather than health services.

There are three broad types of residential rehabilitation: concept houses, religious-based organisations and '12-step' programmes. Lengths of stay range from 4–12 months, with 12-step programmes comprising the majority of those with shorter stays. Concept houses tend to be more challenging: group work is more confrontational and the structure is hierarchical with new residents having to earn privileges. Religious-based organisations are more accepting, less intense, and propound Christian values rather than dogma. Twelve-step programmes are based on the 'Minnesota Model', which is the basis of Alcoholics Anonymous and Narcotics Anonymous. Some drug users have difficulty accepting the Minnesota Model's principles of being afflicted with a lifelong illness from which they will, at best, be forever 'recovering', insistence on abstinence from all drugs, and spiritual 'surrendering to a higher power'. For those who can accept them (and the principles are interpreted with varying degrees of flexibility), 12-step programmes provide a comprehensive treatment package with an excellent network of support, through Narcotics Anonymous groups, after discharge from the programme.

Residential centres are valuable for rehabilitating entrenched drug users, those with poor family support and those who have little chance of remaining drug-free outside a protected environment. All those who stay the course in residential rehabilitation will have 'bought time' and adjusted to being drug-free. For many, the experience produces fundamental changes in attitudes, values, and interpersonal relationships.

Others

Other services for drug users include day centres, hostels, 'drop-ins', crisis intervention centres, self-help and support groups.

'Drop-in' centres are usually confidential services where people can drop in without an appointment – or at least be seen fairly quickly. They provide advice and counselling as well as guiding people towards other types of specialist help.

Day centres are a relatively new development which provide structured day programmes in the community. They offer more rigorous and intensive intervention than 'drop-in' and counselling services, with their patients being expected to attend regularly. Pilot programmes aimed at tackling offending behaviour as well as reducing drug use have recently been commissioned and funded by probation services, and can take on users who are receiving pharmaceutical treatments.

There is also a growing range of self-help support groups. These include groups for those who are still using drugs, those who are in treatment, abstinent drug users, partners of drug users, and parents of drug users. In some instances, these have grown into established voluntary organisations providing services of their own. The longest-established self-help group is Narcotics Anonymous (NA). There are about 300 NA groups meeting each week in the UK but they are mainly established in metropolitan areas, with 100 in London alone. Twelve-step programmes have gained scientific credibility since the outcome of alcoholics undergoing treatment through Alcoholics Anonymous was shown to be similar to that of those treated with conventional psychological treatments by the American Project MATCH.

SERVICE PROVIDERS

Treatment is provided by statutory services, mainly health services through NHS trusts, but also social services and probation services, the non-statutory voluntary sector, and, to a small but growing extent, by the private sector. Most community drug teams and in-patient units are provided by health services, and most residential rehabilitation centres, drop-ins and support groups are provided by the non-statutory sector. Increasingly, services are being provided by partnerships between agencies. Non-statutory services have evolved enormously. From initially relying entirely on volunteers and charitable donations, they now attract funding from health authorities and are staffed mainly by professional staff. The flexibility of non-statutory services has enabled them to complement statutory services by covering gaps in provision, often through innovative practices which have later been widely adopted.

General practice

Like other doctors, most GPs have been reluctant to treat drug users, and users themselves are often keenly aware of this (see Figure 8.1). Surveys show that GPs find drug users more difficult to treat, more time-consuming and more disruptive than any other patients, and they believe that drug dependence requires forms of treatment beyond their competence that are best provided by specialist drug dependence services. Although GPs have always

Figure 8.1. Cartoon highlighting doctors' reluctance to treat drug users. *By Mike Linnell.*

been expected to inform patients of the dangers of drug use and to look after the physical health needs of users, providing specific treatments, and especially maintenance prescribing, has been seen as the job of specialist services. This view has been endorsed by the British Medical Association which excluded methadone maintenance from its proposed definition of 'general medical services', thus making it an optional activity that should attract extra payment. The 1991 UK Health Departments' guidelines for GPs[1] advocated methadone reduction as the treatment of choice for heroin users treated by GPs and recommended that methadone maintenance remained predominantly within the province of specialist services.

Recent years have seen a volte-face in policy, with the prime objective of many purchasers of drug services being to encourage more GPs to treat drug users and, in particular, to provide methadone maintenance. This change has been influenced by several factors: the continued escalation in drug use, an increased awareness of the benefits of treatment, long waiting-lists for treatment at many specialist services, and a complete absence of specialist services in some areas. There has also been a simultaneous shift of emphasis from specialist treatment towards primary care (general practice) throughout the health service.

Increasing the role of GPs has many advantages. Young drug users may be recognised and counselled early on in their drug-using careers – before they are dependent or their use causes problems. Drug problems can be under-stood and managed appropriately to the circumstances of both the individual and the family, whom the GP may have known for many years. GPs also provide local services that are less stigmatising for drug users; and they are able to provide general medical services, such as hepatitis B testing and immunisation, contraceptive advice and cervical screening more easily than specialists.

While studies have shown that GPs' attitudes to treating drug users are largely negative, they do reveal an increased willingness to treat if training and support are made available. Thus, the concept of GPs providing 'shared care' with specialist services seems particularly apt. Shared care is not new. It forms the basis for the treatment of several other conditions including diabetes, asthma and pregnancy and enables the advantages of both primary and specialist services to be combined. Usually, shared care for drug users involves specialist drug workers, often called GP liaison workers, providing support and advice to the primary health care team at GPs' surgeries. The GP has overall responsibility for the patient's treatment, but the liaison worker retains a key role. Shared care must be arranged so that it is flexible enough to allow more or less input by the liaison worker according to the level of expertise in the GP's practice. Not all drug users can be managed within shared care – those with complex needs must remain the responsibility of specialist services. Whether treatment is provided through specialist or shared care, arrangements need to be flexible enough to allow for changes in the patient's condition.

There is no doubt that the concept of shared care has now gained pre-eminence in providing treatment services for drug users. The first recommendation of the Task Force to Review Services for Drug Misusers states that "the process of 'shared care', with appropriate support for GPs, should be available as widely as possible",[6] and, in 1997, the Department of Health directed health authorities to review urgently their shared care arrangements for treating drug users. The 1999 guidelines reinforced the importance of shared care. Recent research has shown that specialised GPs working in shared care arrangements can achieve similar results from methadone treatment to specialist services.

Community pharmacies

Community pharmacies have a key role to play in treating drug misuse. In 1995, half of all pharmacies dispensed controlled drugs to addicts, one-third sold injecting equipment and one fifth provided a needle exchange service. Clearly pharmacists have regular contact both with drug users who are in treatment and those who are not. Their role could be extended with both groups. Pharmacists are in a good position to give information, whether verbally or by distributing leaflets, about general health care measures and treatment services to those not receiving advice from treatment services. For those receiving treatment, pharmacists could have a greater role in monitoring whether patients are following their treatment regime. Many pharmacists already fulfil these roles, but more would do so if their role was made more explicit with protocols and training courses.

Although there has been reluctance in the UK to dispense methadone at the clinics where it is prescribed, some schemes, notably in Glasgow, arrange for methadone to be consumed under supervision at the pharmacy. The 1999 guidelines have placed particular emphasis on developing the pharmacist's role, recommending that, where possible, those starting treatment with methadone should have supervised consumption on a daily basis for at least the first three months.

Detoxification

Withdrawing from heroin is often described as being similar to a heavy bout of flu that lasts a week to 10 days. This might be true for those who have used heroin in small amounts for a short period only, but it understates the intensity of stomach and muscular cramps, aching bones, craving, agitation and restlessness experienced by most who go through 'cold turkey'. There are essentially three methods of opiate detoxification: gradual reduction, abrupt withdrawal and accelerated detoxification.

Gradual detoxification

The most common method of detoxification from opiates is by prescribing reducing doses of methadone. This can be carried out in the community or in a residential setting. In-patient methadone detoxification usually involves reducing the dose of methadone over 10 days. Withdrawal symptoms are most intense at the end of the reduction and diminish over the following ten days. In community detoxification the dose of methadone is gradually withdrawn over a longer period which may range from weeks to months.

The long duration of action of methadone, which makes it an excellent 'maintenance' drug, may prolong withdrawal symptoms after the final dose and other opiates may be at least as effective for gradual detoxification.

Abrupt withdrawal

Abruptly stopping opiates can cause diarrhoea, nausea, and insomnia, but clonidine and lofexidine have proved particularly effective in combatting these symptoms. Clonidine has the disadvantage of lowering blood pressure. Lofexidine has little effect on blood pressure, has been shown to be as effective as methadone reduction in an in-patient setting and is being increasingly used in preference to methadone in community detoxification.

Accelerated detoxification

In order to avoid protracted withdrawal symptoms, to shorten the course of treatment and to increase the proportion of patients completing detoxification, a radically different approach has recently been developed. Accelerated detoxification procedures use opiate-antagonist drugs (naloxone or naltrexone) which displace opiates from their sites of action in the brain. High doses of additional medication are needed to prevent severe withdrawal symptoms. There are several accelerated detoxification regimes, all of which require hospital admission. The quickest procedure uses general anaesthesia to cover the period of most intense withdrawal, but this 'ultra-rapid' detoxification has resulted in some unexpected fatalities.

Naltrexone as an aid to relapse prevention

Naltrexone has enormous potential for preventing patients relapsing as it blocks the action and effects of any opiates taken. It can be safely started immediately after completing accelerated detoxification, but not before a period of at least one week after abrupt or gradual withdrawal, otherwise it will bring on withdrawal symptoms.

Research on the effectiveness of naltrexone in preventing relapse has reported mixed results. All too often, patients stop taking the drug, either because they think they no longer need to or because they want to resume using opiates. A slow-release injection of naltrexone which remains active for several weeks is being developed.

What is the preferred setting for opiate detoxification?

There is considerable variation in patients' rates of completing opiate detoxification in different settings. Between 15% and 20% complete methadone detoxification in the community. Specialist in-patient services report success rates of about 75% for completion of methadone detoxification, with up to half of these being abstinent six months later. Advocates of accelerated detoxification claim up to 100% complete detoxification.

Only one study has compared the effectiveness of opiate detoxification in specialist and general psychiatric in-patient settings. Fifty-nine per cent of those offered admission to the specialist unit were drug-free five months after discharge and 32% had been opiate-free throughout the entire period. The corresponding figures for those randomly allocated to the general psychiatric ward were 10% and 0%. If the poor outcome for in-patients treated on a general ward is confirmed in other studies, the appropriateness of this approach must be reviewed. Both general psychiatric wards and specialist in-patient settings remove the user from their drug-using environment, remove many of the situations that prompt drug use, prevent or at least reduce contact with drug-using friends and dealers, and offer support from health professionals. Clearly, there are features of a specialist unit that are especially beneficial. It is likely that the intensive daily group programmes and individual counselling that are features of specialist in-patient services have a significant effect.

Specialist inpatient services are expensive and cannot satisfy the demand from drug users wanting to detoxify. The protection offered by an inpatient setting is artificial and temporary. How relapse rates for those completing inpatient treatment compare with those detoxified in the community is unknown.

Maintenance treatments for opiate dependence

Methadone maintenance treatment

Methadone has advantages over heroin as a maintenance drug because it can be taken by mouth and produces effects that last over 24 hours, and methadone maintenance has now been adopted by all Western European countries as a valuable tool to treat heroin dependence and reduce the spread of HIV.[14] Since it was first described in 1965, several controlled studies have confirmed its ability to substantially reduce illicit drug use, injecting, and crime while improving physical and mental health and social functioning. Recently research has focused on what types of methadone treatment programmes produce the best results. An American study of six programmes found the proportion of patients who continued to inject drugs varied from 10% to 56%. The most successful programmes retained patients in treatment longer, prescribed higher doses of methadone, did not enforce detoxification after a period of maintenance, provided better counselling and medical services, achieved a good level of clinic attendance by patients, had a close long-term relationship with patients, and low rates of staff turnover.[15]

The importance of the dose of methadone and the provision of ancillary services in addition to merely taking methadone has been confirmed by many studies. A daily dose of 80 mg of methadone results in half the illicit heroin use that a dose of 40 mg does. A minimal service, involving only emergency counselling and advice in addition to methadone, produces some improvement but effectiveness is considerably enhanced by regular supervised counselling and urine testing, and is further improved by adding medical and psychiatric services, social work, family therapy and employment counselling. Cost–benefit analysis has shown that the middle of these three levels of ancillary services produces the most cost-effective outcomes.

The key public health component of methadone maintenance is best exemplified in the Netherlands where 'low-threshold' programmes accessed by the majority of heroin users are run by the metropolitan authorities and 'high-threshold' programmes by the health authorities. Low threshold programmes demand only that service users turn up to take their methadone. Their prime intention is to contact the maximum number of heroin addicts and minimise sharing of injecting equipment. Their impact on illicit drug use is modest but 80% of all the Netherlands' heroin addicts are said to use the service at any one time. High-threshold programmes are more demanding of patients and provide intensive treatment aimed at eliminating illicit drug use and working towards abstinence.

The way methadone maintenance treatment is given in the UK differs fundamentally from the rest of the world. Elsewhere, methadone consumption is supervised at specialist centres with patients usually having to attend every day. In Britain, methadone is usually dispensed from community pharmacies with no supervised consumption. The frequency at which methadone is dispensed also depends on the prescribing doctor. On a national basis, only one-third of UK methadone prescriptions are for daily (or six-days-a-week) dispensing, with no less than one-third being dispensed at weekly or greater intervals. The UK is also unique in having a substantial proportion of patients receiving methadone prescribed by GPs.[16,17]

There are advantages and disadvantages to supervised consumption at a specialist clinic. Advantages include knowing that the methadone is being taken and not sold on to others, preventing methadone overdoses and being able to observe the patient each day. Disadvantages include having drug users congregating together each day, which interferes with their ability to resume normal daily activities. A compromise strongly recommended in the new guidelines is for methadone consumption to be supervised by community pharmacists.

It is widely acknowledged that an unknown but significant amount of prescribed methadone is sold on to others. Claims have even been made that this is not necessarily a bad thing, as it may help reduce drug-related crime and encourage those who buy illicit methadone to come forward for treatment. There has, however, been a steady increase in the number of deaths attributed to methadone overdose and, in some areas of the country, there is evidence that methadone is used by those who have never taken heroin.

Maintenance treatment using other oral opiates

Two other opiates have been evaluated as maintenance treatments for opiate dependence and found to be as effective as methadone. LAAM (L-α-acetylmethadol) is a synthetic opiate that is related to methadone. It has a very long duration of action so need only be taken three times a week. This has considerable advantages in supervised dispensing programmes, as frequency of attendance at clinics can be substantially reduced. One potential disadvantage is that the onset of the effects of LAAM is delayed for several hours after consumption. This could lead to some drug users taking it, being disappointed that there is no immediate effect, using heroin or other opiates, and then experiencing an overdose of opiates when the delayed action of LAAM occurs. Sadly, LAAM is not yet licensed for use in the UK, and it is high time it was.

Buprenorphine (Temgesic) is an opiate analgesic that has several theoretical advantages over methadone. Like LAAM it is longer-acting and so need only be given three or four times a week. It may also be easier to withdraw from than methadone, causing less severe withdrawal symptoms, and is probably safer than methadone in overdose. Buprenorphine acts on opiate receptors in the brain in such a way as to block the actions of other opiates taken subsequently. In some parts of the UK, buprenorphine has been the most popular misused opiate, without apparently blocking the effects of heroin and other opiates. In controlled trials, buprenorphine has proved to be equally effective to methadone.

Buprenorphine is the most common maintenance treatment for opiate dependence in France. It has been formulated in high doses appropriate for treating drug users, and in combination with naloxone, which deters addicts from injecting the drug. It has recently been licensed for the treatment of heroin dependence in the UK, but its use is likely to be restricted as the formulation that deters injecting is, as yet, unavailable.

The 'British System' allows doctors to treat heroin addiction by prescribing whatever drug they believe will be most effective (although prescribing heroin, cocaine and diconal for the treatment of addiction is limited to doctors with a licence from the Home Office). Several other oral opiates are being used as heroin substitutes in maintenance treatment, but none has yet been evaluated.

Maintenance using injectable opiates

Prescribing injectable drugs to treat heroin addiction is another unique feature of the 'British System' and approximately 10% of prescriptions for methadone in the UK are for the injectable form. Rationales for prescribing injectable drugs are that some patients continue to inject regularly when receiving oral methadone and that some are only attracted into treatment because injectables are available. There is no research evidence to support or refute the purported benefits of injectable methadone. The guidelines place prescribing injectables firmly in the arena of the specialist or specialised generalist, since it is generally a treatment of last resort for drug users who will not or cannot stop injecting. These patients' problems are often extremely difficult to treat, and the skills needed are not usually found in general practice. It is therefore worrying that almost as much injectable methadone is prescribed by GPs as by specialist services, and that prescribing injectables is particularly common in the private sector.

How much injectable heroin is prescribed is not known. In 1995, 55 doctors had heroin licences and most of them prescribed heroin to less than 10 patients. Heroin is generally unsuitable as a maintenance drug because it has a short duration of action, has to be injected at least three times daily to avoid withdrawal and is very expensive to prescribe. There are further disadvantages: urine testing is unable to reveal whether those prescribed heroin are 'topping up' by using street heroin; and there is the increased risk of prescribed heroin being sold on the street. Protagonists of heroin maintenance claim that heroin prescribing attracts the highest proportion of opiate addicts into treatment and minimises the additional drug use that is common in methadone treatment. They also believe that prescribing heroin instead of methadone will stop addicts stealing to fund their habit and so help eradicate the illicit heroin trade.

A comparison of injectable heroin and oral methadone carried out in London in the early 1970s found that the best and worst results were among those prescribed methadone with those receiving heroin occupying the middle ground. More recently, a large Swiss trial of heroin maintenance in the treatment of heroin addicts who had failed to improve on oral methadone maintenance produced favourable results over a range of outcomes.[18] It is important to note, though, that all the Swiss subjects had failed to respond to oral methadone treatment programmes and had to attend to inject heroin three times each day under supervision in treatment centres. Nevertheless, there is considerable international interest in heroin maintenance and several further studies are planned. This topic is discussed further in Chapter 10 (pp. 234–236).

Stimulants

After cannabis, amphetamine is the most widely used drug in the UK. For most amphetamine users it is a 'recreational' drug and unlikely to lead to major problems, but there exist an unknown proportion who inject and/or whose amphetamine use is severely dependent. The emergence of smokeable crack cocaine has resulted in exposure to the rapid and short-lived dependence-inducing highs of cocaine that previously only followed injecting the drug.

Services for users of stimulant drugs are poorly developed. This may be owing to a lack of treatments as effective or as attractive to users as those for opiate dependence. There is also good evidence that drug services are viewed as being for heroin addicts and are thus unattractive to those who have problems with stimulants.

There remains a belief that dependence on amphetamine and cocaine is not physical and 'only psychological', and so must be overcome by strength of will rather than medical treatment. Advances in our knowledge of how stimulants work have clearly demonstrated that stimulant withdrawal states, although manifest in altered mood and not observable physical signs, are the result of profound disruption of brain activity.

The actions of amphetamine and cocaine on the brain are similar and account for their common effects and withdrawal syndrome. Although treatment approaches have tended to be drug-specific, similar treatments are likely to be effective for both drugs.

Treatment of amphetamine misuse

In the late 1960s, attempts to treat injecting amphetamine use by prescribing injectable methamphetamine were judged a therapeutic failure. Nevertheless, there is a small but increasing number of treatment agencies that prescribe oral dexamphetamine on a reducing or maintenance basis akin to prescribing methadone for heroin addiction. Such oral amphetamine substitution treatment is highly controversial. Opponents of dexamphetamine treatment point to evidence from animal studies showing that methamphetamine has toxic effects on the brain, and to the dangers of inducing an amphetamine psychosis and of tablets being injected. Proponents of treatment with dexamphetamine cite the absence of evidence that dexamphetamine is neurotoxic to humans, the likelihood of psychosis being reduced by prescribing controlled amounts under medical supervision, the difficulty of preparing tablets for injection and the availability of dexamphetamine as a non-injectable liquid to be drunk.

Alternatives to dexamphetamine substitution are to support users through withdrawal symptoms, if necessary in an in-patient setting, and prescribing antidepressant drugs. The rationale for antidepressants is based on the profoundly depressed mood that is typical of amphetamine withdrawal and claims that some antidepressants (selective serotonin reuptake inhibitors) have properties that should reduce craving.

Evidence for the effectiveness of any treatment approach is scanty. One uncontrolled study of dexamphetamine substitution found significantly reduced injecting, illicit amphetamine use and criminal activity but was limited by its reliance on self-reports. A recent study comparing matched groups receiving dexamphetamine substitution, treatment without dexamphetamine (but often with antidepressants) and a control group not in treatment, found significant improvements across a range of outcomes for both treatment groups, with the greatest benefits resulting from treatment with dexamphetamine.

A barrier to the evaluation of dexamphetamine treatments has been the inability of urine testing to differentiate between prescribed dexamphetamine and illicit amphetamine sulphate. This has now been overcome and should lead to improved monitoring of those in dexamphetamine substitution treatment and better evaluation of treatment programmes. Although the guidelines now recommend that treatment with dexamphetamine is only initiated by specialists or specialised generalists, it is disturbing that of the estimated 1000 individuals receiving treatment with dexamphetamine, almost half are treated by GPs, who are unlikely to have the expertise needed in this area.

Treatment of cocaine misuse

Cocaine leads to more problems in the USA than any other drug and the treatment of cocaine users has consequently received considerable research attention there. As the effects of cocaine (and amphetamine) enhance the activity of dopamine in certain brain areas and withdrawal symptoms are associated with subsequent depletion of dopamine, research has concentrated on drugs affecting this neurotransmitter. Unfortunately, initially promising results have, as yet, not been confirmed.

Drugs that increase dopamine activity (dopamine agonists) might be expected to relieve the craving for cocaine and diminish withdrawal symptoms. Several dopamine agonists have been studied but none has produced sustained benefits. Using the reverse approach, drugs that oppose the actions of dopamine (dopamine antagonists) might be beneficial in blocking the stimulant and euphoric effects when cocaine is taken. Haloperidol is a dopamine antagonist used to treat schizophrenia, but unfortunately such high doses of haloperidol have to be used to block cocaine's activity that the drug's sedating effects render the patient incapable of any useful action.

A different approach involves administering a drug that interacts with cocaine to bring about unpleasant effects (a similar principal to treating alcoholism with Antabuse). Monoamine oxidase inhibitors (MAOIs) are antidepressants whose use has been limited by their interactions with a variety of foods and other drugs. If cocaine is taken by an individual who is receiving treatment with MAOIs, a violent throbbing headache ensues, but may involve a rise in blood pressure that could be fatal.

The most promising results so far have been obtained by using a conventional tricyclic antidepressant, desipramine. Desipramine was chosen because of all antidepressants it has the greatest action on dopamine and is relatively free of side-effects. High doses of desipramine have resulted in diminution of craving and cocaine use, but these effects are delayed for about two weeks after treatment is instigated. Combinations of a dopamine agonist (which acts immediately) and desipramine have failed to show significant prolonged improvement. In-patient admission is often the only practical measure that can be taken to interrupt a cycle of repeated high-dose cocaine use, but relapse soon after discharge is common.

Despite a vast amount of research emanating almost exclusively from the USA, no treatment for cocaine dependence has been conclusively shown to be effective in producing sustained abstinence.

Treatment of benzodiazepine misuse

Benzodiazepines replaced barbiturates in the 1970s as commonly prescribed treatments for anxiety disorders and insomnia. Barbiturates are particularly dangerous in overdose and doctors hoped to prevent the large number of suicides in which they played a part by substituting benzodiazepines. Unfortunately, these drugs also replaced barbiturates as widely misused street drugs used alone or in combination with other substances. Short-acting benzodiazepines like temazepam are the most likely to be misused. Injecting benzodiazepines is common practice among drug users and is associated with particularly high levels of psychopathology, criminality and HIV-risk behaviour. The popularity of temazepam on the streets and the problems of injecting the contents of gel-filled capsules has led to the withdrawal of this preparation in the UK.

Benzodiazepines may be used in combination with other drugs to intensify intoxication, 'take the edge off' the effects of stimulants, or ameliorate withdrawal symptoms. They may be taken in high doses as the main drug used in order to produce profound intoxication. They could be used to self-medicate anxiety disorders or sleep disturbance, and their continued use may be in order to avoid benzodiazepine withdrawal symptoms. In order to treat benzodiazepine misuse it is important to establish the reason or reasons they are taken: this may be difficult as the user's account may be biased towards the response most likely to be rewarded with a prescription.

The only indication for prescribing benzodiazepines to those who misuse the drug is established dependence, which must be confirmed by urine testing. Prescriptions should be for longer acting preparations, such as diazepam, on a reducing basis and issued for daily dispensing. Those who fail to complete benzodiazepine detoxification in the community may fare better if treated in specialist in-patient units. A decision to prescribe benzodiazepines on a long-term basis to anyone with a history of drug misuse should not be taken lightly and only after consultation with specialist services.

Despite widespread misuse of benzodiazepines among the illicit drug using population in the UK and elsewhere, there has been no systematic research into the effectiveness of any treatment.

Ecstasy and related drugs

The enormous increase in the use of ecstasy (MDMA) and the related drugs Adam (MDA or 3,4-methylenedioxyamphetamine) and Eve (MDEA or 3,4-methylenedioxyethylamphetamine) in Britain is intimately related to the 'rave scene'. Deaths from using these drugs have received enormous publicity. Most deaths have resulted from the combined effects of ecstasy or related drugs, vigorous exercise in hot surroundings, and inadequate replacement of lost fluids so that the body overheats. Heeding advice to take breaks from dancing and drink a pint of a non-alcoholic drink every hour while sweating heavily in this environment would have prevented most of the fatalities. Rave clubs should ensure that this information is widely available and that supplies of cheap (or free) non-alcoholic drinks are available. Many clubs have drug workers constantly present during opening hours to give advice and institute emergency treatment if needed.

In addition to advising club and rave attenders how to avoid dehydration when they use the drug, those that take ecstasy should be warned that taking high doses or using cocktails of drugs increases the dangers substantially. The fallacy that pure ecstasy is safe with dangers resulting only from contaminants or 'fake E' should be corrected.

Hallucinogens

Problems caused by LSD, 'magic mushrooms' and other hallucinogens include 'bad trips' and drug-induced psychoses. Bad trips are states of terror induced by the frightening features of an hallucinogenic experience. They may last for up to 12 hours but will subside when the effect of the drug has worn off. They require constant reassurance in a quiet, non-threatening environment. Hallucinogen-induced psychoses resemble acute onset schizophrenia and should be treated with antipsychotic medication.

Cannabis

Most of those who use cannabis do so without sustaining harm beyond that caused by the toxic effects of cannabis and tobacco smoke on their lungs. In countries where cannabis grows naturally and is available cheaply and in potent forms, heavy use may bring about a toxic confusional state characterised by acute onset of delusions and hallucinations, disorientation and amnesia. Cannabis can also bring about an acute psychosis and precipitate relapse of a schizophrenic illness.

Tolerance may develop to the drug's effects and dependence on cannabis develops insidiously in some heavy users. Although cannabis users rarely request help to stop or reduce their use, the numbers doing so are increasing. The minimal demand for treatment may be because no specific treatment is available or because of users' perception that treatment centres are for heroin users. The increasing availability of potent strains of cannabis may result in more users seeking treatment. Those who do request treatment may be helped by counselling and the general measures described earlier.

Performance-enhancing drugs

Use of performance-enhancing drugs, particularly anabolic steroids, is widespread in gyms across the UK. Anabolic steroids are usually injected intramuscularly. Rates of needle-sharing among steroid users may be higher than those of heroin injectors. Needle exchange facilities and information on the dangers of performance enhancing drugs should be readily available and provided in a way that is accessible to this group. Performance-enhancing drugs do not induce dependence, but they have dangerous effects on physical and mental health. The medical profession has a role in minimising harm by monitoring physical and biochemical changes and advising of the dangers to mental and physical health.

TREATMENT OF SPECIFIC GROUPS

Young drug users

The extent of problematic drug use among the young is unknown. In some areas, half of all 16–17-year-olds have taken an illegal drug. Although cannabis is the most common drug used, levels of amphetamine, ecstasy and LSD use are worrying and the 2% who have taken heroin and 3% cocaine especially so. Drug users in treatment frequently date their drug problems back to early adolescence.

Young drug users rarely attend specialist services and, when they do, treatment options are not straightforward. Many specialist services are only allowed to treat those over 18 years old and offering advice, counselling or needle exchange to the under 16s introduces dilemmas over confidentiality. Young drug users may attend for treatment only because of pressure from parents, schools or social services. Their motivation to change may be minimal and there are considerable risks that they may find the lifestyles of the older drug users they meet at the clinic exciting and glamorous. Further, the skills and experience needed to work with young drug users are usually unavailable at adult services.

A report on drug services for young people by the Health Advisory Service, then an inspectorate of the Department of Health, emphasised the need for drug services that are specifically dedicated to young people, but found very few examples of such services and only isolated examples of good practice.[19] The report stressed the importance of young people's services being in convenient sites and open outside school hours with collaboration between youth services, schools, social services, child and adolescent psychiatrists and specialist adult drug services.

Although drug use is common among the young, drug dependence, although increasing, is unusual. Drug dependence in the young is usually accompanied by behavioural and emotional difficulties that necessitate a combined approach with other professionals. It may require residential treatment, but the dearth of specialist services is especially apparent in this area.

Pregnant drug users

Pregnant drug users present particular problems for both specialist and generic services. Fertility is likely to be reduced in untreated dependent drug users. Absent or irregular menstrual cycles may be the result of a drug lifestyle or a direct effect of misused drugs. Improvement brought about at the onset of treatment may catch women who do not use contraception unaware and result in an unwanted pregnancy. Dangers to the foetus include intrauterine growth retardation, infection, obstetric complications and, to the newborn child, drug withdrawal symptoms. Pregnant drug users may be reluctant to attend treatment services or to keep antenatal appointments with GPs and maternity services. Emotions of guilt, embarrassment, or a fear that their baby or other children may be taken into care are common. However, some drug users respond to pregnancy with an increased motivation to change and there have been considerable improvements in the treatment of this group in response. Many drug services have a specialist drug liaison midwife who facilitates liaison between drug services, general practice, maternity services and paediatricians.

Although pregnant drug users still face prejudice from a wide range of professionals, this is becoming markedly less. Social services are more likely to offer support, for instance by providing nursery places for other children, than immediately institute care proceedings. When babies have to stay in hospital for treatment of opiate withdrawal symptoms, staff will encourage the mother to breast feed and visit the baby regularly. Drug services recognise that giving up drugs is not necessarily the most important advice that pregnant drug users should heed. Giving practical advice about diet and lifestyle, including reducing cigarette smoking and alcohol consumption, is frequently overlooked and may be more achievable. For women treated with methadone the dangers to the foetus from relapse into street drug use are far greater than those of continuing with methadone, so reductions in dose, although desirable, may have to be revised or abandoned.

Drug users with mental illness

The frequent coexistence of drug use and mental illness brings additional problems for the management of both conditions. Many drugs, particularly amphetamine and cocaine, can induce severe mental illness in those previously in good health. Drugs may worsen the symptoms of pre-existing mental illness and bring about relapse in recurrent conditions. Drugs may also be used by those with mental illness as a form of self-medication for their symptoms or to counter the side-effects of medication. Therefore, drug use can be both a cause or result of mental illness.

The relevance of drug use to the onset of mental illness is often unclear. Although it is well-known that amphetamine can induce psychosis with symptoms identical to paranoid schizophrenia, amphetamine use is common and the relationship of the two conditions may be coincidental. Patients attending psychiatric services may not disclose information about their drug use for a variety of reasons. Conversely, a patient's accurate account of his or her drug use may not be believed. Urine testing for drugs may clarify the picture but needs careful interpretation. The relationship between mental illness and other drugs is much less clear. Cannabis may be a factor in relapse of schizophrenic disorders, but testing urine for cannabis is unlikely to be helpful as traces of the drug may be present in urine for several weeks after it was last used. Ecstasy may cause depressive and anxiety disorders but, again, the relationship may be entirely coincidental.

In the last decade or so, the misuse of alcohol and drugs by people with chronic psychotic illnesses – mainly young men with chronic or recurrent episodes of schizophrenia – has become an increasingly prominent problem on both sides of the Atlantic. These 'dual diagnosis' or 'comorbid' patients are usually unemployed and often live alone. They rarely seek treatment and tend to 'fall between two stools', partly because both the general psychiatric services and drug services tend to regard them as the other's responsibility. They are also responsible for a high proportion of the violent acts committed by the mentally ill. As yet, no management strategy has been demonstrated to be effective in this singularly difficult population, although the emerging evidence suggests that a single therapeutic team employing 'assertive outreach' methods, and proficient in the management of both psychosis and drug misuse, is more effective than well-intentioned collaboration between separate drug dependence and general psychiatric services.[20]

Whether through possessing drugs, committing crimes to raise funds for drugs or other reasons, drug users are frequently in contact with the criminal justice system. Opportunities for intervention are numerous and exist at several stages of the judicial process: on arrest, at detention in police cells, before trial, at sentencing, in prison and through probation services. Further, the potential for achieving change in drug use may be increased by an element of coercion.

The majority of police forces have arrest referral schemes that operate with varying degrees of sophistication. At a minimum level a police officer may issue a card with information on where an individual can seek help for a drug problem. In some areas, drug workers are assigned to police stations or courts so they are immediately available to see drug users. This proactive model of arrest referral has been evaluated in three areas of the UK.[21] Almost half of those seen by drug workers had had no previous contact with drug agencies, although they typically had long criminal histories with an average of 21 convictions. At a subsequent interview 6–8 months after referral, one-quarter reported not using any illicit drugs and over half had stopped injecting drugs. The average amount of money spent on drugs each week fell from £400 at the time of arrest to £70 at follow up interview. The Anti-Drug Coordinator's 1998/99 annual report states that, by 2002, all police services should operate face-to face arrest referral schemes covering all custody suites.

When confronted with the option of treatment in residential rehabilitation or imprisonment it is not surprising that a drug user will usually choose the former. There is a risk that drug users' stays in residential rehabilitation may last only a few days and their probation officer may chose not to 'breach' them by going back to the courts. Probation orders conditional on treatment in the community may therefore be more realistic. There are now indications that the potential for treating drug users who come before the courts is going to be realised. 'Treatment and Testing Orders' are being developed that will allow an alternative to custody for drug-using offenders who agree to undergo treatment. Supervised by the probation service, progress reports will be submitted to the courts with revocation of the order and imprisonment for those who do not demonstrate improvement. Three UK pilot schemes are currently underway and awaiting evaluation. If they prove effective, Treatment and Testing Orders will almost certainly be adopted on a national basis. Mr Hellawell also announced that £60 million would be available in 1999 to fund this initiative.

Treatment services in prisons have improved substantially over recent years, but there are still wide variations in policy and considerable impediments to developing good practice. Examples of best practice include detoxification programmes, facilities for cleaning injecting equipment, drug-free prison wings, prison drug workers and liaison workers. Impediments to good practice include a lack of training of prison staff, uncertainty as to the fate of remand prisoners, sudden transfer of inmates to other prisons, and poor links with community treatment services that may be far away or have waiting lists. Resolution of these difficulties will certainly be helped by a substantial forthcoming investment by the prison service into new treatment programmes as well as providing "counselling, assessment, referral, advice and throughcare services" (CARATS) for drug-using prisoners. By 2002, CARATS are expected to have an annual case-load of 20 000 with 5000 prisoners placed in treatment programmes each year.

The effectiveness of interventions instigated through all stages of the criminal justice system depends on police officers, probation officers, police surgeons, magistrates, judges and prison staff being trained in identifying drug problems and having some knowledge of treatment procedures. Monitoring response to treatment with hair testing and maintaining abstinence by supervised administration of naltrexone have obvious potential that has not yet been exploited and will require substantial further training of drug workers. Further, if drug users are to be effectively diverted into treatment, drug services must be able to respond rapidly without the impediment of long waiting lists. There is also a risk that the recent and most welcome investment into drug treatment within the criminal justice system might result in quicker and better treatment for offenders than for those who request treatment and are not involved in legal proceedings, and even displacement of those who seek help voluntarily.

Conclusion

This chapter began by describing trends in the treatment of drug use up to publication of the current national strategy and the appointment of Keith Hellawell as the first UK Anti-Drugs Coordinator. Throughout this period, treatment has been influenced by a series of authoritative reports that have been produced in response to threats from drug use, and have been based on what was then current practice and, latterly, research evidence. The 'British System' for treating drug use remains idiosyncratic and as distinct from treatment elsewhere as ever.

Regulations and national policies discourage innovation and the relative freedom of British doctors has enabled some important treatment developments to take place. Heroin maintenance was practised from early in the century although to this day, with the exception of research projects in Switzerland and the Netherlands, in no other country can heroin be used as a treatment for addiction. Needle Exchange Schemes, the cornerstone of harm reduction, were begun by enterprising volunteers in 1960s London and in 1964 a health service maintenance programme with daily dispensing was started in Birmingham. The swift, pragmatic response to the advent of HIV resulted in infection rates amongst injecting drug users that are considerably lower than in most Western countries whereas the USA, for all its research activity, has yet to accept needle exchange.

The biggest failing in Britain's drug services is the persistent failure to evaluate its treatment approaches adequately or to develop practice in response to evidence of efficacy, with training lagging far behind research findings. Injectable opiates and dexamphetamine have been widely prescribed for decades, but we still have no firm evidence either way as to their effectiveness. The emerging predominance of 'shared care' arrangements in methadone treatment may be a good idea but is radically different from the regulated American programmes for which there is the best evidence of major reductions in heroin use. With the National Treatment Outcome Research Study, a tentative beginning has been made to evaluation. This large national study has demonstrated that the main specialist treatments provided in the UK are cost-effective,[22] with every £1 spent on treatment saving more than £3 in costs to the community, but this falls far short of the $7 saving for every $1 spent in the USA.[23] Although treatment should not be rigidly restricted to what has been proved to be effective, in the UK or overseas, it must be subject to rigorous evaluation, so that what really works can be developed and what does not work discontinued.

Chapter 9. Lessons from history

SUMMARY

Throughout history, there have been episodes where drug use has suddenly increased, perhaps through technical innovations, such as cigarette manufacture, or sudden increases in availability. Societies and governments have responded to these 'epidemics' in a number of ways and, despite the disparate historical contexts and drugs involved, certain common themes emerge as to what interventions work to reduce drug-related harm, and under which circumstances.

Price and availability are crucial factors affecting drug consumption, both of which are more easily influenced with legal than illegal substances. The success of an intervention will depend on who makes it, when, and the views and interests of those it affects. Interventions by a discredited and weak body, such as the Soviet state in the 1980s, are less likely to gain the public's support and achieve their aims. If attempts to reduce the availability of a drug are made early enough, before it is well-established within a society or among individual users, they may succeed in curbing an epidemic. Otherwise, as occurred in Japan in the 1940s, users are likely to seek alternative drug supplies with the potential for greater risks to their health and of encouraging a black market. Public support repeatedly emerges as vital to success – despite its eventual repeal, alcohol Prohibition was strictly observed in those American states and Canadian provinces that backed it strongly, achieving considerable reductions in alcohol related diseases. Vested interests in encouraging consumption, such as Japanese organised crime in the 1970s, can push in the opposite direction; as one drug falls from favour, they may even provide new drugs for future epidemics. Interventions are only part of the story, since many of the changes in patterns of drug consumption seem to owe more to wider social and economic changes, and unpredictable fashions can draw users from one drug to another.

INTRODUCTION

Throughout history, drug use has ebbed and flowed. Episodes of greatly increased use – epidemics – follow a technical innovation, such as the flue-curing of tobacco leaves and the mass production of cigarettes, or the isolation of cocaine from coca leaves, or from a sudden drop in a drug's price, as happened with gin in 18th-century England. As Chapter 3 described, drug use in Britain is higher now than at any time in living memory and at the turn of the millennium we are facing a resurgence of heroin use in particular. Past epidemics of drug use have been met with varying responses both from governments and the governed, so what can the successes and failures of these interventions teach us about policy options today?

An 'epidemic' is simply a marked increase in incidence, and although the term is often associated with infectious diseases, it is not used here to imply that drug use is passed from person to person like a germ, without any conscious action, (although such a metaphor has been used in the past, perhaps unhelpfully, to describe drug addiction). The term 'epidemic' is sometimes used in an alarmist way, singling out a particular type of drug use from wider trends, as a special phenomenon that requires urgent action. It is therefore important to be aware of the reasons for focusing on one particular form of drug use and not another that may be occurring at the same time.

There are reasons for caution in drawing direct comparisons between the epidemics of the past and contemporary drug use. First, motives for drug use vary considerably and today most use, such as taking cannabis, ecstasy or heroin, is hedonistic, with neither religious significance nor any intended medicinal benefit. This is not to say that religion and medicine have no part in contemporary drug use – the misuse of minor tranquillisers, such as benzodiazepines, spans medical and recreational use, and those seeking spiritual insight may have experimented with LSD or other hallucinogens.

Second, harm arising from drug use should not be measured by the scale of the public, media or professional outcry which surrounds it. New drugs, new methods of use, and the involvement of people seen as threats to the social order, such as the young, ethnic minorities and the socially deprived, tend to arouse disproportionate attention. This raises questions about who is defining a particular drug-using phenomenon as a problem and why. For instance, the smoking of crack cocaine by young, unemployed Blacks in the USA in the 1980s combined several of these elements and aroused huge public contro-versy, while wealthy White Americans snorting cocaine a decade earlier tended to be regarded as 'chic' and their behaviour as of much less signifi-cance. The scapegoating of a particular group for the wider problems of society may be one of the mechanisms at work here.

Finally, another factor which makes direct comparisons between the past and present difficult is the difference in historical definitions. The concept of 'addiction', for instance, was not an important part of 19th-century concepts of drug taking, even with opium use. Opium had the same pharmacological properties then as now and its addictive properties were described in great detail by De Quincey at the beginning of the 19th century, but with so little concern or record of this at that time, it is difficult to assess historically what is one of our main preoccupations with drug use today.

Opium in 19th-century England

The position of opium in 19th-century England illustrates some of the differences between current drug use and some previous epidemics, and the different dangers perceived then and now. In the early-19th century, opium and laudanum (tincture of opium made with distilled water and alcohol) were legal, cheap and freely available. With the lack of regular medical care affordable to the working classes (and often of limited effectiveness for those who could afford it) and little in the way of effective pain relief, opium and laudanum were used as 'cure-alls', providing pain relief, a general feeling of well-being, and easing a range of common symptoms.[1,2]

Nowadays, when faced with patients who need treatment for their drug use, one of the first things the doctor will try to determine is whether they are dependent on the drugs they use. Yet, for much of the 19th century, the emphasis was quite different. Excessive opium-eating was regarded as overindulgence, rather like gluttony, and long-term use seemed to be of little concern. Dean Isaac Milner told William Wilberforce (who had originally started taking opium in 1788 to relieve a stomach ulcer):

> "Be not afraid of the *habit* of such medicine, the *habit* of growling guts is infinitely worse. There is nothing injurious to the constitution in the medicines and if you use them all your life there is no great harm. But paroxysms of laxity or pain leave permanent evil".

Distinguishing between the physical and mental relief opium brought is difficult, since it provided both.[3] Overtly recreational use was mainly restricted to small groups such as the Romantic writers and poets, and this 'luxurious' use of opium seems to have been disapproved of by 'respectable' society, although no more so than over-indulgence in alcohol.

Even here, there was some cross-over, as Thomas De Quincey, who persisted in using opium for its power "over the grander and more shadowy world of dreams" had initially taken opium to relieve the "terrific curse" of chronic toothache.[2] The origins and reasons for continuing opium use became a source of argument between Coleridge, another literary opium eater, and De Quincey, and after the former's death, De Quincey publicly claimed that, while they had both become involved in opium innocently, they had knowingly persisted. Coleridge, he stated, had taken opium "not as a relief from any bodily pains or nervous irritations – for his constitution was strong and excellent – but as a source of luxurious sensations".

Opium use did present medical problems by today's definitions. A high number of both infants and adults died from opium overdoses, and opium poisoning was a frequent occurrence, yet it was not until the end of the century that the public regarded moderate use of opium as detrimental to health. Those who led concern over the use of opium, in particular the public health movement, and the medical and pharmacy professions who eventually persuaded Parliament to place restrictions on its sale, revealed their political motives in the way they pursued control over its use.

The 1868 Pharmacy Act reflected the efforts of the emerging medical and pharmacy professions who were defining their areas of competence. Up until 1868 drugs were sold by people with varying levels of qualifications or none at all and before 1840 the profession of pharmacy hardly existed. The Act was intended to place the sale of opiates under pharmaceutical control (although in practice it had little impact), but was mainly effective in drawing a line between medical and non-medical opiate use and helped shape our current view of drug use as either recreational or medical.

These variations in the role of a particular drug – its social and medical significance – reveal some of the difficulties in matching epidemics of drug use to different contexts. Finally, while many historical facts can be stated with confidence, it is much harder to determine whether one event caused another. The use of 'control' groups employed in scientific experiments is rarely possible in the study of historical or contemporary society. It is unlikely, for instance, for a policy or event to occur in one community, and an identical community where this did not occur to be available for comparison. This means that most of our conclusions are 'best guesses'. Bearing in mind these difficulties, there are still some patterns that seem to recur through history, and there are a range of historical drug epidemics in which these can be traced.

GIN AND DISTILLED SPIRITS IN ENGLAND, 1650–1760

As Chapters 2 and 3 show, compared to drugs with a more established history, new drugs or formulations tend to excite attention disproportionate to the harm they cause, but the fact that their use has not been integrated into accepted social behaviour can cause real problems. The story of gin shows how a combination of increased availability and reduced prices led to a problem that could not be reversed by changing either of these factors. However, it is also a story of consumption by the poor arousing disproportionate attention compared with heavy drinking by the middle and upper classes. Efforts to reduce drinking were hampered by the vested interests of gin producers and the Exchequer, and the unpopular methods used to control the trade. Consumption eventually fell after moderate price and licensing controls were brought in, acceptable methods of law enforcement were used, the brewing industry reemerged as a strengthened competitor, and drinking fashions changed.

The traditional drink of British working people and the poor of all ages had, for many centuries, been beer, which provided a staple ingredient and essential nutrients in a poor diet. In the 18th century the 'small beer' drunk at every meal had an alcohol content as low as 2–3%. In 1688, two and a half barrels of beer and ale were produced for every man, woman and child. Even when production had fallen from this peak, almost a third of the arable land of England in 1695 was devoted to barley for beer and ale. Its sale had been firmly controlled since the reign of Edward VI in the middle of the 16th century who had made it illegal to sell ale and beer except at licensed houses.

Gin and other distilled spirits were first introduced into England from the Netherlands through the contact with Dutch wares, customs and tastes that resulted from frequent wars, commerce and immigration. The process for distilling gin was perfected in the mid-17th century and imported brandy and rum had gained popularity by the 1680s, but it was not until the following century that distilled spirits came within reach of anyone other than the wealthy. A sudden price reduction in distilled alcohol brought distilled spirits to a level affordable by the labouring classes and demand rose.

During the reign of William and Mary (1689–1702), the monopoly on the production of spirits of the London Distillers Guild was broken, encouraging the widespread distillation and retail sale of spirits made from English grain on payment of a duty. At the same time, taxation was added to beer and other fermented drinks. Wine was too expensive for ordinary people because of the high transportation costs from continental Europe. By 1688, distillers were thriving with duty levied on 0.5 million gallons (2.3 million litres) of British spirits, but, by 1720, the amount was around 2.5 million gallons (11.4 million litres) and still rising.

Domestic production of spirits was beneficial to the British economy and Exchequer and therefore encouraged by government, partly by removal of licence requirements for retail. The result was to make gin cheaper than beer, increasing consumption to 3.5 million gallons (15.9 million litres) per year and arousing the concern of Parliament and London magistrates. The brewing industry, which was in the hands of a few large producers, and burdened by greater taxation and the heavily regulated alehouse trade, found it hard to compete. Fashion, too, was an element in the popularity of spirits.[4] The tide then began to turn against spirit drinking, particularly by the poor, and 1729 saw the first Gin Act. This was the first stage of the government's movement back and forth between control and *laisser-faire* as concern about excessive drinking alternated with the need for taxation and exports.

In the light of this concern, what evidence was there for a medical or social problem associated with distilled liquor? Much of the high London death rate, where spirit drinking was common, was attributed to alcohol related diseases. In 1726, the Royal College of Physicians presented its concerns to Parliament, stating:

> "We have with concern observed for some years past, the fatal effects of the frequent use of several sorts of distilled spirituous liquors upon great numbers of both sexes rendering them diseased, not fit for business, poor, a burden to themselves and neighbours and too often the cause of weak, feeble and distempered children".[5]

Certainly statistics for the population of London showed a decline in 1747, in spite of a regular influx of immigrants (675 000 in 1750), and this was thought to be due in part to gin-related deaths during a period of very heavy consumption. However, the high ratio of deaths to births may have been a result of recording methods and certainly preceded the gin epidemic by many years.

Infant mortality, too, was attributed to the practice of giving gin to infants. However, it may well have resulted mainly from overcrowded, insanitary living conditions and the endemic levels of smallpox and typhus.[4] Supporting the second explanation is the fact that London's infant mortality rates dropped as London improved its water supplies and parents supplemented their infants' diets with cow's milk.[6]

Crime was blamed on gin (and poverty), like heroin today, and reported as a serious problem in London during the 1730s and 1740s, but, without reliable figures, this cannot be proven or disproven, and contemporary reporting was often exaggerated and sensationalist (see Figure 9.1). A well-known story circulating at the time described a gin shop advertising "Drunk for a penny, dead drunk for twopence, clean straw for nothing", and, although immortalised by Hogarth in his print 'Gin Lane' (1751) depicting the degraded lives of the London poor, it was acknowledged to be apocryphal at the time.[4]

Figure 9.1. Gin was seen as the cause of crime and poverty. Image courtesy of the National Addiction Centre, London.

With a market for strong spirits now well-established, a series of laws were passed to try to reduce consumption. The first Gin Act raised the price of gin, by imposing heavy licence requirements on retailers and duty on gin sold. Critics successfully campaigned for the Act's repeal, claiming that it had damaged the legal trade and encouraged illicit retailers. Imported and smuggled spirits may have filled the gap in demand, and after repeal spirit drinking rose substantially.

The offensive was taken once again by those campaigning for greater controls and in 1736 resulted in the second Gin Act. This aimed to raise the price of spirits out of the range of excessive use by the poor, but also proved unsuccessful. Those responsible for enforcement had not been consulted during its hasty drafting, and a subsequent measure was brought in to allow the payment of informers. This ultimately proved fatal to the Act because the distrust and suspicion it created across different sectors of the community was seen as too high a price to pay for enforcement. Riots against the Act, the onset of war against Spain, a disastrous harvest bringing fears of further public unrest, and the death of two key figures supporting the Act all contributed to its demise.[7]

Spirit consumption then fluctuated until 1751, when it fell sharply. Gin consumption declined from an annual 11 million gallons (50 million litres) to less than 2 million gallons (9.1 million litres) by 1758. Although beer drinking increased for a while, the lowering of the tax on tea to a nominal sum towards the end of the century preceded its replacing beer as the national drink of working people, particularly in the south of England.

While much of the legislation passed earlier in the century had failed to reduce either consumption or demand, the 1751 Act "for more effectually restraining the retailing of distilled spirituous liquors", which reimposed the original provisions of the 1743 Act, and the Disorderly Houses Act of 1752, were more successful. From then on, licences for the sale of spirits were only granted to alehouse holders and distillers were forbidden to be retailers. The licence fees and duties imposed by the Act were high enough to have a real effect on consumption, but not so excessive as to lose public support or encourage an illicit trade. Support for the Act may also have been strengthened by a greater national consensus about the seriousness of the problem resulting from the spread of large-scale gin retailing to the provinces.[4] Breweries also drew drinkers away from spirits through a strengthened system of distribution and the popular new 'porter' ale.

Alcohol in Britain during the First World War (1914–1918)

Another example of successful government intervention that reduced harm from alcohol was seen during World War One. Here, reduced availability, but not prohibition, supported by the population and leadership from the top, as well as a pre-existing downward trend in drinking produced sustained reductions in the whole range of drink related problems, including public drunkenness and cirrhosis deaths.

For many years before the war, concerns had been voiced about the social ill effects of alcohol, not least by a powerful temperance movement. At the beginning of the war, munitions and ship building managers complained that drunkenness was an important cause of low productivity. Instead of taking up the calls for total prohibition, as the Canadian Government did, the British Government set up the Central Control Board and this body imposed a wide range of restrictions. In 1915, for certain areas of the country, particularly where alcohol consumption was high, these measures included reducing the hours of sale of alcohol, lowering the alcohol content of some drinks, and outlawing the sale of alcohol on credit. From 1916–1918, beer and spirit production was reduced by 50% and wine importation by the same measure, which affected the whole of Britain.

The 1914–1918 conflict was a watershed in military history in that it was the first 'total war' experienced by the British, where the whole population and economy were involved in the effort. It was a time when ordinary people experienced and tolerated a remarkable degree of interference in their everyday lives under the banner of patriotism. Britons were deprived of many of the civil liberties they had enjoyed when the jingoistically titled Defence of the Realm Act was passed with little opposition, introducing a wide range of wartime controls.

Liver cirrhosis deaths are a good measure of the amount a population is drinking, and since most result from excessive drinking, they can provide an indication of the extent of the problem (see Table 9.1). After the Board had introduced its restrictions, liver cirrhosis death rates dropped dramatically, as did overall alcohol consumption and convictions for drunkenness among civilians both in areas affected by the Board's controls and outside them. Reductions were greater in the restricted areas, although substantial reductions also occurred in the non-restricted areas. Removing youthful recruits from the civilian population may have reduced the amount of drunkenness, but this is unlikely to have accounted for the drop in deaths from liver cirrhosis, as few die from the condition before their mid-forties.

Table 9.1. Alcohol consumption and liver cirrhosis deaths in Britain, 1914–1918. Data drom: Smart, R. G. (1974) The effect of licencing restrictions during 1914–1918 on drunkenness and liver cirrhosis deaths in Britain. *British Journal of Addiction*, **64**, 109–121.

Year	Consumption of spirits in gallons	Consumption of wine in gallons	Consumption of beer in million gallons	Liver cirrhosis deaths per million population
1914	31 660	10 360	1230	152
1917		7099		
1918	15 108		460	56

The possibility that background factors could have been responsible for these changes also needs consideration. People may have had less time to drink as unemployment diminished, and working hours lengthened; they may have felt sympathetic to calls from Lord Kitchener and the King who had reduced their own drinking for the war effort; consumption had already been falling slowly since 1900 and the detection of drunkenness and liver cirrhosis may have diminished because of a shortage of policemen and doctors. Perhaps most important were the limitations on alcohol production and importation and increases in price during the war which affected the whole country.

Overall, the controls introduced by the Central Control Board succeeded in reducing alcohol-related problems and alcohol consumption, but they were crucially assisted by the unusual wartime conditions under which they were passed. Consumption remained relatively low, however, for over 40 years until the controls were finally relaxed in the 1950s and 60s.[8]

ALCOHOL DURING PROHIBITION IN THE USA, 1920–1933

A more radical approach to alcohol was seen in America's nationwide prohibition which began in 1920, following the passing of the 18th Amendment to the American Constitution and its subsequent enactment in the Volstead Act. It is often held up as the classic example of the law's inability to stop any form of drug use when the users themselves have no intention of stopping, but this is not the whole story. Alcohol consumption had begun to fall before Prohibition in 1915, but most Americans continued to drink less during Prohibition, and after its repeal alcohol-related diseases rose once more. Furthermore, in areas where there was public support for the laws, such as the rural South and West, they were effectively enforced. On the negative side, organised crime and political corruption flourished and deaths from poisonous illicit alcohol increased (to 4 per 100 000 population per year). The end of Prohibition also owed a great deal to the Great Depression which took hold from 1929. The prospect of substantial revenue from taxing alcohol, during a time when the taxable economy had shrunk, was hard for the government to resist, as in 18th-century England.

One of the best predictors for continued drug use is how ingrained its use by an individual citizen has become, not only in terms of dependence but involvement in a drug-using lifestyle. The degree to which drug or alcohol use can be changed in a society is also influenced by how well-established it is, not only as a part of social, religious or medical activities, but also in the network of economic interests that supply, distribute, and tax it.

Prohibition was not an isolated experiment; rather, it was the culmination of a long and well-organised political movement, joining together a range of interests, and its eventual repeal reflected not only discontent with the regulations and their enforcement, but a change in the political landscape of the USA. It was preceded by many local experiments with individual 'dry' states bringing in their own regulations many years before the Volstead Act was passed.

A majority of Americans may never have been in favour of the regulations: while a majority of states voted in favour of the 18th Amendment, as was required by the constitution, it was the less populous states who tended to support it. Those campaigning for compulsory temperance represented for the most part an older, Protestant order of rural interests, whose puritan lifestyle was marked, among other things, by abstinence, and whose position of influence was being eroded by rapid urban industrial growth and increased immigration during the 1880s and 1890s. The support of industrialists, believing alcohol to be responsible for industrial injuries and absenteeism, was gained in the early 1900s, and the women's movement also played an important part through its campaigns.

In contrast, alcohol was central to the political and economic life of a large part of the American population. The industrialised cities, where Prohibition was most openly flouted, housed the bulk of the new immigrant populations, many of whom were Italian or Irish Catholics, and used saloons as the centre of their trade unionist activities. Thus, the political, cultural and ethnic divisions in the country were expressed in their differences in alcohol use.

Gender differences may also have played a part – while alcohol was not greatly drunk by women before Prohibition, their emancipation during the 1920s and greater participation in previously male-only preserves brought forward a new group of drinkers with different habits, and saw the end of the old-time saloon with its macho heavy drinking culture.[9]

Because alcohol was so interwoven in the fabric of American life, a total ban was impractical, but the resulting complicated licensing system provided many loopholes: alcohol could be produced for scientific, industrial, medicinal and sacramental purposes. Some doctors exploited this and profited by writing prescriptions for whiskey.

Within the first six months of Prohibition, five sources of illicit alcohol appeared: medicinal, illegal beer, smuggled liquor, industrial alcohol, and production from illicit stills. Even so, in the early 1920s consumption dropped greatly to about 30% of pre-Prohibition levels – an historic low point.[9] By 1925, however, the illegal trade was well-established, with speakeasies and similar establishments appearing in large numbers to supply the increasing demand, but although drinking and prices increased throughout this time, by 1927, it was still only two-thirds that of 1911 and 1914 levels.

Canada's less well known Prohibition experiment ran a similar course. With the exception of the French-speaking, predominantly Catholic Quebec, Prohibition was a large-scale national movement, which, despite wide support and early success, brought unanticipated problems and was eventually rejected. Like the USA, temperance was more popular in rural areas than in the big cities and among a larger proportion of Protestants than Catholics. Its nationwide introduction was achieved in 1915 under a patriotic wartime banner, but disillusion quickly set in as loopholes in the law allowed physicians to enrich themselves by prescribing alcohol, breweries to produce the confusingly named 'temperance beer' (2.5% alcohol), officials to be corrupted and the police and special agents to resort to Draconian methods of enforcement. More positively, deaths from liver cirrhosis, where they were recorded, dropped dramatically, and, more visibly, public drunkenness melted away; but Prohibition failed to deliver the great society promised by the temperance movement, where poverty, crime and disease would be banished. Like their American counterparts, Canadian politicians in need of taxation revenues were eventually content to declare the policy unenforceable.

Although American and Canadian Prohibition failed to achieve abstinence in the whole population, they cannot be declared complete failures. For those seeking to achieve change, the areas in which it failed show the importance of taking account of the role of a drug within an established lifestyle and of developing policies that work in the same direction. Unless the drug using population is willing to change its lifestyle and attitudes, a simple ban rarely appears to be effective, and indeed may produce greater harm, either to individual or public health, social relationships, or through the development of a criminal black market, whereas restrictions that limit use with a degree of public support may reduce overall harm. Whether more are harmed by a ban or by controlled availability will depend in part on how widespread is the drug's use in the first place.

STIMULANTS IN JAPAN AFTER 1945

Between 1945 and 1954, the number of people using amphetamine in Japan grew from almost none to 550 000 as huge supplies of the drug, originally manufactured for military use, were released onto the market. Two-million people are said to have used amphetamine overall. Users first bought the drug from chemists, but once the Government restricted these sales, they turned to the black market to supply their needs. Yet by 1956, the epidemic had waned.

The experience of post-war Japan shows how sudden, unrestricted availability in conditions of hardship and great social turmoil can create a huge demand and growth in drug use which is then difficult to reverse. Imposing restrictions on availability without a simultaneous drop in demand can result in people taking dangerous risks to obtain and use drugs, with consequent harm to themselves and the rest of society. A whole range of interventions and conditions have been identified as key to bringing an end to the epidemic, but the truth is, there is not enough evidence to draw firm conclusions. Perhaps the social background against which control measures were introduced were critical to their success – certainly the destitution that had fuelled the epidemic's rise had largely been left behind by the mid-50s. Or more randomly, the single, well-publicised incident described below, which apparently galvanised the public mood against these drugs, may have made stimulant use unacceptable.

Until 1945, there are thought to have been fewer alcoholics in Japan than in most Western countries and there were very few drug users, either dependent or otherwise, with less than 400 (mainly opium) addicts in a population of around 73 million. Amphetamine was available without prescription from 1941, but its use was not considered a matter for concern.[10] During the war, the military had distributed amphetamine among troops to enable them to remain alert for long periods of time, to boost morale, and to increase the productivity of workers in the military support industries. It was these soldiers and workers who were the first 'misusers' of the drug after the war.

As the Second World War drew to a close, it is difficult to understate the devastation that faced the defeated Japanese nation and the upheavals its people were to experience in all aspects of their lives. Many faced destitution and hunger as the demands of the war economy had bled dry the countryside. The Japanese people, never before defeated, were now under US military occupation.

Into this context of vast social and political change and economic distress, pharmaceutical companies released onto the market large stocks of amphetamine. Army stocks of the drug were also released and there was no awareness of its dangers. Manufacturers promoted amphetamine to "fight sleepiness and enhance vitality" and it was not until 1946 that the first cases of dependence were noticed in the major commercial and industrial centres.

Between 1948 and 1957, a series of laws was passed attempting to control the epidemic, but, in the absence of any reduction in demand, these were either ineffective or worsened the situation: a total ban on stimulant production in 1950 resulted in continued illicit production by both pharmaceutical companies and secret laboratories. Illicit stimulants were sold in ampoules for injection, a high proportion of which were contaminated with bacteria and, as law enforcement became more effective, the substances sold became less pure; eventually police seizures contained only caffeine, ephedrine or inactive substances.[11] Despite criminalising the possession, import, production, sale, receipt and use of amphetamines the following year, with penalties of up to three years' imprisonment, users were not deterred. By 1953, the Japanese police force had been reorganised from a regional to a national structure to cope with the increasingly sophisticated criminal organisations supplying the illicit stimulant market.

By its peak in 1954 there were said to be 550 000 users in a population of 88.5 million, with 55 664 arrests that year for stimulant-related offences and a high level of injecting. Yet by 1957, those arrested for stimulant related offences numbered only about 500 people, and the epidemic was largely over. After this dramatic diminution, Japan did not revert to its previous status as a country almost free from drug use, but neither did it see epidemics on such a scale again. Heroin, although never as popular as amphetamine had been, emerged between the mid-1950s and the 1960s. At its peak, this epidemic saw 40 000–50 000 users, at most one-twentieth of the highest number of amphetamine users, and was followed by outbreaks of solvent misuse.

Following the amphetamine epidemic, the range of drugs used widened, alcohol consumption rose and in the 1970s stimulant use rose again.

These developments raise the question of whether one epidemic paves the way for the next. In 1954 10-30% of Japanese amphetamine addicts were also addicted to heroin, and in the next decade it was found that 40% of all heroin users had also been previously involved in amphetamine use,[11] suggesting that, on an individual level, an initiation into dependence may be the start of a varied career of drug use. Furthermore, the policy changes were not without long-term effects: in the 1970s criminal gangs were involved in the traffic of stimulants from other Asian countries, with Japan then becoming the transit point for international drug trafficking between South-East Asia and North America.

Part of the Government's efforts to control use included a massive education campaign against amphetamine during the 1950s, which has been credited with bringing the first epidemic to an end, but there seems to be little evidence to support this claim. Such health education messages have a poor success rate in most Western countries, leading to skepticism about the impact of this campaign. Furthermore, the outcome of any such campaign would depend upon the target audience, that is, who was using the drugs. The first users in 1946 were those who had been given the drug during the war – soldiers and military support workers, reportedly followed by writers, journalists, factory workers and students who worked or studied overnight. The purpose of use then changed as recreational stimulant use became common among juvenile delinquents. Up until 1951, it was estimated that 5% of those aged 15–25 were using amphetamine, but a change in the law marked a move away from 'ordinary citizens' to antisocial and alienated people, usually men, including criminal gang members. Much of this information comes from arrest records, raising the possibility that these groups were more likely to be arrested than more established members of society, and so more likely to be caught with the drug. The overall picture remains unclear, but if most use was among delinquents and alienated people, it is unlikely that they would have been receptive to government campaigns and authority figures. A change in public opinion against stimulants has also been linked to the widespread outrage at a widely reported incident in 1954, when a youth with a history of amphetamine use murdered a 10-year-old girl while intoxicated.

Some researchers have pointed to the introduction of compulsory treatment for chronic addicts as contributing to the decline in use, but without more detailed information about those using stimulants at the time or evaluation of the treatment given, it is very difficult to draw conclusions about what made people stop.

During this epidemic of stimulant use (1945–1956), the condition of the Japanese people changed dramatically, and as the economy recovered, unemployment fell and the standard of living rose. Although not everyone benefited equally from these developments, the destitution that had faced so many in 1945 was generally a thing of the past. Perhaps it was this change in circumstances and the resulting optimism, rather than the policy initiatives against stimulant use, that drew the majority of users away from problematic, injecting drug use.

The involvement of criminal gangs in the drugs trade may have important implications for the continuance of drug use in the local population, as their investment in production facilities and expertise and distribution networks mean that when one drug epidemic wanes they have a vested interest in stimulating demand for other drugs.

The development of a black market in amphetamine therefore not only had implications for continuing drug use, but consequences too for other criminal activities. Japanese police estimated that during the 1970s half of criminal gangs' income came from drugs trafficking and dealing, enabling their continued business expansion into gun running, prostitution, gambling, fraud and money laundering, linking up with other criminal gangs in Thailand, Hong Kong and the Philippines. During the early 1970s, workers in res-taurants and bars, bar hostesses and escorts were drawn into the distribution of amphetamine in what has been described as the spread of the gangster culture in Japan.

US SOLDIERS RETURNING FROM THE VIETNAM WAR, 1970S

A remarkable example of an epidemic which all but vanished, or was replaced by less harmful forms of drug use, took place among American servicemen, who used heroin and other drugs in Vietnam but stopped on their return home from the war. Before 1969, only low-grade heroin was available in Vietnam, but that year, with production and distribution allegedly aided and protected by corrupt South Vietnamese government officials, large quantities of low priced, high-quality heroin suddenly became available to the US army.[12] More than 80% of soldiers were offered heroin while in Vietnam, and usually within a week of arrival.[13] Furthermore, because it was so pure and cheap, soldiers deterred by the need to inject could smoke it with tobacco or snort it instead. This sudden drug availability, perhaps combined with the stress of being combatants in an unpopular and potentially dangerous war, created a huge demand. Yet a high risk of being caught and punished for use, followed by a change in environment, and the availability of alternative drugs appear to have enabled most addicts to successfully give up heroin.

In September 1970, surveys by army medical officers found that about 12% of soldiers had tried heroin since arriving in Vietnam, and about half of these were regular users. Up until this time, use or possession of heroin in the US armed forces was dealt with by court martial, which could lead to a dishonorable discharge, but in spite of this, the number using heroin kept rising. President Nixon responded by ordering all soldiers to submit to urine tests for drug use prior to departure for home, and, from June 1971, being found positive for heroin resulted in two weeks' compulsory treatment in Vietnam before returning to the USA. Testing of soldiers was universal, although because their precise date of departure was uncertain the test date was unpredictable. Testing appeared to have a deterrent effect as the numbers using heroin in Vietnam in the first six months after its introduction fell, although there was no evidence that supplies were less prevalent.

What of the former users who returned home? Academic researchers from outside the army conducted a study of randomly chosen enlisted men returning home from Vietnam: 43% had used an opiate (mainly heroin and opium) while in Vietnam, and almost half had used opiates regularly there. One out of five of the enlisted men returning from Vietnam to the USA felt that they had been addicted to heroin during their time in Vietnam, but within a year of their return home, only 5% of those who had been addicted to opiates in Vietnam were, to some degree, still addicted. This remarkable recovery rate did not even necessarily involve giving up opiates completely. Although nearly half the men who considered themselves addicted in Vietnam tried opiates again after their return, only 6% overall became addicted again, and very few men received any treatment for their drug use.[14,15]

There are many possible factors, both environmental and individual, that could have influenced this remarkable recovery rate. In Vietnam, soldiers were separated geographically from their usual environment and were also involved in the unusual and stressful situation of war. It is possible that they perceived their tours of duty as a 'special' period divorced from the rest of their lives and from the usual social rules. This is borne out by the fact that those who had not used drugs before their posting were least likely to continue on their return, despite the ready availability of heroin in the USA. The ability of people to compartmentalise different types of behaviour according to context can mean that drug use, while acceptable at one time, may cease without treatment, despite some degree of addiction, when the acceptability of the drug changes.

Perhaps the most striking characteristic of those who used drugs in Vietnam was their drug experience before their postings. Two-thirds of drug users in Vietnam had tried cannabis before being sent there, compared with less than one-fifth of those who did not use drugs in Vietnam, and while there almost 80% of enlisted men used cannabis.[13] Part of the change to safer forms of drug use among those returning home was the widespread use of cannabis rather than opiates. Among those not found to be positive for drugs when tested at the end of their service (many of whom had nonetheless used drugs during their time in Vietnam) 45% had used cannabis since their return, whereas among those testing positive for drugs when due for discharge, 81% had used cannabis a year of their return.

It is possible that those who had previously been using opiates felt that cannabis, which had been sufficient before their tour of duty, provided an adequate replacement form of drug use on their return. There had been changes at home, too, during their absence as cannabis smoking had become much more common, and was particularly favoured by the youthful counter culture of the time.

So if Vietnam veterans were apparently able either to give up dependent opiate use or change to less harmful, non-dependent use, why are relapse rates so high for most patients treated for opiate dependence? The fact is that many opiate users do give up spontaneously without professional help. Those who come into treatment are users who have been unable to stop on their own and are probably not representative of the wider heroin-using or dependent population.[13] They often have additional psychological and social problems and are less likely to have the support of a network of non-users. The severity or duration of their dependence may also play a part, and the army's early intervention in the epidemic may have been crucial. The small number of addicts from Vietnam who did come into treatment afterwards relapsed as rapidly as other young men in treatment.[13]

ALCOHOL IN RUSSIA AND THE SOVIET UNION – 1980s AND 90s

The experience of Russia and the then Soviet Union during the 1980s and 90s illustrates once more the difficulties in reducing consumption in the long term of a well-established drug through control of supply without public support and against a backdrop of economic and social upheaval. Initially, restrictions brought substantial improvements in the nation's health, but these could not be sustained. Then the removal of price controls reduced the cost of alcohol, encouraging greater consumption to disastrous effect.

Alcohol, and particularly binge drinking, has long played an important part in Russian life, most notably among men, who are the heaviest drinkers,[16] although there is great regional variation across the Russian Federation.[17] Since the 1960s, drinking had increased considerably with resulting medical and social problems, including premature deaths, injuries while drunk, loss of economic productivity, and alcohol-related crime. A number of studies identified alcohol as the single most important cause of divorce and family breakdown, with up to 80% of cases attributed to its influence.[18]

Until the late 1970s, life expectancy in the Soviet Union had been increasing, but then began to fall, from 64.5 years for men and 73.6 years for women in the early 1970s, to 62.5 for men and 72.6 for women by the end of the decade, with the lowest levels in Russia itself. This downward trend continued until the anti-alcohol campaign started in 1985, backed by the authority of Mikhail Gorbachev himself. Although this pattern was also seen in some East European countries, nowhere else in the industrialised world has experienced such a decline during peacetime, and the gap between men and women's life expectancy is unparalleled. It is estimated that between 1960 and 1985, between 30 and 35 million people died as a result of alcohol misuse in the Soviet Union.[18]

There are many other horrifying statistics, such as alcohol being implicated in 80% of road deaths, constituting the most important single cause of suicide and of drowning, and being involved in about a third of all rural accidents. So many crimes seemed to have been committed under the influence of alcohol, and so many workers seemed to spend their time drinking or recovering from the effects, it is hard not to see Russian men in particular as having spent more time drunk than sober.

Some steps were taken in the 1960s to address this problem, when a network of labour rehabilitation centres were set up giving compulsory treatment, and fines were introduced for public drunkenness. In 1972, there were campaigns and education against drinking, an attempt to reduce the production of vodka and other spirits and to compensate with increased wine, beer and non-alcoholic drink production. But the output of strong drink actually increased, as did violations of anti-drinking legislation. In 1976, the Ministry of Health made further attempts to curtail the problem by establishing prevention and treatment centres across the USSR, but to little effect.

By the late 1970s, many officials saw the problem as insurmountable. During this time, two of Russia's leaders, Leonid Brezhnev (General Secretary 1964–1982) and Konstantin Chernenko (1984–1985) were known for their heavy drinking and Chernenko's death in 1985 was attributed to liver cirrhosis. With such leadership, it would seem unlikely that any campaign would be conducted with much energy or conviction.

In 1984, Gorbachev introduced the first of a new set of restrictions to limit the availability of alcohol and launched a mass anti-drinking campaign, the biggest ever in the Soviet Union. Two years later, vodka and cognac production were cut, the sale of alcoholic drinks was prohibited in many public places, and on working days was prohibited until after 2pm. At the same time, the number of places selling non-alcoholic drinks was increased. Prices for spirits were raised sharply, and more moderately for beer and wine. Advertising alcoholic drinks was banned and the campaign for temperance continued.

The campaign against alcohol followed a pattern identifiable in many other failed Soviet campaigns. Calls for action about the problem would appear prominently in the official press, a sign that a substantial section of the leadership had decided that action was needed. The leadership would respond to this 'cue' and launch its campaign. Local officials then competed with each other to report 'successes' to central government, establishing as many 'sobriety zones' as possible, zealously closing down wine shops more rapidly than was planned and promoting mass following for the temperance society (even if newly conscripted members continued drinking). Stories of individual redemption filled the press. After this, the gap between the fabricated reports and the reality of widespread evasion of regulations would emerge, along with the negative side-effects of the policies. Government would acknowledge that 'not everywhere' had the required changes been made, and that a 'more complex' long-term strategy would be needed.[18]

Party secretaries and other bureaucrats charged with implementing such policies were well accustomed to these cycles and by this stage had already transferred their attentions to more pressing, and for their careers, more promising objectives. The campaign against alcohol misuse became part of a more diffuse movement in favour of a healthy lifestyle, and the specific legislation was either reversed or quietly abandoned.

However, like American Prohibition, the campaign did achieve some striking early successes. Although home brew consumption went up, overall levels of drinking fell, with the result that fewer people died from alcohol-related causes (mortality fell from 23 per 100 000 population in 1984 to 9.1 per 100 000 in 1987), and life expectancy increased sharply for both genders between 1984 and 1987.[16,19] But this success was short-lived. Russians once again began to drink more and although they did not reach 1984 levels until 1992, there was a substantial increase in all the principal causes of death from 1987 to 1992, which has been convincingly linked to rising alcohol consumption and the poor quality of illegally produced drink in which there was a large trade. Another parallel with the USA's experience of the 1920s was the shift to a greater proportion of alcohol drunk in the form of spirits. As an illicit commodity, spirits are more profitable and less risky than beer or wine because their higher alcohol content means that for the same effect they take up less space and are therefore easier to conceal.

Within the overall rise in deaths, there was a disproportionate increase in those caused directly by alcohol, with acute alcohol poisoning leading the way.[19] Between 1988 and 1993, there was a near doubling in the incidence of delirium tremens, a syndrome of alcohol withdrawal. In 1993, Russians gained the dubious accolade of becoming the world's heaviest drinkers.

Why then was the Russian drinking problem so resistant to change? In a country with a centrally controlled economy, control of supply would initially seem to be fairly easy to achieve, but this would overlook the fact that the Soviet Union already had a well-developed black market capable of supplying considerable demand. Furthermore, the later stages of the campaign coincided with a freeing up of the economy, which meant an end to the government's official monopoly on alcohol production and an increase in poor quality alcohol on public sale.

Under Boris Yeltsin's leadership, many economic controls were relaxed, including those on prices, with the result that most other consumer goods, including basic foods, rose in price more steeply than alcoholic drinks. For instance, in 1984 a bottle of vodka cost twice as much as a kilo of sausages, but 10 years later, the vodka cost less than half as much as the sausages. This was accentuated by the rise in real value of average wages between 1992 and 1994 so that the unit cost of alcohol fell relative to income. Popular opposition to alcohol restrictions made greater inroads during this time, as first Perestroika and then multi-party democracy were introduced.

With alcohol playing such a central role in the life of Russians, and the lack of hard currency, vodka was often used as a form of payment or incentive. Doctors were reported to have offered a bottle of vodka to every three blood donors who presented themselves and were overwhelmed by the public response, and factory workers were paid in vodka when no money was available.

Not only did the bureaucracy charged with implementing Russia's anti-alcohol campaign carry out its duties inefficiently and inconsistently, it was also fighting a losing battle against the conditions of the day. The social and economic turmoil experienced during this period conspired to increase the importance of alcohol in daily life as well as increasing its availability and effectively reducing its price.

DRUG USE DURING THE 1980S IN THE USA

While the Russian Government was trying to tackle alcohol, its rival superpower, the USA, was waging a 'War on Drugs'. Drug use in America in the mid-1980s, although high, was falling, after reaching its peak in the late 1970s and early 1980s.[20] Yet this downward trend did not stop concern fuelling an evangelical campaign, first against cocaine, then heroin, generating one of the biggest government programmes, which absorbed $11 billion in a single year.

The technological innovation that produced 'crack', and a new marketing strategy, brought cocaine to poorer consumers who were more likely to encounter problems with their drug use (see Chapter 3). Although the overall prevalence of cocaine use in the American population fell during the 1980s, problem use became more common, and was often concentrated in particular geographical areas. The enormous efforts to stem the flow of drugs into the country – the main plank of the 'War on Drugs' – failed because of the continued domestic demand, the massive profits for suppliers, corruption of some of those responsible for preventing the trade both in the USA and abroad, the producer countries' economic dependence on the drug economy, and an American foreign policy.

From 1969 to the early 1980s, there was a sustained increase in the use of cocaine powder, mainly by sniffing, particularly among affluent Whites. Although there was some concern over cocaine overdose deaths of young people, it was generally seen as an acceptable, non-addictive drug. The fatal overdose of Len Bias, a basketball star, deterred casual users from what they had seen as a benign drug, but the most radical change in public opinion came in 1985 when crack cocaine arrived, surrounded by enormous media and public attention. Cocaine then acquired a new reputation as a uniquely dangerous and addictive substance.

As mentioned before, public attitudes to drug use depend on the character-istics of the consumers.[21] Instead of prosperous, 'respectable' White users, crack cocaine, sold cheaply in $10–15 chunks, opened up the market to those who were already feared by White middle-class society – poor African–Americans and Latin–Americans living in the inner cities. Crack undoubtedly contributed significantly to the already considerable problems of these areas, but media coverage and political debate often portrayed it as the sole agent of harm.

Amid the public furore of the 1980s, President Reagan called for "a national crusade against drugs", involving drug testing at schools and workplaces, improved treatment and rehabilitation, and greater public intolerance of drug use – typified by Nancy Reagan's "Just say no" motto – and heightened enforcement against domestic and international trafficking. Most of the $4 billion released by the Anti-Drug Abuse Act, which was passed just prior to the 1986 national elections, was destined for law enforcement. The tolerance of drug use seen during the 1970s and early 1980s had evaporated and many ordinary citizens found their lives affected by the campaign, by, for instance, roadside drug testing. Then, just before the 1988 general election, Congress passed a second bill including severe penalties for dealing, personal use and possession.

The use of harsh criminal sanctions was part of a trend particularly notable since the 1970s that saw state politicians competing with each other to push through ever more stringent legislation making the sale or possession of even small amounts of certain drugs punishable by severe mandatory prison sentences. The effect was to greatly increase the number of people imprisoned, so that by the late 1990s the USA had a higher percentage of its population in prison than any other nation and was spending $24 billion annually on the 1.2 million prisoners serving sentences for non-violent drug-related crimes. The difference in Reagan's approach compared with his predecessors was the move away from treatment in favour of such criminal sanctions, law enforcement, border policing and international control efforts.

President George Bush continued this policy in 1989, officially declaring it the 'War on Drugs' (see Figure 9.2). The bulk of funding continued to go to enforcement. Activities against cocaine consisted of pressure on Latin–American source countries to stop growing coca, cutting the flow of drugs northward from the Caribbean and Mexico, and Draconian law enforcement for users and dealers at home.

Although the total number of Americans using drugs continued to decline during the 1980s and 1990s, the harm experienced both by users and the rest of society intensified. From 1988, casual cocaine users became fewer, but addicts and heavy users, whose need was so great or who had little to lose, and so were willing to face extreme penalties and a greater likelihood of being caught, retained their habits. The National Household Survey on Drug Abuse estimated that between 1988 and 1990, there was a 29% fall in the number of occasional cocaine users, but that the number of daily cocaine users rose from 292 000 to 336 000, and cocaine related deaths rose by 10% over the same period.

The move away from drugs, tobacco and alcohol, which had preceded the campaign, became a way of identifying oneself with respectability and aspiration, increasingly marginalising drug users, particularly those unable to stop. By segregating the problem among those with the least resources to help themselves, failing to address the harsh social conditions in inner-city ghettos, and emphasising enforcement above treatment, the problem of impoverished, heavy drug users living in areas with few prospects worsened.

Emergency room (accident and emergency department) visits are an indicator of problem drug use and those resulting from cocaine increased from 8 831 in 1984 to 46 020 in 1988, despite the decline in overall numbers of users. Although the media exaggerated the problem of 'crack babies' (infants born addicted to cocaine), cocaine use during pregnancy did increase during this

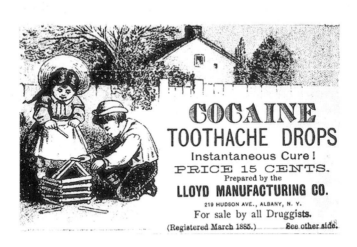

Figure 9.2.   Cocaine, which was a common ingredient in patent medicines
a century ago, became the focus of the American government's
'War on Drugs' in the 1980s and 90s.

period. For instance, 5.3 babies out of every 1000 born in New York City in 1985 had been exposed to cocaine, but by 1990 the number had risen to 17.6 per 1000, most of whom were Black (66.3%) or Puerto Rican (20.3%), the poorest groups in American society. The highly profitable crack trade attracted those without other economic prospects or status, particularly poor African-Americans, and became known for its extreme violence, devastating urban communities.

After the federal government had spent $13 billion over 10 years on interdiction the General Accounting Office concluded in 1991 that the estimated volume of drugs entering the country in the previous two years had not declined, and for cocaine in particular there was no indication, either in price, purity or consumption, that the American cocaine supply had been reduced. Although the overall number of drug users diminished during the 'War on Drugs', the amount of drugs consumed did not, because, although relatively few in number, the heaviest users account for the bulk of the drugs used, and their numbers increased.[22] Casual, occasional users have relatively little impact on the drug economy and it was the frequent users who maintained the high level of demand from producers.

Operations in the Andes against production of drug crops were ineffective for both geographic and economic reasons. Colombia produced around 310 tons of cocaine in 1988, employing 300 000 workers and earning 20% of the country's foreign exchange, worth $1.5 billion – almost as much as coffee, the country's largest legal export, which earned $1.6 billion that year. It is estimated that cocaine played an even more important economic role at that time in Bolivia and Peru, which also depended on coca production for their survival. Opium and coca are ideal cash crops for remote regions as they grow easily, are lightweight and so can be transported without difficulty across long distances, and the demand is strong. Furthermore, attempts to encourage these countries to grow alternative crops such as citrus fruits and soya beans were hindered by American agricultural interests concerned about competition.

Conflict between America's anti-drug and anti-Communist foreign policy goals also hampered the effort to reduce production of drug crops. During the Cold War, those controlling drug production and trafficking offered considerable influence in their countries, often outside the control of their governments, and American intelligence agencies are known to have made alliances with such individuals, effectively protecting the drugs trade[22] (see Chapter 6).

If the War on Drugs could be credited with lowering society's tolerance of drug use, and reducing the overall prevalence of drug use (see Figure 7.3), it could be deemed a success. On most other counts it failed. Indeed, it worsened the situation: the supply of drugs remained plentiful, producer countries expanded their crops and increased their economic dependence on these harvests, problem drug use increased at home with a consequent rise in deaths of users, and violence, particularly associated with the crack trade, escalated.

Large numbers of people were imprisoned for long periods during the 1980s and 90s, deprived of their liberty at huge expense to the tax payer. Many are likely to have lost educational and career opportunities and may face a bleak future on their release. Sixty-six per cent of released American prisoners go on committing crimes. The prolonged incarceration of chronic predatory criminals probably has a significant impact on crime rates and other people's quality of life, but it is difficult to show an impact on either crime or drug use from prolonged incarceration of non-violent drug users arrested solely for possession of small amounts of drugs.

Could this failure have been predicted? Past experience of taking on the global drugs trade has shown that even when there is some success in reducing production, as Nixon achieved with the Turkish poppy crop, the drop in availability of drugs to Americans is short-lived. In that case, discussed in Chapter 7 (p. 135), a major increase in opium production in South-East Asia swiftly made up Turkey's shortfall. High levels of drug use, particularly heroin and cocaine, were reported by the media as if it was a new problem, fueling a sense of crisis and calls for immediate action to bring about a swift resolution.

Attention was focused more on the drugs themselves than on the social and economic factors that compounded these problems and made drug dealing an attractive option, such as a lack of alternative leisure activities for young people, poor housing, racial discrimination and a lack of legal job prospects. In the drive to eliminate all drug use, policy makers and enforcers did not distinguish between casual users who did little harm to themselves or others, and those whose drug use was likely to dominate their existence and that of those around them.

CONCLUSION

Before generalising from the past to the present, it is important to bear in mind the very different contexts of drug and alcohol use in these disparate historical examples, but there are some threads that can be woven together. In a given epidemic, changes in patterns of use can come about through interventions aimed specifically at the problem, from other social or economic changes or from a combination of the two. It can, though, be difficult to distinguish which should claim the credit or the blame.

In the cases of American Prohibition, British restrictions on drinking in the First World War and the American War on Drugs, falls in the number of drinkers or overall consumption had already started before the policies credited with achieving change were introduced. Where there is support for restrictive policies, it is likely that the society has already become less tolerant of excessive (or any) alcohol or drug use. At the same time, without this support it is rare for restrictive policies to succeed.

The effectiveness of interventions to reduce the harm from drug use depends on the characteristics of the epidemic, the nature of the interventions, and the point in time at which they are made. How one defines 'harm' is also pertinent. For instance, where an intervention results in improvements in the health of the majority this is a reduction in harm, but the same intervention might increase the risks for those resorting to other sources of supply. 'Success' therefore depends on which part of the total picture is under examination.

Restrictions on the availability of drugs may prove ineffective if a large number of people oppose them, or a substantial minority have a vested interest in continued use or have little to lose, as occurred in the earlier stages of Japan's amphetamine epidemic. A total ban, or prohibition, may reduce the overall numbers of people using these substances, as with alcohol in American and Canadian Prohibition, and in the American drugs policies of the 1980s. These abolished the direct effects of drugs and alcohol on the abstainers, but for those persisting, the consequences for themselves, in terms of health and legal problems, were likely to be more severe than before. Furthermore, the persistence of this smaller group of users could lead to unanticipated consequences for the rest of society in the form of crime and political corruption.

Administrative sanctions – those that encourage certain forms of behaviour without criminalising contraventions – acknowledge the existence of particular forms of drug use, but attempt to shape patterns of consumption. For such measures to be effective, they must have either the support of the public, as was the case with the restrictions introduced in Britain during the First World War, and at least acquiescence from the economic interests involved in supplying drugs or alcohol. Successful and unsuccessful interventions can depend upon subtle differences in framing and enforcing the law. For instance, many of those responsible for policing the 1736 Gin Act considered the social tensions created by the use of paid informers too great and this helped make the Act unworkable.

In the case of Russia during the 1980s and 90s, limits on the availability of alcohol were imposed suddenly, without public support, by a weakening and discredited state. Where demand is strong, attempts at prohibition or sudden restriction of availability through price or other means are often countered by users turning to the black market to supply their needs. Yet even where there is powerful opposition, as in America in the 1920s and Russia in the 1980s, the early stages of a ban are often accompanied by overall benefits to the population before alternative sources of supply emerge.

The degree of need, both social and psychological, plays a part in the lengths to which people will go to avoid restrictions, with consequent social and health sequelae. Where drug use is ingrained in religious or secular traditions, or at an individual level is part of an established lifestyle or dependence, demand may be very strong. Equally, where particular circumstances increase people's desire for a drug, perhaps in the case of extreme stress due to poverty or unemployment, the strength of demand may be particularly great. Attitudes to the law and authority will also determine how willing people are to resort to an illicit market for supplies. Even where it is clear that there are advantages to public health from restrictions, as was seen during US Prohibition and Russia in the 1980s, people may prefer to live with the harmful consequences of freedom of choice.

The availability of alternative drugs or formulations is a recurring theme in reducing harm from drug use. By the mid-18th century, the English brewing industry was regaining its competitive position against the distillers by marketing a new high quality beer named 'porter', the real price of which fell steadily. The fickleness of fashion too, which helped porter to dominate the market, is perhaps the factor least open to policy interventions and is as unpredictable as sudden shifts in public sentiment, which may be of horror or outrage at one widely reported murder or death linked to drug use.

The availability of a substitute drug or formulation can also influence how effective legislative restrictions prove to be. Cannabis, which was relatively freely available in the USA during the 1970s, replaced heroin use for many of the opiate-using soldiers returning from Vietnam, and may partly explain why they did not carry on using heroin. The economics of the supply system are crucial to the level of demand as it influences price and availability. Evidence suggests that where this is outside the law, it is particularly resistant to government intervention. But where a drug is regulated rather than prohibited, as with alcohol in Britain today, demand can be influenced beneficially, or otherwise. Excessive taxation can lead to the development of an illicit market, but set at a realistic level can serve to limit the consumption of legally produced alcohol. Distribution is also important: the domination of alehouses by the breweries with the emergence of tied house networks in London and southern England in the mid-18th century helped brewers rather than distillers to control the drink trade.

The development of a black market with strong criminal organisations to supply it was important in the emergence of drug use as a problem in Japan after 1945. Perhaps, too, it was significant that conditions that had previously protected the country before the war – its traditional social structure and the relatively slow pace of change – had gone forever. Changes that have underpinned the increasing and more diverse use of drugs in Britain and the USA can also be traced in post-war Japan, and include a widening 'generation gap', with elders receiving less respect from young people, a greater questioning of authority, the growth of consumerism and individualism, and, compared with the pre-war generations, a more hedonistic and less spiritual approach to life.

Finally, the point during a drug epidemic at which an intervention is made is likely to be important in determining whether the drug has a chance to become established and integrated into people's lives. If drug use occurs during a 'special' period of time, such as during war, or in a delinquent adolescence, it might be expected that a change of environment or growing older could achieve a reduction in drug use. Efforts are more likely to succeed if they are made before illicit suppliers have invested in production and distribution networks, and developed as criminal organisations with wide influence.

Chapter 10. The key issues

Summary

The distribution of government expenditure on drugs

At present, 75% of UK expenditure on 'Tackling Drug Misuse' is devoted to enforcement activities and international supply reduction, with little evidence that this is money well-spent. In view of the proven cost-effectiveness of methadone maintenance and abstinence-based programmes for heroin addicts, a higher proportion of the overall budget should be spent on effective treatments. The number of addicts receiving methadone and residential treatment could probably be doubled. There are perverse incentives for NHS drug clinics to lower their prescribing costs by giving addicts prescriptions for a whole week's supply of methadone, and too many addicts are being given intravenous rather than oral methadone, often by private or GPs. In this context, the announcement of an extra £50 million for treatment by the year 2002 is extremely welcome. However, Keith Hellawell, the 'Drug Czar', will need to make sure that the this funding is allocated to treatments of proven effectiveness. These, at present, are often over-subscribed, and the quality of care needs improvement (see 'Improving the value of treatment' below). Mr Hellawell will need to resist calls for expanding unproven and often untested treatments, despite the fervour of their advocates.

Since treatment has been shown to reduce the criminal behaviour of previously untreated heroin addicts, there may be considerable scope for funding improved treatment through the criminal justice system. This could involve courts enforcing participation in treatment.

Although the UK spends almost as much on drugs education as on treatment there is little evidence that the kinds of educational programmes mounted in this country actually change behaviour. The implications of extensive American research need to be taken on board, and much better evaluations built into future educational programmes.

Research expenditure

UK expenditure on drugs research does not begin to match the magnitude and urgency of the problem, and as a result, many basic questions remain unanswered. There is a pressing need for stable research monies to fund at least two permanent, multi-disciplinary research teams. Just 1% of the annual drugs budget would inject £14 million a year into drugs research, several times the current expenditure.

Improving the value of treatment

In comparison with the USA, the improvement rates obtained by some UK treatment centres are rather disappointing, possibly because of lower standards of staff training, less investment in staff training and monitoring of patients and fewer essential support services and complementary social care. A more systematic approach is needed to integrate improvements into UK treatment – both those already recognised and innovations as they emerge from research. More investment is needed to bring UK drug treatment up to standard, but this does not imply a 'bottomless pit' of spending since, in terms of the intensity of treatment per patient, there may be an optimal level of investment and benefit beyond which improvements plateau out.

Treatment and harm reduction

The publication by the Department of Health of guidelines for the clinical management of drug misusers is welcome, though observance of these guidelines will probably need to be monitored. There are, though, unresolved issues about the relative importance of the health of the user, the health of the wider public and crime reduction. Better and more extensive treatment facilities are needed for adolescents for whom there is currently very little provision.

Prescribing heroin to addicts

Until recently, Britain was the only country where heroin was prescribed to addicts, although the practice is rare, but over the last decade, several European countries have introduced heroin maintenance programmes. Carefully regulated trials in Switzerland have shown encouraging results in patients who have failed to benefit from other treatments.

Private prescribing

The private prescribing of substitute drugs is an area with considerable scope for poor practice, including the provision of large quantities of drugs to patients in what can amount to little more than 'buying a prescription'. Unlike most other areas of private medicine, doctors treating drug users outside the health service are not required to have any special training in the addictions field, nor is there equivalent monitoring or regulation.

Drugs and social exclusion

Although there is a strong relationship between the use of heroin, other major drug problems and deprivation, unemployment and delinquency, the relationship is complex and at least partly due to selective migration in and out of deprived neighbourhoods. Government policies for reducing poverty and unemployment and renovating run down housing estates are welcome on both political and economic grounds, but may not have a major impact on the prevalence of heroin or other injecting drug misuse.

Drug testing by employers

The technology now exists for detecting the use of a wide range of drugs over a period of several months by the analysis of samples of hair. It is expensive, and obviously raises important ethical and legal issues, but the widespread adoption of hair testing, by employers and even by schools and universities, might have a major impact on the prevalence of drug use in the future.

Ecstasy and recreational drug use

Regular, non-dependent use of substances such as ecstasy and LSD has become increasingly common among young people. Despite widely published information on the dangers of ecstasy, and its status as a class A drug, many continue to use it, and some drugs education campaigns may have even proved counter-productive. Health advice needs to be given taking into account its potential impact both on those who will be deterred and those who continue to use drugs.

Amphetamine dependence

Amphetamine dependence, particularly where injecting is involved, probably carries more risks to the user and to public health than heroin addiction. Very little research has been carried out into how amphetamine dependence develops or into treatment.

Cannabis dilemmas

Cannabis is not a harmless drug. It may contribute significantly to road traffic and other accidents, long-term use often leads to dependence, and smoking cannabis may prove to have similar long-term effects on the lungs to smoking tobacco. Even so, its ill effects on health are almost certainly less than those of the legal substances tobacco and alcohol and it is used, in defiance of the law, by a high proportion of adolescents and young adults. As a result, many governments have reduced the penalties for use or possession, or abolished them altogether. Although there is increasing pressure for 'legalisation' of cannabis and a clear need for a more open and better informed debate on the issue, legalising the production and sale of cannabis would have important adverse effects as well as benefits. Police and criminal justice costs would be reduced and important new sources of revenue would be available to government – but consumption, accident rates and long-term damage to health, with associated NHS and social services costs, would all rise. More research is needed into both the medicinal benefits and the long-term ill effects of cannabis, and legislative experiments, as in Holland, should be encouraged rather than discouraged. In the meantime, the medicinal use of cannabis on a named patient basis should be allowed for specific conditions if supported by well-designed clinical trials. People requiring cannabis to relieve disabling conditions should not be prosecuted.

Policy options for heroin

The results of legalising heroin would be likely to be similar, but much more extreme, than for cannabis. Addicts would benefit from a regulated, cheaper supply, and acquisitive crime, with all its consequences, would diminish, but addiction would be likely to become more widespread, with possibly serious effects on the economy and the population's health. A more likely scenario is the spread of heroin prescribing unofficially tolerated because of its beneficial impact on crime by addicts.

Current trends and implications for the future

Consumption of cannabis, amphetamines, heroin and cocaine has been increasing relentlessly in Britain and many other countries for the past 30 years. Attempts to curb international trade, and thereby the supply of these and other drugs, have consistently failed and will probably continue to do so. Consumption will only fall if demand is reduced. Although steadily rising consumption of an increasingly wide range of drugs is not inevitable the forces driving increasing consumption seem more powerful than those capable of reducing it. If the prevalence of drug use and drug-related crime do continue to rise, the pressure on the UK and other governments to change policies that are clearly failing is bound to increase. It is possible, too, that the size and wealth of the drugs industry, and the consequences of the associated money laundering and corruption for the world economy, will alarm governments more than more visible social ills like acquisitive and violent crime and eventually result in a radical review of international legislation.

INTRODUCTION

In the previous chapters of this book we have described or discussed most aspects of the use of psychoactive drugs. We have described the widely used drugs and their pharmacological properties, and summarised the complex history of drug use in different cultures and the progressive rise of drug use in 20th-century Britain. We have discussed the social and developmental antecedents of contemporary drug use and its medical and social consequences and explored the development and subsequent decline of several previous epidemics. We have also discussed in some detail the prevention and control policies available for restricting alcohol, tobacco and drug use, and the role of treatment. Several broad conclusions can be drawn.

Drug problems have long aroused concern from the public and government but the attention individual drug epidemics receive cannot be used as a reliable measure of either their scale or severity. The emergence of a new form of drug use may prompt urgent calls for stricter controls, especially if it involves a sector of society perceived to be the source of other problems, such as young people or ethnic minorities. Middle class drug users, on the other hand, may be tolerated or overlooked. It is also important to appreciate that some groups are likely to get into greater difficulties with drugs than others – particularly if they have few resources to cope with ill health or reduced income, but complacency about the risks of a more accepted drug can pose an equal danger.

The type of drug also affects the publicity it receives. Britain's steadily growing heroin consumption in the early 1990s was eclipsed by fears about a newer drug – ecstasy. Reports of a resurgence of heroin use at the end of the millennium have returned the spotlight to a problem which never really went away. Novel drugs or ways of taking them are particularly newsworthy, and prone to exaggerated reactions, but it is also true that because their dangers are not fully understood they may have greater potential to cause harm. Such substances may be blamed for a variety of social ills, including crime, violence and family breakdown. Yet if a substance with a long history, like alcohol, is well accepted by society, the same adverse effects tend to be blamed on the 'irresponsible' user rather than on alcohol itself.

Where there is some consensus that action is needed, there are a wide range of possible approaches lying between the extremes of total prohibition or unfettered legalisation. Small details in the framing or enforcement of an act can have a significant impact on its effect, both positive and negative. For instance, the use of informers to detect offenders may prove so divisive that the costs of enforcement are considered too high to be acceptable. And the question of what makes a law 'unworkable' will depend on how much personal freedom society is willing to relinquish to reduce crime and ill health.

We now in this final chapter focus on a number of key issues: in particular, the difficult policy decisions facing present and future governments, and social and technological developments likely to influence the future nature and scale of the international drug problem. Some of these issues have been discussed already; others are raised here for the first time. We address issues both at the forefront of current debate, such as the use of ecstasy, and the possible legalisation of cannabis, and others such as amphetamine dependence which attract little public interest.

TARGETING RESOURCES BETWEEN EFFORTS TO REDUCE DEMAND
AND TO REDUCE SUPPLY

The Government's £1.4 billion portfolio of expenditure on attempts to curb the UK's drug problems was described and discussed in Chapter 7. We believe that the balance of investment between approaches that aim to reduce demand for drugs, for instance by preventing initiation into drug use and by facilitating routes out of drug use, and those intended to reduce their supply, such as law enforcement and international measures, should be altered. The allocation debate should not be driven by preconceived ideas: it should focus wherever possible on evidence. In most areas, research findings are now available to influence conclusions about the relative effectiveness and cost-effectiveness of the various measures available to the Government, and in areas where such information is lacking it is important that the requisite research should be undertaken.

The distribution of funding between measures aimed at law enforcement and those directed towards treatment and rehabilitation is clearly a priority issue. Three-quarters of the current £1.4 billion budget is spent on law enforcement within the UK and attempts to discourage or prevent illicit international trade in drugs. 'Success' is measured in terms of numbers of arrests or quantities and hypothetical 'street values' of drugs seized, without any accompanying evidence that this is having an effect on overall use or black market prices. There is little scrutiny of the actual impact of this huge investment, despite the fact that the street price of heroin has been falling for the last decade, and its purity rising, and Customs and Excise estimates that they only succeed in intercepting 5–10% of the drugs entering the country. Substantial resources obviously have to be devoted to international control efforts to prevent the country being flooded with drugs, but it is by no means obvious that 75% of the total drug budget should be spent in this way.

By contrast, in the treatment field, there is now strong evidence of benefit resulting from the treatment of at least one important group of drug takers – those who have become addicted to heroin. The results of the National Treatment Outcome Research Study (NTORS) indicate that treatment succeeds in improving a range of behaviours (see Table 10.1). Furthermore, the costs of each day of treatment are more than adequately paid for by the reduced costs to society from the preceding drug-related damage and associated criminal behaviour.

If the requisite funding were available to provide sufficient NHS and voluntary sector drug treatment clinics and associated facilities, we believe that perhaps twice as many opiate addicts could be drawn into formal drug treatment programmes, with resulting benefits both to themselves and to society. As an initial step, we consider that there is a compelling financial as well as humanitarian case for an immediate 50% increase in treatment capacity for heroin addicts, with subsequent further expansion based on the speed with which these new and expanded treatment opportunities are taken up.

The UK Anti-Drugs Coordinator, Mr Keith Hellawell, delivered his first annual report in mid-1999, in which he announced plans for a doubling of treatment capacity over the next decade. Mr Hellawell deserves to be congratulated on the boldness and wisdom of the proposal, which will relieve much individual and family suffering, and will also go a considerable way to reducing the power of the drug–crime link. He has also appropriately singled out heroin and cocaine as the main focus of attention. However, careful attention will need to be paid to the implementation of these recommendations to ensure that they produce the envisaged gains, and in our view, the following additions to Mr Hellawell's recommendations are necessary.

First, it will be important that any expansion of treatment should be 'index linked' to the rise in the numbers with drug problems. To illustrate this point, if we were to consider the last decade, there has been more than a doubling of the numbers of people who have become addicted to heroin – so a doubling of treatment capacity would not even have kept pace with the expansion of the problem and would certainly not have been sufficient to make greater inroads into the potential treatment deficit. Hence we strongly recommend that mechanisms are established to make sure that the doubling in treatment availability is a doubling of the service capacity index-linked to increases or decreases in the size of the target population.

Table 10.1.   Results of the National Treatment Outcome Research Study (NTORS). Source: Gossop, M., Marsden, J. & Stewart, D. (1998) *NTORS at One Year. Changes in Substance Use, Health and Criminal Behaviour One Year after Intake*. London: Department of Health.

Results of treatment in community settings (478 patients)

	At intake	After one year
Proportion of patients abstaining from illicit opiates	5%	22%
Proportion of patients injecting	62%	45%
Proportion of patients involved in shoplifting	37%	22%

Results of treatment in residential settings (275 patients)

	At intake	After one year
Proportion of patients abstaining from illicit opiates	22%	50%
Proportion of patients injecting	61%	33%
Proportion of patients involved in shoplifting	36%	20%

Second, a more critical examination should be undertaken of the evidence base supporting different treatments. It would be a mistake to consider that all treatments are intrinsically beneficial and of equal worth. Consequently, it would be wasteful merely to try to increase treatment capacity. New funding should be focused on treatments of demonstrable effectiveness that are applicable to the population in need. We now have good evidence of the major benefits to individuals and society that result for some types of treatment of specific disorders, but a blanket approval (and funding) of all treatments would be as inappropriate as an indiscriminate assumption that 'surgery works'. Treatments that currently lack an adequate evidence base should perhaps continue to be supported, but need to be considered as research or exploratory initiatives for which better evidence from well-designed studies will allow considered funding decisions to be made in the future.

Although targets have been set in relation to the number of drug users, specific ones could also be set for treatment, such as hepatitis B immunisation, prevention of hepatitis C infection, or prevention of overdose deaths by reducing the large UK market in diverted pharmaceutical drugs like methadone.

Treatment has been shown to reduce the criminal behaviour of previously untreated heroin addicts, and, if major decisions are to be made to devote more resources to the treatment of addicts, and relatively less to law enforcement, there may be merit in considering interventions that act as a bridge between these approaches.

Although increasing numbers of heroin addicts are undergoing detoxification in jail, provision to encourage continued abstinence is lacking. Many prisons have established drug-free wings, where prisoners wanting to remain abstinent voluntarily submit to drug tests in return for privileges, but there are frequently waiting lists to enter them. Moreover, treatment within prison seldom involves specialist expertise, and continued treatment on release is far from adequate.

There is considerable potential for using prison funding to treat offenders through early conditional release from prison and participation in treatment as an alternative to custodial sentences. Few such initiatives are in place in the UK, although three pilot studies of 'Treatment and Testing Orders' are currently in progress (see Chapter 8, page 182). Heroin addicts, having pleaded guilty to, for example, charges of burglary or shoplifting, may be referred to a special drug treatment programme which periodically reports back to the court on the therapeutic progress of the addict and any continuing heroin use and criminal behaviour. This could be supported by supervised prescription of the opiate-blocking drug naltrexone which, taken three times weekly, prevents relapse into heroin dependence.

Such initiatives are welcome but will not be problem-free. The courts will have to decide, for instance, how to respond to drug users who fail to cease using heroin completely but achieve major improvements in other areas. The judicial system will need to develop a fuller understanding of the nature of drug dependence and the complexity and often extended time-course of treatment. With both early release arrangements and Treatment and Testing Orders the element of compulsion should be more fully exploited.

With estimates of between 20% and 50% of all acquisitive crime attributed to drug users raising funds to buy their drugs, and reductions in drug use resulting from treatment, it is easy to get carried away by the potential for treatment to reduce crime. Although a significant impact of treatment programmes on crime rates can be expected, dependent drug users frequently have criminal histories unrelated to drug taking that are likely to persist despite treatment. In grasping opportunities for funding through the criminal justice system, treatment services must be realistic about what can be achieved.

Nearly £170 million, 12% of the UK's overall drug budget, was spent on drugs education in 1997–98, almost as much as on treatment and rehabilitation. Despite the scale of the expenditure involved, educational programmes have been evaluated much less fully and rigorously than treatment, particularly in this country. Some American programmes have been shown to be successful when they have gone beyond simple educational initiatives to include sustained interventions on many levels, such as trying to change attitudes in the whole community in tandem with school-based programmes. In this country, though, there is little evidence of beneficial results. The few educational programmes that have been adequately evaluated have produced only short-lived improvements in knowledge and attitudes, and have failed to produce any evidence of what really matters – change in behaviour. If the primary purpose of drugs education is to deter or reduce drug use, it is questionable whether such a significant proportion of funding should continue to be invested in the absence of evidence that it is making a worthwhile difference.

Clearly, it would be inappropriate to abandon all drugs education. For one thing, it is important that accurate factual information should be available to all drug users and potential users, and presented in such a way that they will believe it. Much more attention needs to be paid, though, to the lessons of American research, particularly through commissioning the development and evaluation of multi-level educational programmes in this country.

THE CONTRIBUTION OF RESEARCH

Informed debate and decision-making need good evidence. While writing this book we frequently encountered questions that could have been answered by conducting research, but the research evidence was not there. For example, although large-scale surveys have told us what overall proportion of the population reports using different kinds of drugs, little is known about the medical and social problems, if any, that these users are currently encountering. There are many uncertainties about the long-term physical and mental health consequences of prolonged use of several of the commonly taken drugs. It is not even possible to estimate with any precision the most extreme outcome – how many people die each year from drug-related causes. There is considerable doubt about 'what works' in prevention. Many therapeutic measures and programmes are also under-researched. Even less is known about the effectiveness of the many law enforcement approaches that aim to reduce the supply of and demand for drugs, despite the fact that the bulk of government expenditure is devoted to law enforcement. This lack of basic evidence makes very difficult the task of assessing the effectiveness of potential alternative drug policies, or of predicting the consequences of alternative policy options.

Much of what we do know is based on research in other countries, particularly in the USA, which supports over 85% of the world's research on drug use and drug addiction.[1] Reliance on other countries' research is relatively safe when it is concerned with the biological actions of drugs and mechanisms of dependence. It is also possible to generalise to some extent from one country to another about the effectiveness of different enforcement, prevention and treatment approaches. But the more one moves from the biological to the social realm, the more hazardous it becomes to extrapolate from one setting to another. This is because the kinds of drugs that are used, the way they are used, and the problems that result differ considerably from country to country. Enforcement, prevention and treatment programmes also differ markedly between countries. Treatment programmes in Europe, Australia and the USA may appear to be similar because they have similar names (methadone maintenance, for example). But similarities begin to dissolve in the light of variations in where, how and by whom the treatment is provided, the way the treatment is perceived by patients, the ability of patients to opt for other competing treatments, and the degree of formal or informal coercion to enter into and remain in treatment. Where good, transferable evidence does exist, it has led to, for instance, improvements in the quality of treatment provided for patients and shown how resources can most effectively be spent (see below).

It is difficult to calculate how much is currently spent on drugs research in the UK. The last two Government White Papers (*Tackling Drugs Together*[2] and *Tackling Drugs to Build a Better Britain*[3]) identified the money spent on deterrence, prevention and treatment, but did not reveal how much was spent on research. Our enquiries suggest that the total annual UK expenditure on research on drug problems by government departments, research councils and the major charitable foundations amounted to between £2.5 and £3 million in 1998. That sum is just 0.02% of the £1.4 billion that the Government estimates is spent overall on drugs problems in the UK each year. Between them, the two largest sources of funding for medical research – the Wellcome Trust and the Medical Research Council – spend over £600 million a year, but only a tiny fraction of this is devoted to research that is directly relevant to drug problems.

Tackling Drugs to Build a Better Britain includes a commitment to research, and Mr Hellawell has already identified some additional funds for research and information gathering. The £2 million a year over the next three years announced in his First Annual Report and National Plan is a welcome addition to the current meagre drugs research budget, as is the £2.5 million that the Department of Health will be spending over the next five years. Research funded by government departments usually and understandably focuses on issues directly relevant to their policies, and this new money will be spent on research that informs the Government's drugs strategy. However, research that is not directly funded by government departments and is driven by scientific questions, or that can independently analyse drugs problems and policy options, is equally important.

In addition to the obvious need for more research into what is a major and rapidly growing social problem, there has to be a long-term, stable income stream. The reasons for this are twofold. First, some of the research questions that need to be answered require long-term or ongoing data collection. For example, studies of the effectiveness of treatments require follow-up of patients over a period of several years, as do studies of the impact of drug use on physical and mental health. Second, without long-term financial security, it is difficult to develop research groups with a critical mass of inter-disciplinary expertise, and hard to attract the best intellects. Unstable funding also makes it extremely difficult to create a climate in which people can develop careers as specialists in addiction research and drug problems. It is equally difficult to encourage a research culture within hard pressed treatment agencies, or in drugs education or law enforcement. For all these reasons, there is an urgent need for funding at least two stable, multidisciplinary research teams. This is not special pleading: it is merely a plea for funding appropriate to the importance and complexity of the problem.

What would be a reasonable level of research expenditure on drugs in the UK? One way to consider this question is to look at how much is spent elsewhere. In 1995, the American Government spent $542 million on drugs research, amounting to 4% of their total government expenditure on drugs. Even this level of expenditure was criticised as inadequate by the USA's General Accounting Office, and it is estimated that the equivalent sum for 1998 was in the region of $850 million to $1 billion. Another way of considering the question is to look at expenditure on research and development in other fields. At one extreme, the pharmaceutical industry is a high investor with an average of 20% of annual output spent on research and development. On a more modest scale, when the NHS Research and Development programme was established in the late 1980s in response to the criticisms of the House of Lords Sub-Committee on Science and Technology, the aim of successive Secretaries of State was to commit 1.5% of the total NHS budget to research and development.

Whatever comparison is used, it is clear that current UK research expenditure is trivial compared with the scale and importance of the phenomenon. Research is the most under-funded component of the UK's response to drugs. As a starting point, 1% of the annual drugs budget would inject £14 million a year into drugs research.

IMPROVING THE VALUE OF TREATMENT

While there is a clear need for treatment services to expand to attract more problem users into treatment, much more also needs to be done to improve the outcome for each drug user who enters treatment – to the benefit of the individual, his or her family and the wider society. When insufficient attention is paid to the way treatment is provided, or when the intensity of the treatment is below a certain level, it has much less impact. A recent American study gave methadone maintenance patients extra support at three levels of intensity and cost. Those receiving the cheapest and lowest intensity treatment did least well with 71% still using street drugs after one year. By spending a little more on treatment, patients at the intermediate level of intensity did markedly better, with only 53% still using street drugs a year later. The highest-cost, highest-intensity treatment patients, although they did best of all, led only by a very small margin (51% were still using street drugs after a year).[4] Methadone maintenance is better researched than any other area of drug treatment,[1,5] and this is a clear demonstration of a plateauing out of the benefit from increasing the intensity of treatment per patient. This suggests that there is a limit beyond which greater investment in more intensive treatment programmes is less cost-effective. If the North American evidence also applied to UK treatment, this country would benefit from bringing its treatment up to the optimal middle level at which the greatest cost-effectiveness is seen.

NTORS, the biggest study of drug treatment ever conducted in the UK, demonstrated the considerable benefits to the individual and to society that result from bringing dependent drug users into treatment and these were described in Chapter 8. However, it is worthy of note that the rates of improvement described in NTORS are modest when compared with treatment programmes in the USA. It is not clear why this is so. However, there are substantial differences between the kinds of treatment provided in the two countries, and it is highly likely that these differences contribute substantially to the more modest benefits observed in the UK.

The clearest comparisons can be made between methadone treatment programmes in the two countries. In the USA, all methadone maintenance programmes incorporate employment, housing, counselling and medical care, and are given according to approved treatment manuals and by trained and supervised counsellors. In the UK, methadone treatment is often little more than the provision of a methadone prescription, sometimes accompanied by an invitation to talk to a counsellor. American treatment programmes have explored the most influential ways of using urine testing to discourage patients from continuing to use street drugs and to determine the extent to which they are following their prescribed treatment, but this is rarely done in their UK equivalents. Similarly, methadone treatment in the UK rarely takes a systematic approach to privileges – such as whether patients are allowed to take home their methadone supply or have to consume it in the clinic – and so loses a useful mechanism for encouraging patients to work towards agreed objectives of treatment. Indeed, for much of UK methadone treatment, it is difficult to see how such influence could be brought to bear by drugs counsellors since they are in contact with their patients so infrequently and there are few independent sources of information about patients' drug use.

Britain also lags behind in the actual doses of methadone that are prescribed. Well-conducted research studies have shown that higher-maintenance doses of methadone are associated with reduced levels of continued injecting, less use of street drugs and reduced levels of continued criminal behaviour. Responding to this evidence, the USA and Australia, among others, have moved to higher-dose maintenance prescribing, although such increases bring the added risk that patients will take more than one dose at once and overdose, or will sell any surplus on the black market. These risks have been dealt with by widespread supervision of methadone consumption and the use of urine testing and other objective measures to ensure the regimen is being followed. In the UK, in contrast, virtually all methadone is being dispensed in 'take-home doses' (i.e. with no supervised consumption), and with a third of all methadone prescriptions being dispensed in bulk for a week or longer. Consequently, doctors are cautious about increasing their patients' daily dose for fear of increasing the overdose risk and feeding the black market. The absence of any central control or coordination over methadone prescribing in the UK also makes it extremely difficult to bring about change: thus, concerns expressed by the Department of Health in 1991 about the dangerous practice of prescribing methadone in tablet form (it is believed often to be crushed and injected) have probably had little impact on the field, with 10% of methadone still being prescribed in this form.

When patients start a course of methadone treatment, there are particular risks of overdose resulting from errors in prescribing the appropriate dose for that individual. Patients who continue to use street drugs on top of their prescribed methadone and are not experienced in combining them are also more likely to overdose. Even for this crucial early stage of treatment, no standard arrangements exist for supervision of methadone consumption to reduce these dangers. In most other countries, clinicians can be confident that patients follow the agreed methadone prescribing regime (since the patient usually takes the methadone under supervision) while in the UK it is a matter of faith and speculation. In these circumstances it seems highly likely that greater benefit to all concerned would result from a more disciplined and organised approach to methadone treatment through:

- wider adherence to treatment protocols by treatment staff;

- ensuring a safe chain of custody and consumption for the prescribed drug from the prescription pad to the named patient (for instance with supervised consumption);

- the universal incorporation of monitoring (such as urine testing) and feedback of the results into the treatment process;

- changes to the treatment system to allow new research findings to be quickly and efficiently implemented across the whole country; and

- focusing on integrating methadone treatments with essential support services such as housing and employment.

In some cases, quite simple alterations to the way existing services are funded could increase their efficacy considerably. For a long time now, it has been standard practice in the treatment of heroin addicts for the patient to visit a local pharmacy to collect a single day's supply of his or her substitute drug (usually methadone) at a time – thereby increasing the likelihood that the prescribed supply would be taken as intended and reducing the scope for diversion to the black market (because the black market value of each single day's supply is unlikely to be sufficient to cover the risk and inconvenience involved in selling it). This practice was already more liberal than in most other countries, where the patient was required to take his or her methadone under supervision, at least until he or she had demonstrated stability, drug-free urine tests and adherence to the treatment programme. However, in recent years, the increasing financial pressures on NHS drug services have compelled them to reduce their prescribing costs and the associated fees paid to community pharmacists. As a result, many drug services are now forced to issue prescriptions for a whole week's supply of these drugs in order to reduce the cost of pharmacists' fees – recently found to be the case with a third of all methadone prescriptions across England and Wales and with up to three-quarters of methadone prescriptions in some parts of the country.

The costs to society of this enforced drift into inadequately monitored dispensing are probably far greater than the modest savings made by the treatment programmes themselves, but the treatment service is faced with little choice when its prescribing budget is capped despite an increase in number of patients. The problem is that the costs of this change are costs to a different government department. Reducing pharmacists' fees saves money for the health departments; the cost of increased leakage of prescribed methadone onto the black market are borne by the Home Office through the criminal justice system and by the community as a whole. This undesirable change in clinical practice could be easily corrected by transferring the responsibility for the costs of substitute prescribing and pharmacists' dispensing fees into a different budget, with immediate benefits both to patients and the neighbourhoods in which they live.

Longer-term planning would lead to a further improvement in the quality of services provided. Mr Hellawell's recommendation that additional money for treatment might be obtained from the seized assets of drug dealers would need to be carefully thought through. If it merely led to an unpredictable fluctuating flow of additional monies it would not be possible to establish stable and dependable services for those in need of treatment. Hence, if such money is to be used, it would be more appropriate for it to be pooled centrally and distributed as part of the regular funding for drug treatments, rather than being used for specific projects whose funding would expire when the sequestered assets ran out.

There are also important manpower issues if treatment services are to be expanded. At the level of the general drug worker, there will be a need to increase recruitment from a range of disciplines into work in the drugs field. There is also a major need to fund further training and career development opportunities for those who can assume a leadership role in the expanded addiction treatment services. For this reason, the anticipated establishment of addiction psychiatry as a separate speciality with its own training programme will be a welcome development. If the Government's plans and our own proposals for expanding and strengthening treatment services are to be realised, every sizeable community is going to need a fully trained and experienced addiction specialist to plan and help organise the whole range of services, voluntary and statutory, in the locality, and to help train the staff of these services.

The recent establishment in England and Wales of the National Institute for Clinical Excellence (NICE) and the Commission for Health Improvement (CHI) offers an opportunity for addressing some of these issues, and we consider that there is a compelling case for methadone treatment provision to be taken up urgently as an area requiring special attention by this new National Institute. Sensible advice on safeguards, against the diversion of methadone onto the black market and injudicious prescribing of injectable drugs by doctors untrained in managing drug dependence, have already been given by the UK Health Departments' guidelines.[6] However, guidelines alone have limited impact. It may be necessary to assign a monitoring function to health authorities or CHI to ensure that the guidelines are followed.

TREATMENT AND HARM REDUCTION

There is now good evidence that certain treatments of drug misuse work, and that the view that nothing can be done for drug problems is unjustified. Like many other medical conditions, drug misuse is neither completely preventable nor instantly curable, but the effectiveness of treatment compares favourably with that of many other chronic disorders.

Treatment benefits the individual drug user in many ways, but the effect of treatment on the prevalence of drug misuse in the rest of the population is less certain. There is no doubt that it enables many individuals to stop using drugs, but drug users may also become abstinent without any treatment. The direct impact on the prevalence of drug misuse is not likely to be great, although it may have a larger indirect effect by reducing the recruitment of new users. There is also some evidence that increasing the numbers of drug users in treatment reduces the perceived glamour of drug use and decreases the amount of drug dealing by users.

Chapter 8 described the massive influence of 'harm reduction' approaches on the treatment of drug dependence in the UK in the late 1980s and 1990s. These measures were adopted as an urgent, pragmatic response to the threat of an HIV epidemic. There is now a need to define our concepts of harm reduction more clearly, and to decide what can be achieved by this approach, and at what cost both to the individual drug user and to society. Harm reduction in its broadest sense encompasses a wide spectrum of activities. Indeed, it could be considered to be simply what the treatment of most chronic medical conditions involves – minimising suffering and ill health indefinitely or until such time as the condition, if curable, is cured. At the other extreme, harm reduction can be viewed narrowly as being quite distinct from treatment and simply as a means of enabling drug users to take drugs with the minimum danger to themselves and others. This narrow interpretation has more to do with social policy than medical treatment and leads on to consideration of changes in the drug laws.

What emphasis should there be on drug treatment as a public health measure as opposed to a means of improving the health of individuals, and to what extent should treatment encompass crime reduction as a goal? Although needle exchange has rightly become fundamental to treatment, the rationale for prescribing substitute drugs is often unclear. If crime reduction is the prime objective of treatment the widespread provision of a range of drugs, including injectable heroin, may be appropriate. If improving public health is the main objective, a priority would be to ensure the ready availability to drug users of methadone or other oral opiate substitutes in order to reduce intravenous injection and needle sharing. If treatment is directed at the health of the individual drug user, the focus would be on moving through the intermediate goals of stopping sharing, injecting and using street drugs, to eventual abstinence.

In practice, a compromise position is generally adopted where methadone is prescribed, but this prescribing is not conditional on moving towards abstinence or stopping all drug use. Nevertheless, within this middle ground, there are still wide variations, largely determined by the prescribing doctor and the influence of the local health authority. With the move towards wider GP (as opposed to specialist) prescribing, primary care group (as opposed to health authority) funding, and the advent of courts commissioning treatment through probation services, objectives and practice will become even more diffuse. As long as treatment remains under-resourced and its objectives undefined, treatment services will continue to grapple with dilemmas about where their priorities should lie.

The Netherlands have addressed the problem by adopting an approach that separates the public health and to some extent criminal justice objectives from those of individual health by providing two distinct treatment services funded respectively by the metropolitan authorities and health authorities (see Chapter 7, p. 171). There is considerable potential in the UK for following this course and aligning treatment objectives with specific sources of funding.

Most drug use is recreational and carries only a small risk to health. By far the most commonly used drug, cannabis, is relatively safe in the short term. Most drug users do not want to stop taking drugs and see no reason for doing so. They do, though, want accurate information about the risks involved and how these may be minimised. Since the advent of HIV/AIDS, the potential for influencing the behaviour of those who choose to take drugs by health initiatives directed both at the general population and specific sub-groups like injecting drug users has been extensively and effectively exploited. This approach is not, however, without its detractors who believe this is 'soft on drugs' and implicitly condones their use. But to revert to simplistic messages like "Just say no" would be a grave mistake. Being truthful about drugs and their effects must remain the foundation of drug policy, even if it sometimes results in greater acceptance of drugs and more widespread drug use.

The most serious medical consequences of drug use arise from injecting and dependence. By disseminating information on AIDS and other blood-borne diseases, providing needle exchange schemes, and increasing the availability of treatment with methadone, the spread of HIV was contained – one of the greatest recent public health achievements. However, the majority of heroin injectors are now infected with hepatitis C. This will have major consequences for health service resources in years to come, one reason why interventions aimed at minimising the spread of blood-borne infections must be intensified.

Pressure for the funding of methadone programmes has resulted in decreased availability of abstinence-orientated treatments, and many specialist in-patient treatment facilities and residential rehabilitation units have been forced to close in recent years. There have also been advances in the effectiveness of detoxification procedures that have not been fully exploited. Poor planning of drug services has kept some addicts who want to abstain on methadone maintenance longer than necessary. This is, in part, the result of a commonly held misconception among health service purchasers that residential detox-ification is an expensive alternative to maintenance. Irrespective of the perceived financial costs, it is unethical to encourage drug users to remain dependent on prescribed methadone without providing necessary assistance with detoxification, so that the user can become drug-free if he or she wishes to.

Recent evidence of widespread heroin dependence among adolescents in many areas of the country emphasises the urgent need to develop services for treating young drug users. The Health Advisory Service has described the woeful inadequacy of such services and the rarity of examples of good practice. Treating adolescents requires specialist skills from a range of disciplines. There are very few residential places for treating young drug users in the whole of the UK. Usually such youngsters, for lack of any alternative, have to be accommodated in secure units under the care of social services departments. With expertise in this area so limited, health authorities and Drug Action Teams should be encouraged to consider establishing regional adolescent drug problem teams, incorporating specialists from drug dependence, adolescent psychiatry, social work, youth work and education.

Coexistence of serious psychiatric disorder and harmful drug use is common. Such 'dual diagnosis' patients or 'comorbidity' is associated with especially high levels of use of psychiatric and other resources. Both drug treatment services and general psychiatric services serve these patients poorly. The management of problem drug and alcohol misuse must therefore become more central to the training of all mental health professionals, particularly for those working in community psychiatric services. The establishment of integrated treatment services specifically for those with serious mental illness and substance misuse should also be considered.[7]

More could also be done to prevent unintended drug overdose deaths. Drug users themselves, their families and partners should be educated about the dangers of overdosing and how to avoid them. They should also be trained in resuscitation techniques and encouraged and empowered to use them when an overdose occurs, without fear of reprimand or inappropriate police investigation. It has recently been proposed that, alongside this training, the opiate antagonist naloxone should be provided. This injectable antidote quickly neutralises the effects of any opiate, even in overdose. We are satisfied that such new initiatives should now be the subject of carefully designed preventive treatment trials to establish their true worth and the best way of bringing their benefits to drug users and their families.

Although we know that the treatment of heroin dependence is, or can be, effective, we know little about the relative effectiveness of different therapeutic regimes, or which treatments are most appropriate for which individuals. Indeed, Britain has a lamentable record in researching treatments for drug dependence, and there are dangers in relying on research findings from abroad where circumstances are inevitably different. One unexplored area is the potential for self-treatment. It is important not to lose sight of the fact that most of those who stop using drugs do so without recourse to health professionals. Little is known about the individual, family, social and environmental factors that are conducive to becoming abstinent without the help of formal treatment services, so there is much scope for research.

PRESCRIBING HEROIN TO ADDICTS

The possibility of treating heroin addicts by the provision of a prescribed supply of heroin has often been considered by the international community. Until recently, the UK was the only country in which this practice was possible, and it had become progressively rarer here within the broad sweep of drug treatment, so that by the mid-1990s it comprised only 1% of all drug prescribing to addicts for the treatment of their addiction. However, the feasibility and possible advantages of this approach have been actively considered over the last decade by Australia, and Switzerland introduced heroin maintenance programmes on an experimental basis during the early 1990s. Clinical trials have also started in the Netherlands. These initiatives have not required changes to the international laws on drugs.

Methadone maintenance has repeatedly been shown to reduce users' street drug use and other criminal activities, and to improve health and social behaviour, so what need is there to prescribe heroin or other injectable drugs? Approaches based either on oral methadone or abstinence both have a major contribution to make, but do not work for all addicts. Indeed patients were only enrolled onto the Swiss trial if they had failed in methadone and drug-free treatment several times. Furthermore, some drug users' injecting behaviour is so entrenched that they are unwilling or unable to give it up, yet may benefit from a controlled supply of injectable drugs.

So far, evaluations of the Swiss treatment have shown very impressive results: addicts' health has improved, they took part in less criminal activity, reported less use of illicit heroin and improved their social functioning. However, the debate about prescribing heroin to addicts has widened beyond a simple consideration of the possible benefits to patients.[8] It might, goes the argument, be interpreted as the government weakening its stance on drug use, so encouraging drug taking among the young; this was the reason cited by the Australian Government when it blocked a proposed clinical trial of heroin prescription in 1997. Similar concerns that it would open the door to wider legalisation failed to be realised, when Swiss voters approved the continuation and expansion of heroin prescription for opiate addicts, but rejected the legalisation of heroin in referenda in 1998.[9]

The leakage of heroin from patients to the black market is another potentially important issue raised in the debate. The Swiss programme incorporates a high level of security with tight supervision of consumption of all supplies of heroin, minimising leakage. However, the UK, with its long history of heroin pre-scribing, has traditionally taken a laxer approach and most patients receiving prescribed heroin do not have to take the drug under supervision. The degree of control exercised by the Swiss programme is expensive to provide, but the overall savings from reduced crime and other costs outweigh the expense.

In Britain, where the most commonly prescribed injectable opiate is not heroin but methadone, a similar controversy over the wisdom of prescribing injectable methadone needs to be resolved. In 1995, a national survey showed that 10% of all opiate prescriptions issued to addicts for the treatment of their addiction was for injectable methadone. No serious study of this form of treatment has yet been undertaken, in the UK or elsewhere. In the absence of research evidence to inform decision-making, we support the introduction of a graded system of prescribing, as recently recommended in the new guide-lines from the Department of Health,[6] in which the responsibility is placed with those treatment centres with greater resources and greater expertise. At present, intravenous methadone is provided as frequently by GPs as by drug misuse specialists. Specialist treatment centres should more readily accept responsibility for drug-dependent patients for whom this type of treatment is considered necessary, while GPs should be encouraged to work on a 'shared care' basis in the management of more straightforward cases using oral methadone. This proposal may, however, require legislation.

Private practice in the addictions field is unusual and warrants special consideration. Much good work of high standard is undertaken in private practice. However, the private prescribing of drugs raises important issues. The process of going to a private doctor, paying a fortnightly appointment fee of perhaps £30–50, and coming away with a substantial supply of substitute drugs is regarded by some observers and by many drug users themselves as little more than buying a prescription. The private doctors would no doubt point out that NHS and private practice coexist in virtually all areas of health care in the UK, and might also point to waiting lists and the stretched resources of drug treatment services in the NHS. But the private prescribing of drugs to drug addicts is different.

Across NHS and private practice generally, the medical profession considers that the actual treatments provided should be broadly the same, but with private prescribing to addicts this is not the case. Doctors providing private prescriptions typically give twice the normal daily dose, are four times as likely to give prescriptions in a form that can be injected, and virtually always give prescriptions to be collected in a single, large weekly or fortnightly instalment, instead of setting up arrangements for daily dispensing. Furthermore, such private prescribers often include other misusable drugs, such as amphetamines, on the prescription, and often prescribe in this manner with no adequate checks that the patient needs and is taking the prescribed supply and is following the treatment. In most other areas of medical practice, the private specialist holds his or her position as a result of substantial training in a specialist field and the gradual establishment of a worthy reputation. In contrast, the doctor prescribing drugs to addicts as part of private practice often has no special expertise or training in this field: he or she has simply established a booming private practice once his or her reputation has spread among the drug-misusing community as an 'easy touch'. This is what the *Junkie* author, and real-life heroin addict, William Burrows called a 'croaker' – a doctor who in a reversal of the usual patient–doctor exchange could be relied upon when handled with the right 'bedside manner' to provide a prescription.

There is no doubt that some private practitioners in the addictions field provide responsible, ethical care, but the scope for poor practice is too wide because at present private prescribers are largely unmonitored and unregulated. As in other areas of health care, NHS and private practice should be broadly equivalent, and the 'unacceptable face of private practice' should either be tackled by banning prescribing to addicts by such independent operators, as in many other countries, or alternatively be brought firmly into the same framework for monitoring and regulation as NHS practice.

DRUGS AND SOCIAL EXCLUSION

The uses of particular drugs and how people take them can be described in terms of their socio-economic status, age, gender and locality. Patterns change over time, depending on fashion, availability, cost and other factors. More consistently, once a form of drug use gains an undesirable reputation, such as smoking crack cocaine, injecting drugs, or, in the 18th century, drinking gin, it is likely to find its way into deprived neighbourhoods.

Social deprivation, certain types of criminal behaviour and unemployment are all closely linked with problem drug use. We cannot pinpoint any one of these as deserving the 'blame' for drug use, or claim that drug use 'causes' crime, poverty or unemployment in isolation, but the three do tend to cluster together and reinforce one another.

Links between problem drug use and adverse social circumstances are much stronger in neighbourhoods than in individuals. In deprived areas with their multiple social problems, drug use may be simply one part of a wider spectrum of delinquency, perhaps involving gang fighting, unemployment, and an underground economy where a whole range of commodities are traded, and of which drugs are only a part. A ready system of supply is therefore waiting to respond to demand, and the criminal lifestyle that can accompany dependent heroin use may be more attractive in the absence of legitimate opportunities or occupations. People living in poverty who try to stop using drugs usually also have fewer social supports, or lack the money needed to move away to a new area for a fresh start, cutting ties with their old drug using world.

However, if one studies individuals living in socially deprived circumstances, rather than the neighbourhood as a whole, they are not more likely to use or experiment with drugs, and only somewhat more likely to develop problems as a result of their drug use, than those who are much better off. Why should this be? One possibility is that individual drug use, and more especially drug problems, are, at least to some degree, determined by an inherited vulnerability or relative invulnerability that is not linked to social deprivation. This implies that the people most likely to misuse drugs are those who are both genetically vulnerable and also living in socially deprived neighbourhoods.

There has been a marked increase in drug consumption over the last 30 years (see Chapter 3). To what degree can this be related to social changes occurring over this period? It is well-documented that the economic recession in the early 1980s had an adverse effect on social cohesion, especially in industrial areas of the UK. At the same time, in many cases beginning before that recession, there has been an increase in family breakdown. The number of children living in lone parent families doubled, and the rate of divorce markedly increased (see Figures 10.1 and 10.2) as did the frequency of conduct disorders, delinquency and school exclusions.

As the genetic composition of a population does not change significantly within one or two generations, the likelihood is that unfavourable social changes were at least partly responsible for the progressive increase in problem drug use since 1970, although once a drug culture becomes established, it doubtless develops its own momentum.

It will never be possible fully to disentangle what is cause and what is consequence where the link between drugs and social deprivation is concerned. Nevertheless, it is reasonable to suggest that any measures that combat social deprivation successfully will also tend to reduce problem drug use, and any measures that reduce problem drug use will almost certainly result in a diminution of social disruption. Government initiatives to provide increased financial support to families with children, to improve the quality of parenting, to raise the standard of child care in the crucial early years, to improve educational standards, to increase the provision of leisure facilities, and to combat social exclusion through increased resourcing of disorganised neighbourhoods are therefore to be wholeheartedly welcomed. We cannot be sure though that, even if successful, these initiatives will have a major impact on the prevalence of problem drug use.

If they succeed, these initiatives can be expected to have a favourable effect on the frequency of drug problems. The extent of their impact cannot, however, be calculated. Indeed, their effects will be strongly influenced by accompanying changes such as the level of resources put into treatment facilities, by changes in legislation, by the success of measures to limit the availability of drugs and, perhaps above all, by global social and economic changes difficult for any national government to predict or influence.

DRUG TESTING BY EMPLOYERS

Drug screening by employers started in the USA in the 1980s either as a routine component of the assessment of potential new employees or in

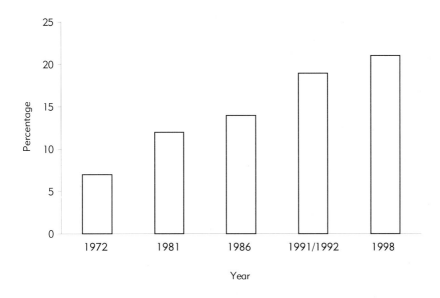

Figure 10.1. Proportion of dependent children living in lone parent families. Source for Figures 10.1 and 10.2: Office of National Statistics (1999) Personal communication.

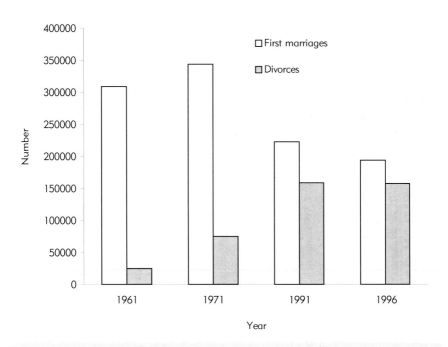

Figure 10.2. First marriages and divorces in England and Wales, 1961–1996.

response to behaviour raising the suspicion of drug use. Initially, it was restricted to industries where intoxication could obviously have devastating consequences – the military, the nuclear and oil industries, airlines and other forms of public transport. It then started to spread to a broad range of other companies and organisations for reasons that were partly economic (the assumption that drug users would tend to be inefficient and have high sickness absence and turnover rates), and partly political (drug taking involves criminal activity and we don't want to employ criminals). British industry started to follow suit a few years later. Drug testing now takes place in the railway, oil and nuclear industries, and in the armed forces. It is also starting to spread, as in the USA, into other sectors, including electricity supply companies, financial institutions, manufacturing, and the food industry.

Most of this testing, both routine screening pre-employment and in response to suspicious behaviour, is on urine samples. Several commercial laboratories provide a comprehensive drug screening service, mainly based on immunoassays employing a range of antibodies specific to particular drugs or classes of drugs. Immunoassay 'dipstick' kits for individual drugs can also be used 'on site', with relatively little equipment or training. For most drugs urine testing will detect any significant use within the last 24–72 hours, and because of their slow excretion use of cannabis and of some long acting barbiturates and benzodiazepines can often be detected for up to a week (see Table 7.1). Urine samples can be stored for weeks without deterioration, and although false positive results may occasionally occur as a result of cross reactivity of the antibody with proprietary analgesics, cold remedies and prescribed drugs, testing is usually accurate and reasonably cheap. Despite the fact that it is impossible to detect most drugs other than cannabis used more than 48–72 hours beforehand, there is evidence from at least one prospective American study that new employees who tested positive for cannabis or cocaine had a raised incidence of absenteeism, accidents, injuries and premature termination of employment subsequently, and that the financial savings that would have accrued if these drug-positive individuals had not been given jobs would have exceeded the cost of the drug screening programme.[10] However, other studies have shown that detected drug use prior to employment is associated with no increased likelihood of industrial accidents. Studies of absenteeism did not take account of the fact that those who use drugs most often (young men) are more likely to be absent from work whether they use drugs or not. Research on the relationship with staff turnover or termination of employment rates suffers from the same problem of not adjusting for the effects of age and gender.[11]

In the last decade the deposition of drugs in hair has also been extensively studied and extremely sensitive means of detection have been developed. Minute quantities of drug are incorporated into newly formed hair in the hair follicles in the skin while the drug is in the blood stream shortly after its ingestion. It then remains in that precise segment of hair as the hair continues to grow, and so slowly moves along the hair at a rate of about 1 cm per month. Analysis of a sample of about 20 hairs from the back of the head makes it possible to detect the use of most of the commonly used drugs (apart from LSD) over a period of up to several months, and even to determine when during that time period individual drugs were used. Although there are a number of technical problems (drug detection is easier in dark than in fair hair and the rate of hair growth varies somewhat from person to person and between different areas of skin), the drug content of hair is usually little affected by washing, dyeing, bleaching or the application of perming solutions. Because individual chemical compounds can be detected with a high degree of specificity it is also possible to distinguish between a drug incorporated into the matrix of the hair and surface contamination, by smoke from other people's cannabis joints, for example, because ingested drugs are metabolised into different, and detectably different, chemical compounds.

Although the capital costs of the equipment are high, and a high level of technical skill is needed to operate it, the equipment can be configured to detect a range of drugs from an individual hair sample in a single analysis, and if large numbers of samples are processed sequentially, the cost per sample, although higher than that of urine testing, is not exorbitant.

Hair analysis is already being used clinically in this country to monitor the drug use of psychiatric patients, and in that setting it has proved to be reliable and acceptable to the subjects (removing a small sample of head hair is simple, painless and cosmetically undetectable even if repeated regularly). In principle, therefore, it could be used by employers, probation officers, the police or even by schools, universities, and doctors' employers, and it is already being used instead of, or as well as, urine testing by some American companies.

There are, of course, important issues of civil liberty and obvious ethical problems. It is questionable whether drug taking before someone is even hired, or during vacations or weekends when there is no real possibility of residual effects impairing work performance, is any concern of an employer, still less of a headmaster or university vice chancellor. Furthermore, the detection and prevention of wrong doing are the responsibility of the police, not of employers or educational institutions. The greater ease of drug detection in dark than in fair hair could also give grounds for arguing that hair analysis discriminated against dark skinned people. And, minor though they are, remaining technical questions over the effects of surface contamination, dyeing, bleaching and perming, and variable rates of hair growth, may make clear legal decisions difficult. Nor does hair analysis detect drug use within the previous week or so, because the hair follicle itself, the site of hair formation, is left in the scalp. Even so, the attractions of hair analysis to employers persuaded, either by economic or safety considerations, or simply by their own moral convictions, that it was essential to have a completely drug-free work force are obvious.

It seems likely, therefore, that hair testing will be adopted in some industries and by some employers in this country over the next few years. In recent decades, breathalysing drivers to measure their alcohol levels has produced major reductions in drink driving. If hairtesting became widespread, as urine testing has already started to do, and was tolerated by public opinion, it might deter recreational drug use among employees and have the potential to reduce the prevalence of drug use by the working population as a whole. Such a scenario might follow a major industrial disaster prompting increased public concern and increased intolerance of drug use. Conversely, it has been suggested that drug screening might add to the pressure for the legalisation of cannabis, as the extent of its use becomes more visible, with employers possibly wishing to concentrate on more harmful drugs. Unfortunately, the recreational drug which poses the greatest threat both to productivity and to safety in the workplace – alcohol – is not detected by hair analysis because it is soon converted to compounds which are normal bodily constituents.

ECSTASY AND RECREATIONAL DRUG USE

Large and increasing numbers of young people are using drugs recreationally without becoming dependent or breaking the law, other than the Misuse of Drugs Act. One recent survey[12] indicates that, by the time they are 18, over half of young people have taken a drug at least once, and up to a quarter do so regularly, while a study of over 3000 second-year university students in the UK reported that 13% had used ecstasy (MDMA). International comparisons suggest that a higher proportion of British youngsters use drugs, and do so more often, than their European contemporaries,[13] particularly ecstasy. However, other countries are catching up, notably Germany, the Netherlands, Spain and the USA, which have all seen recent increases in ecstasy use.

The type of contemporary drug use which has emerged from the 'rave' scene cuts across all Britain's social classes, incorporates many different substances and tends to involve women as much as men. Polydrug use is not a new phenomenon, but the range of drugs to choose from is wider today than 20 years ago. In what has been termed a 'pick and mix' culture, young people are taking combinations of drugs, often preparing for a whole weekend's drug use. This might include cannabis and alcohol before going to a club, ecstasy (or amphetamine and LSD) possibly with amyl nitrite (poppers) or cocaine while at the club, followed by benzodiazepines (such as temazepam) and cannabis later. New drugs are being introduced into these drug repertoires as they appear: fluoxetine (the widely prescribed antidepressant Prozac) may be taken to enhance the action of ecstasy, despite rendering the user vulnerable to a wider range of health hazards. Within weeks of sildenafil (Viagra) being licensed as a prescription-only drug for the treatment of impotence, researchers reported its recreational use, raising concerns of potentially fatal drops in blood pressure when taken together with 'poppers' (amyl nitrate), although how commonly this combination is used in practice has yet to be established.

People respond to health warnings to different degrees, choosing to ignore some and changing their behaviour in response to others. While some recreational drug users may have been deterred from using ecstasy following the warnings about deaths, many have continued but heed advice about reducing the dangers, for instance by drinking water to avoid dehydration. Clubs, too, have acted to improve safety by providing 'chill out' areas to prevent people becoming overheated and exhausted. Users are largely informed, concerned, and want accurate information about the drugs they are taking, particularly about the possible long-term effects of ecstasy.

Loss of life, particularly a young person's, is always a tragedy. Idiosyncratic reactions to MDMA cannot at present be predicted, and the consumption of only one tablet may be enough to kill a vulnerable individual. By comparison, immediate deaths from alcohol intoxication usually involve large quantities consumed over a short period. While obviously a cause for concern, deaths from ecstasy are rare compared with the large numbers of users. Many more people may be at risk from long-term effects, but the latest research gives an inconclusive picture (see Chapter 1). The results of this research are worrying, but do not yet prove that harmful, long-term consequences are likely. The effects of polydrug use, which often involves ecstasy, are also very difficult to measure owing to the wide range of interactions between different substances of unknown composition. So how should policy-makers respond?

A few reports have been received of occupational, relationship and financial problems related to ecstasy, but these seem to be rare and usually minor; the main concerns relate to users' health. Policy could take several approaches: to reduce the availability of ecstasy, to reduce demand by increasing the penalties for users, to improve the safety of the drugs taken, and to provide help for those encountering health problems.

In principle, efforts to 'crack down' on the drug's availability could involve a number of approaches. At an international level, greater efforts could perhaps be made to control the precursor chemicals from which ecstasy is synthesised. Where this approach is not accompanied by a reduction in demand, there is a danger that alternative chemicals may be substituted by manufacturers with the risk of more harmful drugs being produced, or indeed new drugs being developed for which legislation is not in place. Greater efforts to detect smuggled imports are unlikely to make a significant impact on price or availability. Furthermore, ecstasy, amphetamines and LSD are already manufactured within the UK.

The severity of the penalties for possession could be increased so that more users are deterred. However, ecstasy is already a class A drug, so that the strongest penalties under the Misuse of Drugs Act can already be applied to anyone possessing, dealing in or manufacturing it. Existing laws against possession could be enforced more strongly, so that the risks of use outweighed the benefits to a larger proportion of current users. The drawback of this approach is that young people who are not significantly involved in any other criminal activity would become involved in the criminal justice system at great cost to the tax-payer and to themselves.

There have been calls for clubs to provide pill-testing facilities where a small scraping is taken from a tablet and mixed with a reagent to show whether it contains a hallucinogenic amphetamine, such as MDMA, MDA or MDEA. Leaving aside the question of whether this could be seen to condone drug use, the presence of an amphetamine-like drug may be desirable to the user but does not indicate safety. Neither can the currently available test identify other foreign and potentially harmful substances or predict idiosyncratic reactions.

At present, most drug services and GPs are uncertain how best to help ecstasy users, and despite the reportedly high levels of adverse effects suffered by ecstasy users, they rarely seek help from these agencies. Services that provide help and advice specifically for those suffering its adverse effects, or worried about long-term consequences, may therefore need to be provided, possibly as a telephone helpline. Doctors and other professionals providing such services may find themselves torn between warning users not to take ecstasy and suggesting how best to reduce the risks if they choose to ignore the advice about stopping. This conflict has already been overcome with other harm reduction approaches such as the provision of sterile injecting equipment to drug injectors. Needle exchanges provide information to deter users from injecting, but also sterile injecting equipment in recognition of the fact that many will continue to inject, and have succeeded in reducing the harm – such as contracting HIV – from sharing injecting equipment.

The way in which health information about ecstasy should be given needs careful consideration. There are well-documented instances where health warnings, such as those about certain types of contraceptive pill, have resulted in people taking greater risks than those they were trying to avoid. Recent evidence also suggests that the publicity campaign against ecstasy after the death of Leah Betts has created a distorted view of the drug's risks: some young people deterred by these warnings have instead been taking cocaine, mistakenly believing it to be a safer alternative. Information on risks therefore needs to be carefully framed to calculate its effect on users who continue to take drugs, as well as those who are successfully deterred.

The methods of passing on information also need some thought. Originally, advice on how to avoid overheating with ecstasy was circulated to clubs and specialist rave music shops, but for several years now, recreational drug use has been widely discussed in mainstream lifestyle magazines as well as in the media. Health professionals and researchers therefore need to work with the disseminators of information to ensure that it is accurate and conveyed in a way likely to reduce harm among users.

AMPHETAMINE DEPENDENCE

Amphetamine is not only taken by those most commonly involved in drug use, such as young people socialising together, but also by individuals using it to control their weight or obtain extra energy for heavy tasks such as construction work. Across the UK, amphetamine is the second most commonly taken drug (after cannabis). More people inject it than any other drug except heroin, and it is second only to heroin in the number of users who are dependent.

While much amphetamine use is relatively unproblematic, the associated problems increase greatly when regular use develops into dependence. The chemical properties of amphetamine are more harmful to physical and mental health than those of heroin. People who inject it do so more frequently than heroin injectors, with increased damage to veins, and other attendant risks, and amphetamine injectors are more likely to be sexually active and have multiple partners, so are at increased risk from sexually transmitted diseases. Amphetamine is also more likely to be associated with acts of violence than heroin, as a consequence either of the drug's stimulant action or of the development of an amphetamine psychosis. The potential consequences of amphetamine dependence to public and individual health are therefore substantial and, other than in the area of acquisitive crime (amphetamine is much cheaper than heroin), may be of similar magnitude to those from heroin dependence.

Despite these risks, there has been relatively little research on treatment of amphetamine dependence either in the USA or Europe. Nor do we know what proportion of amphetamine users do become dependent, or what factors increase the chance of this happening. As the policy agenda shifts away from health towards reducing acquisitive crime, there is a danger that amphetamine-related problems may continue to be neglected.

CANNABIS: THE POLICY OPTIONS

For the past 30 years, there have been repeated demands in most Western democracies, mainly by the young and the educated, for the 'legalisation' of cannabis. Originally these demands came mainly from publicity seekers and rock stars, but increasingly they come from respected individuals and institutions, from members of Parliament and from broadsheet newspapers. Regardless of their source, they are met either by a stony silence or by blunt statements by government ministers that there is not the faintest chance that UK drug policies will change. An intelligent public dialogue about the potential risks and attractions of legalisation is conspicuously lacking, particularly in Britain and the USA.

Several quite good arguments have been advanced in favour of legalisation. Cannabis is less obviously harmful to health than the legal substances, tobacco and alcohol. Although it is estimated that 120 000 people die in the UK every year from smoking and around 30 000 from alcohol misuse there are very few recorded deaths attributable to cannabis[14] despite its increasingly widespread use. This widespread use has itself been used as an argument for legalisation. Survey data consistently suggest that more than a third of British adults under the age of 30 have smoked cannabis at least once, and that one-third of these had used it in the last month, and several other countries have produced similar or even higher figures. To insist that an activity that is so widespread, particularly among the best-educated, must continue to be a criminal offence is – so the argument goes – ill-advised and dangerous. It brings the law and its institutions into disrepute and potentially brands as criminals large numbers of otherwise law-abiding citizens. It also places a huge and costly burden on the police, the courts and the prisons. In 1997, over 45 000 people were cautioned, almost 30 000 were prosecuted, over 15 000 were fined and over 1000 were imprisoned for possession of cannabis. In addition, the fact that so widely used and popular a commodity is denied to legitimate farmers and traders means that a lucrative market and huge profits are reserved for criminals; and these profits are then used to increase their power and extend their influence into other fields.

These arguments are, however, less compelling than they seem. Cannabis is certainly not a safe drug even though its dangers may be less obvious than those of tobacco and alcohol. The evidence that it produces dependence is now beyond dispute. Long term, regular use leads to tolerance and increasing difficulty stopping despite wishing or attempting to do so, and North American population surveys consistently suggest that 5–10% of those who have used cannabis more than once eventually become dependent. Experimental studies have established that sudden cessation of use is followed by withdrawal symptoms, and drug dependence clinics in the UK, USA, Australia, Sweden and The Netherlands report increasing numbers of patients whose main complaint is their inability to give up cannabis use. Although the risk of dependence is substantially less than for nicotine or opiates, it is comparable with that of alcohol, and there is no doubting the magnitude of the burden alcohol dependence places on British society.[15] Cannabis is also an intoxicant that impairs coordination, short-term memory and judgement, and so inevitably increases the risk of road traffic and other accidents. The magnitude of that risk is very difficult to estimate, partly because cannabis and alcohol are so often taken together, but the effects of a single cannabis joint on the performance of pilots in experimental situations are alarming. It is also important to recognise that because cannabis is metabolised much more slowly than alcohol its effects on coordination and judgement may be considerably longer-lasting.

Large amounts of cannabis, taken by whatever route, can produce alarming psychotic episodes lasting several days, and there are links with schizophrenia (see Chapter 1). It is also important to appreciate that the smoke from a cannabis joint contains most of the same constituents as tobacco smoke, including the carcinogens. It is not surprising, therefore, that regular cannabis smokers develop chronic bronchitis and squamous metaplasia (a precancerous change) of the respiratory tract, and it is likely that in time it will become apparent that they are also at increased risk of cancer of the lung.

It is clear, therefore, that the reputation of cannabis for being a 'safe' drug is unjustified. There are three reasons for this misplaced view. It is not immediately lethal in the way that alcohol and opiates may be; its capacity to produce dependence is slow and insidious, like alcohol, and therefore easily missed; and because it has only been widely used in Western countries for 20–30 years, its long-term effects are not yet apparent. It is also important to recognise three other things. The plant *Cannabis sativa* contains over 400 chemical compounds, including over 60 different cannabinoids, and the pharmacology and toxicology of most of these is still unknown. Selective breeding in the last decade has also greatly increased the potency of some strains of cannabis. In the early 1980s a typical joint contained about 10 mgm of the main active ingredient, delta-9-tetrahydrocannabinol (THC), whereas a modern joint made from 'skunk' or grown under hydroponic conditions may contain several times as much. Even though these high potency strains are still only responsible for 5–10% of the British market, they raise the possibility that much of the research carried out in the 1960s and 70s with its relatively reassuring results may no longer be relevant to current circumstances. Finally, far too little research has been done into the long-term effects of cannabis use, either the harmful effects or indeed the possible beneficial effects. Since about 1977, there has been a dearth of serious research into cannabis, mainly because, once their alarm at the rise of cannabis use in the 1960s and early 1970s had abated, governments throughout the world have been reluctant to fund cannabis research. They did not want either to think or to know about this troublesome substance, and perhaps they hoped that if they tried to ignore it it would go away.

Although few governments anywhere in the world have yet indicated that they are even contemplating legalising cannabis, and most of them, including our own, are bound by international agreements (mainly the Single Convention of 1961) not to do so, it is still worth discussing what the consequences of legalisation would be.

Cannabis would become a psychoactive substance like tobacco and alcohol, which could be grown, processed, marketed and sold quite openly both within and between individual countries. Indeed, if cannabis were taken out of the Single Convention, the World Trade Organisation would regard it as illegal for any individual country to seek to restrain international trade in cannabis or its derivatives. It is likely, though, that, as with tobacco and alcoholic beverages, legal restraints would be placed on both production and sale, with licensed premises, opening hours, a ban on sales to minors, restrictions on advertising and special taxes. Established industries – perhaps the tobacco industry itself – would move in. At the same time the existing criminal importers and distributors might re-emerge as legitimate businesses as some successful bootleggers did at the repeal of Prohibition in the USA. Either way, a commercial market with an ambition to increase sales would quickly be established and, even if special taxes were levied on cannabis products, as they probably would be, consumption would almost certainly rise. This would happen for many reasons, but primarily because that substantial proportion of the population that had previously been deterred from using cannabis by its illegality would no longer have that deterrent. They would probably also be influenced by the covert message accompanying the change in the law – that the government had now decided that cannabis was not particularly dangerous after all. This rise in consumption would almost certainly involve adolescents and would be accompanied by an increase in adverse effects, both immediate and long-term. This is what invariably happens with all psychoactive substances.

At the same time, there would be a number of beneficial effects. Much police time would be saved; many court appearances would no longer occur; and the costs of the prison service and the overcrowding of prisons would be reduced a little. The government would obtain substantial additional revenue from the special taxes it levied on cannabis products; the UK Government currently nets £7.3 billion a year on tobacco products and £5.7 billion a year on alcoholic beverages (1995–96 figures). Research would also be stimulated, because it would become much easier to find out how much cannabis was being consumed by whom, and what the effects were. Perhaps most important of all, a lucrative criminal activity with its associated ills like blackmail, money laundering and the corruption of police and customs officials, would be wiped out.

It is almost impossible to predict, even in limited financial terms, whether the benefits of legalisation would outweigh the costs. All that is certain is that ill effects on health and health care costs would rise and that police and criminal justice costs would fall. Much would depend on two things: how important the poorly understood long-term effects of heavy cannabis use proved to be; and whether the increased consumption of cannabis was additional to or instead of consumption of other psychoactive substances, particularly alcohol – and here the available evidence is not encouraging. There has already been a huge increase in the use of cannabis and other drugs by adolescents and young adults in the last 20 years, and this increase has not been accompanied by any reduction in their alcohol consumption. Indeed, their consumption has risen, particularly that of young women.

It is easy to agree that the League of Nations had insufficient evidence to justify including cannabis in its legislative framework for curbing international trade in opiates and cocaine, as it did in 1925. That decision was made, primarily at the request of the Egyptian Government, on the grounds that smoking hashish was a frequent precursor of insanity, even though no causal relationship had been established. Indeed, it remains uncertain to this day whether cannabis precipitates schizophrenia, or any other chronic psychosis, in people who would not develop the condition otherwise, and, even if it does, it is not responsible for more than a tiny proportion of cases. But although it might have been preferable had the League of Nations never included cannabis in the Geneva Convention, governments have to respond to the situation they find themselves in now at the start of the 21st century, not the situation that might have existed if their predecessors had been wiser or better informed.

Faced with a rising consumption of cannabis which they seemed powerless to control, an increasing number of governments have, overtly or covertly and with varying degrees of reluctance, adopted a policy of decriminalising or depenalising the use or possession of cannabis. While continuing to treat importation or sale as criminal offences (as they are bound to do by the Single Convention), they have ceased to regard the possession of small quantities of cannabis, or its use, as offences, or have reduced the penalty from imprisonment to a fine, or simply allowed their police to turn a blind eye. Possession or use of cannabis is now only punishable by fines in several American and Australian states, and in Spain and Italy this is so not just for cannabis but for all drugs. In the UK, cautioning has already quietly replaced prosecution for most individuals caught in possession of small quantities of cannabis and it is now official policy that first offenders will only be cautioned, and will only be prosecuted if they are caught in possession of cannabis on at least two further occasions. This reduces the burden on the police, reduces the risk to the occasional user of acquiring a criminal record and probably increases consumption somewhat, but it does little else. In particular, it does nothing to reduce the lucrative criminal trade in cannabis.

The boldest and most interesting legislative innovation in the last 30 years has been by the Dutch Government. In 1976 it adopted a formal policy of tolerating possession or sale of up to 30 g of cannabis – a sizeable quantity, as few users consume more than 10 g a month.[16] It also gradually adopted a policy of tolerating the establishment of 'coffee shops' selling cannabis openly, provided (and this was strictly enforced) they did not advertise or sell to minors and did not sell other prohibited substances. As a result, between 1200 and 1500 'coffee shops' eventually came into existence, and cannabis became readily available, risk free, to most Dutch adults. For the first eight years there was little change in cannabis consumption. After 1984, however, there was a progressive increase both in the number of 'coffee shops' and in cannabis consumption – although even in Amsterdam consumption levels were still no higher than in Copenhagen (where the law remained unchanged) or in several American cities. This delayed rise in consumption seems to have been a result not of depenalisation itself, but of the commercialisation and de facto legalisation that developed subsequently, and in 1995, partly in response to increasing pressure from the French and German governments, the tolerated limit for sale or possession was lowered from 30 g to 5g and a 500 g limit placed on trade stocks.

Like many of the other 'facts' used to clinch simplistic arguments in the debate over cannabis this Dutch experiment is quoted both as evidence that removing the penalties for use and possession of cannabis is safe and harmless, and as proof that any relaxation of the law leads inevitably to rising consumption and social disorder. The truth lies somewhere in between. Depenalisation in 1976 did eventually lead to a substantial increase in consumption, but there was little evidence that this was accompanied by any increase in ill effects, medical or social, and Dutch consumption never rose beyond the levels already reached in the USA and some other parts of Europe. Substantial numbers of drug takers were, however, attracted from other neighbouring countries, and the governments of those countries became increasingly hostile to the experiment.

What conclusions should be drawn from all this – either by governments or by their electorates? It is clear that there are no easy answers. Present policies, which are based on international agreements, are failing to curb rising consumption and generating huge social costs. Legalisation would substantially reduce those social costs but would increase consumption even further and generate significant health care costs, and it is by no means clear that this would be preferable. On the basis of our present knowledge, only four conclusions seem justified. First, there needs to be a well-informed public debate about the policy options available to us. Although it is possible that the UK Government's present stance with regard to cannabis is the least unsatisfactory policy available, this is not self-evident and the issues are too important to society as a whole to be left to government departments and their formal advisers. Second, we need to know much more about the long-term effects of cannabis use and about the contribution of cannabis intoxication to motor vehicle and other accidents. That information is essential to any rational appraisal of the relative merits of different policies, and it is the responsibility of governments to fund the necessary research. Third, social experiments such as that conducted by the Dutch government should be encouraged, not discouraged. If any future policy change is not to be a step into the dark, we need as much information as possible about the consequences of legislative innovations, particularly in countries with a similar social structure to our own. Finally, it is difficult to justify ever imprisoning someone simply for the possession or personal use of cannabis. Its international treaty obligations do not oblige the UK government to do so and in the USA, where several states reduced the maximum penalty for possession in the 1970s from imprisonment to a fine, there was no evidence that this led to any significant increase in consumption.[17]

Therapeutic uses of cannabis

The issues raised by the therapeutic use of cannabis and cannabis derivatives are more straightforward. Cannabis has been widely used as a medicament for over 5000 years – in China, India, the Middle East, Latin America, Africa and Europe. It was widely prescribed by British physicians in the second half of the 19th century; indeed, it was regularly prescribed by Queen Victoria's personal physician, Sir Robert Russell, and recommended for migraine by the great Sir William Osler. There is also at least suggestive evidence that it is effective against nausea and vomiting and as a painkiller, and that it may be valuable for combating the loss of appetite and weight commonly experienced by patients suffering from AIDS and certain cancers, for the relief of muscle spasms in patients with multiple sclerosis, and in the treatment of glaucoma, a common cause of blindness. Nor does the medical use of cannabis raise any fundamental issue of principle. Heroin, despite its dangers, its widespread misuse and the Single Convention, is available to all licensed medical practitioners in the UK, subject to certain safeguards. So too is cocaine.

Understanding of the complex pharmacology of cannabis is developing rapidly, thus raising the possibility that cannabinoids might be identified in cannabis extracts or that synthetic cannabinoids might be developed with valuable therapeutic effects without any psychoactive effects.

Existing therapies for nausea and vomiting, for the muscle spasms of multiple sclerosis and for the loss of appetite and weight in AIDS and advanced cancer are far from satisfactory. There should therefore be no obstacle to the conduct of random allocation clinical trials designed to compare cannabis with existing treatments for these and other conditions; and if cannabis proves superior to these existing remedies, there should be no bar to its prescription to appropriate patients. Living with AIDS or multiple sclerosis is hard enough anyway, and it should be possible for doctors to relieve avoidable suffering without being handicapped by inappropriate legislative obstacles. We therefore share the view of the Lords' Select Committee that cannabis should be in Schedule 2 rather than Schedule 1 of the Misuse of Drugs Regulations.

However, treatment with a pure substance, targeted on a known receptor, is always preferable to the use of what is essentially a 'herbal remedy' containing dozens of different substances, and smoking cannabis long-term must be assumed to involve comparable hazards to smoking tobacco. Smoking joints, or indeed the oral or rectal administration of cannabis extracts, should therefore always be regarded as less satisfactory than the administration of a pure cannabinoid. One such cannabinoid, nabilone, is already licensed in the UK for the treatment of nausea and vomiting unresponsive to conventional anti-emetics, and in time it is likely that other synthetic cannabinoids will be marketed and licensed for a range of specific purposes. Although there would be significant problems in prescribing herbal cannabis or resin, until a range of synthetic cannabinoids is generally available there should be no obstacle to the prescription of cannabis itself on a named patient basis, if its efficacy in specific conditions is demonstrated by clinical trials. It is particularly undesirable that people requiring cannabis for medicinal purposes should be prosecuted.

Policy recommendations, very similar to our own, regarding the medical use of cannabis have recently been published by the USA's Institute of Medicine (IoM), an authoritative and highly respected body. Medical use has also recently received legal sanction in Canada.

The IoM recommended that further research should be conducted on cannabis and cannabinoids. Owing to the harmful substances delivered by smoked cannabis, it was not the preferred method of administration, and should not generally be prescribed for long-term medical use. However, for certain patients, such as the terminally ill or those with debilitating symptoms, these long-term medical risks were not of great concern. Therefore, until a safe, reliable and fast delivery system for cannabis has been developed, the IoM considered that it should be possible to prescribe smokeable cannabis to such patients to relieve symptoms where other approved medications had failed. Such patients should be informed of the risks, and their treatment carefully supervised and assessed.[18]

We therefore hope that the UK Government will be prepared to reconsider the position it adopted in its response to the recommendations of the House of Lords' Select Committee on Science and Technology.

POLICY OPTIONS FOR HEROIN

Cannabis and heroin can conveniently be taken as representing the least and most dangerous poles of the spectrum of drugs. We have already discussed the likely consequences of the legalisation of cannabis. Although no government has yet even contemplated the possibility of legalising opiates, and is debarred from doing so by the Single Convention, it might still be instructive to explore the likely consequences if a country were ever to do so.

The government in question would presumably attempt to prevent consumption of heroin from rising by replacing the existing criminal market in adulterated heroin derived from illegal imports with an equivalent or lesser quantity of pure heroin, imported by the government itself, for sale by strictly controlled 'licensed premises' at a price that was lower than the previous street price. This would have major benefits for existing heroin addicts. They would have access to a regular, secure supply of pure heroin, and presumably of clean needles and syringes as well, at a price that was significantly lower than they were previously paying to criminal dealers. As a result, their lives would be less disrupted and the risks to their health would be greatly reduced. They would still be dependent on a highly addictive substance, but they would be at less risk of contracting hepatitis or AIDS, or of dying of an overdose (a fairly common result of using street heroin, particularly when returning to a previous dose level after a period of enforced abstinence in prison). They would also be more accessible to social and medical services and more likely to be capable of holding down jobs. The government would make a very large profit on the heroin it sold, presumably in the form of an excise duty. Prostitution and acquisitive crime, including shoplifting and housebreaking, would be reduced, much police and judicial time would be saved, and fewer prisons would be needed. More important still, the income of a huge, criminal industry would be drastically reduced, the power of the 'Mafia' would wane, and money laundering and the corruption of public servants would diminish.

It would, though, be extremely difficult and probably impossible for the government to prevent the consumption of heroin from rising, because its new status as a legal substance tolerated by the state would tempt many more people to experiment with it, and quickly become dependent on increasingly high doses. If the government set the price of heroin too high and made the associated controls too strict, a parallel black market would still survive; and if it set the price too low and allowed the licensing controls to become lax heroin use would spread rapidly. Moreover, if existing addicts were expected to pay the same high price as everyone else, many would still have to resort to theft or prostitution to pay for their habit; and if they paid a special reduced price, or obtained drugs on prescription, they would still have financial motives for selling part of their supply to others. It would also be virtually impossible to prevent some use of heroin by teenagers, whatever formal restrictions were placed on its availability. At present, there are few countries in which more than 1–2% of the population has ever used heroin, and the majority of these present users have few marketable skills and little education. If heroin were a legal substance this proportion might easily increase 10-fold within a decade, with serious consequences for the labour market, health services and, ultimately, the national economy.

In general terms, the pattern of gains and losses would be similar to those resulting from the legalisation of cannabis. There would be lower social costs because of a reduction in criminal activity, and higher health service costs because of an increase in consumption and in the number of addicts needing treatment. Both the gains and the losses would be considerably greater, however, and the balance between the two even more unpredictable. There would also be a serious risk that the lives of many previously stable, skilled and productive people would be so transformed by their newly acquired dependence on heroin that they became liabilities to their families, their employers and the state.

In reality, a more likely scenario is a local medical decision to prescribe heroin rather than methadone to addicts, followed by a police decision to turn a blind eye to evidence that an illegal market in this prescribed heroin was replacing the local market in imported street heroin – because they were convinced that this change was accompanied by falling crime rates in the neighbourhood. If the consequences of a series of unofficial local initiatives of this kind appeared to be largely benign, a government might be prepared to contemplate adopting a national policy of prescribing heroin rather than methadone to addicts, and this could be done without formally legalising heroin or breaching the Single Convention. The end result might then be a de facto legalisation of heroin comparable to the de facto legalisation of cannabis in the Netherlands, with the twin attractions of ready reversibility if ill effects started to mount or public opinion swung against the experiment and the avoidance of any formal breach of international obligations.

It is always rash to try to predict future events, and detailed predictions almost invariably prove mistaken. It is important, nevertheless, to try to anticipate the likely consequences of contemporary trends and policies. The past is the best guide we have to the future and extrapolation of the serial changes of the last few decades is likely to give us advance warning of at least some aspects of the 'drug scene', and their political consequences, in the early decades of the 21st century.

Consumption of cannabis, of amphetamines, of heroin and of cocaine have all been increasing relentlessly in Britain and in most other industrial countries for the past 30 years. Moreover, so far only a very small proportion of the population (1–3%) has been prepared to try using heroin or cocaine even once, whereas we know that if social conditions are conducive to drug use it can become widespread even though possession is illegal. In Vietnam in the late 1960s, for example, the prevalence of heroin use by American servicemen was estimated to be close to 40%. In simple economic terms, therefore, the market for heroin and cocaine looks far from saturated.

It is also clear that any control policy based primarily on preventing drugs from getting into the country is bound to fail. Hundreds of planes, ships and trains and tens of thousands of passengers enter the UK every day. Less than 1% of these international travellers are or could be interviewed or searched, and their numbers are rising every decade. At the same time, they are becoming increasingly cosmopolitan as tourism and international trade expand, settled immigrant communities strengthen their links with their kinsfolk in Southern Asia and the Caribbean, and new immigrant communities from Africa and the Middle East expand. Any of these millions of travellers could be transporting drugs and the profits involved ensure that every day some of them will be. Since the start of the era of mass international travel 30–40 years ago, no country has succeeded in reducing the illicit importation of any drug except very temporarily, and Customs and Excise estimate that, year on year, they only succeed in seizing 5–10% of the drugs entering the UK. The fact that the street price of heroin has been falling in Britain for the last 20 years, and its purity rising (see Figure 7.9), is eloquent testimony to the failure of our attempts to reduce supply. Indeed, we are unable to prevent drugs entering our prisons despite their being purpose-built to prevent unauthorised entries and exits and the Draconian powers of prison officers. In 1996–98, there were over 17 000 separate 'drug finds' in English and Welsh prisons.[19]

It is almost inevitable, too, that more new 'designer drugs' will be developed over the next 20 years and manufactured in small, illicit laboratories scattered across Europe. LSD, amphetamines, ecstasy and gamma-hydroxbutyrate (GHB) will not be the last psychoactive substances to be discovered, synthesised illegally and exploited commercially. There are too many well-trained chemists and pharmacologists, and the potential profits from manufacturing and distributing popular psychoactive substances far exceed those of any legitimate industry. Indeed, the illicit manufacture within the industrial world of an increasingly wide range of stimulants, sedatives and hallucinogens may eventually largely replace the commercially inefficient importation of plant extracts like heroin, cocaine and cannabis from distant countries in Latin America and Asia.

Even so, steadily rising consumption of drugs is not inevitable. Opiate consumption in China fell very substantially between 1906 and the 1930s, and has remained low ever since. Major changes in per capita consumption of alcohol have taken place in Britain in the last 300 years and there have been large, sustained reductions – in the mid-18th century and the first half of the 20th century – as well as increases. The prevalence of cocaine use, although probably not the associated ill effects, also fell steeply in the USA in the mid-1980s, when it became widely appreciated that the drug was not the harmless and socially acceptable stimulant many casual users had naively assumed it to be. If drug use does fall significantly, though, it will be because of a reduction in demand, not because of any reduction in supply.

Several influences might lead to a reduction in demand. The present UK Government is committed to a sustained campaign to combat poverty and long-term unemployment and to eliminate substandard housing, and there is a well-established association between all these social ills and heroin and other major drug problems. Unfortunately, American evidence suggests that this association is only partially causal. It is partly a result of selective migration of those who are already using drugs and becoming unemployable into poverty-stricken, crime-ridden areas, and a simultaneous selective migration of people with regular jobs and incomes out of these areas. Moreover, reducing or even eliminating these social disadvantages will not necessarily result in the disappearance of drug misuse that has already become firmly established. For both these reasons, therefore, the effect on the prevalence of heroin use of reducing income differentials and the unemployment rate and renovating derelict housing estates is uncertain.

Other influences, though, might have a greater effect on demand. If urine and hair testing by employers, and even by schools and universities, became widespread it might reduce consumption by those concerned about the risk of detection. School-based educational campaigns might slowly become more effective, and increasing awareness of the real risks associated with drug taking, coupled with the dramatisation by the media of tragic events like the death of Leah Betts, might lead to major changes in the attitudes and behaviour of adolescents and young adults comparable to those that have already taken place in their elders towards smoking. There might also be a selective reduction in intravenous drug use as the long-term consequences of hepatitis C infection become increasingly apparent, although it is a sobering fact that many people who take heroin regularly by 'chasing the dragon' end up as injecting users despite an initial determination not to do so.

We can probably assume with some confidence that over the next 10 or 20 years, laboratory research will start to decipher the neural pathways underlying drug dependence, and perhaps give us some understanding of the fundamental biological mechanisms that make psychoactive drugs so attractive and dangerous. It is probable, too, that genes will be identified that make individuals particularly likely, or unlikely, to misuse or to become dependent on particular drugs or classes of drugs, and these genes may create valuable opportunities for genetic counselling. At the same time, pharmaco-logical research will almost certainly lead to new and more effective therapies for at least some forms of dependence. It is unlikely, though, that this increased understanding of the biological basis of drug dependence or these new therapies will provide simple solutions to many of our current diffi-culties, or remove our present policy dilemmas. Medical science does not often provide simple answers to our complex social problems.

The National Plan published by the Government in 1999 set targets for reducing the proportion of young people using heroin and cocaine by 25% by 2005 and by 50% by 2008. These are very ambitious targets, but the modest initiatives outlined in the plan are unlikely on their own to reverse the steadily rising consumption of the last three decades. Indeed, the factors tending to increase the prevalence of drug taking even further over the next two or three decades seem considerably more powerful and inexorable than those that might reduce it. It is therefore important to consider the likely effect on public opinion of visibly rising consumption of an increasingly wide range of illicit substances. Doubtless, there would be demands for harsher penalties, particularly for 'drug barons', as well as calls for the abandonment of outdated legislation, and the balance between the two would be influenced by whose drug consumption was more conspicuous – the alienated unemployed or the otherwise law abiding middle classes. It seems likely, though, that relentlessly rising consumption would lead to increasingly powerful demands for radical legislative changes by the UK Government or the international community. Electorates and governments would be bound to conclude sooner or later that policies that were visibly failing, decade after decade, must be changed, and the most obvious alternative to the comprehensive prohibitions embodied in the original Geneva Conventions and the 1961 Single Convention is some form of legalisation.

The result of such a change would almost certainly be a further increase both in consumption and in the associated ill effects on health, but there would be a reduction in both violent and acquisitive crime, in money laundering and in the corruption of public servants, and legitimate governments would at last be able to share in the huge profits of the industry, by taxing consumption or licensing manufacture and sale. We cannot be confident that this would necessarily be regarded as an improvement, for it would involve a complex mixture of gains and losses against a background of strongly held conflicting beliefs. But if drug consumption and the conspicuous social ills associated with a vast, illegal international industry continue to rise, a policy change of this kind seems inevitable sooner or later. We have already reached the stage at which sober and presumably well-informed bodies, like the Financial Action Task Force of the seven leading industrial nations (the G7), estimate that international trade in drugs generates between $1500 and $5000 billion a year, a sum that exceeds the entire gross domestic product of every nation in the world other than the USA and Japan, and that at least $120 billion (£73 billion) of this vast amount is laundered through the world's banking systems every year. Indeed, it may be the implications of this for the world economy, rather than crime rates and other more visible social ills, that finally persuades governments that radical changes have to be contemplated.

Only one thing is certain. In the long run, society will only be at ease with its drug control policies if they are based on a rational assessment of the risks associated with different psychoactive substances and an objective appraisal of the consequences of previous policy changes, rather than on moral postures, the mistaken assumptions of the past and the accidents of history.

Glossary

NB These are not formal definitions but descriptions of the meaning attributed to these terms as they are used in the book.

addict: convenient shorthand term for someone dependent on one or more drugs; in everyday use, the term has acquired pejorative overtones.

addiction: *see dependence*

alcoholic: convenient shorthand term for someone who has become dependent on alcohol.

analogue (of a drug): a modification of the original chemical structure retaining essentially the same pharmacological actions.

communicable disease: disease that is capable of being transmitted from person to person (in this context mainly by drug users sharing infected needles).

dependence: broadly equivalent to addiction, meaning that the user has adapted physically and/or psychologically to the presence of the drug and would suffer if it were withdrawn abruptly.

designer drug: drug specifically created with the intention of evading drug control legislation.

detoxification: the process by which drug withdrawal is managed in a dependent user, usually under medical supervision.

drug: in both scientific and ordinary usage this word can have a number of meanings. Strictly speaking, most of the medicines prescribed by doctors are drugs. So are many widely used substances like aspirin which are available 'over the counter'. In most instances in this book the term is used in a more restricted sense to refer only to psychoactive substances, both illegal substances such as cannabis and heroin, and legal substances, like solvents and tranquillisers, used in an unsanctioned way. (This definition excludes alcohol and tobacco purely for convenience. In reality, alcohol and nicotine are both psychoactive substances).

drug misuse: drug use that is harmful or hazardous to the individual or others.

drug use: a neutral term that does not imply either the absence or presence of harm or hazard.

endorphin: a substance produced by the body itself with similar pharmacological effects to opiates.

hallucination: sensory perception in the absence of sensory stimulation, e.g. seeing scorpions on the bedspread or hearing voices.

hallucinogen: a drug that produces hallucinations *(q.v.)* or perceptual distortions, such as an altered sense of the passage of time.

opiate: a drug extracted from the opium poppy (such as morphine or codeine), or derived from one of these (such as heroin). Also commonly used to describe a similar synthetic drug (such as methadone).

narcotic: a term widely used in the USA to describe opiates or cocaine but sometimes, as in international legislation, it refers to any illicit drug.

neurotransmitter: a chemical by which a nerve cell communicates with another nerve cell or with a muscle fibre.

noradrenalin (known as norepinephrine in some countries): a neurotransmitter (q.v.) and hormone that increases blood pressure and the heart rate.

polydrug use: use of more than one drug by the same individual, either in a drug 'cocktail', or one after the other, or because the user's preferred drug is unavailable. Drugs may be combined to enhance their sought after effects or minimise unwanted ones.

problem drug use: implies that either the pattern of drug taking, or the route of administration, is causing significant physical, psychological, or social problems for the user. Generally implies greater harm than 'drug misuse' *(q.v.)*.

psychoactive drug: any drug that affects mood, thought processes or perception.

psychosis: a form of mental illness characterised by delusions (irrational beliefs), hallucinations, and bizarre behaviour. Drug-induced psychoses are usually short-lived.

recreational drug use: a term describing the hedonistic use of drugs and implying, not always correctly, that there is no significant associated harm.

relapse: a return to drug use after a period of abstinence by someone attempting to remain drug-free.

schizophrenia: a severe and often long-lasting mental illness characterised by particular psychotic symptoms (cf. psychosis).

stimulant: a drug that elevates mood, increases wakefulness and gives an increased sense of mental and physical energy.

tolerance: a state in which the same dose of a drug produces a reduced effect or higher doses are needed to maintain the same effect as a result of the body's adaptation to the repeated use of the drug.

toxicity: the harmful medical effects, immediate or slowly progressive, of a drug.

volatile substance abuse: sniffing or inhaling solvents or vapours for their psychoactive effects.

withdrawal syndrome: the physiological and psychological response to the sudden absence of a drug on which the individual had become dependent. Symptoms are usually the opposite of those produced by the drug itself, and usually unpleasant.

References by chapter

CHAPTER 1

1 Edwards, G. & Gross, M. (1976) Alcohol dependence: provisional description of a clinical syndrome. *British Medical Journal*, i, 1058–1061.

2 Joint Working Group, Royal College of Physicians, Royal College of Psychiatrists & Royal College of General Practitioners (1995) *Alcohol and the Heart in Perspective; Sensible Limits Reaffirmed*. London: Royal College of Physicians.

3 MacAuley, D. (1996) Drugs in sport. *British Medical Journal*, 313, 211–215.

4 Ruben, S. M. & Morrison, C. L. (1992) Temazepam misuse in a group of injecting drug users. *British Journal of Addiction*, 87, 1387–1392.

5 Hall, W. & Solowij, N. (1997) Long-term cannabis use and mental health. *British Journal of Psychiatry*, 171, 107–108.

6 House of Lords Select Committee on Science and Technology (1998) *Cannabis the Scientific and Medical Evidence*. London: The Stationery Office.

7 Henry, J. A., Jeffreys, K. J. & Dawling, S. (1992) Toxicity from 3,4-methylene-dioxymethamphetamine ('ecstasy'). *Lancet*, 340, 384–387.

8 Henry, J. A., Fallon, J. K., Kicman, A. T., *et al* (1998) Low dose MDMA ('ecstasy') induces vasopressin secretion. *Lancet*, 351, 1784.

9 Green, A. R., Cross, A. J. & Goodwin, G. M. (1995) Review of the pharmacology and clinical pharmacology of 3,4-methylenedioxymethamphetamine (MDMA or 'Ecstasy'). *Psychopharmacology*, 119, 247–260.

10 McCann, E. D., Szabo, X., Scheffel, U., *et al* (1998) Positron emission tomographic evidence of toxic effect of MDMA ('Ecstasy') on brain serotonin neurons in human beings. *Lancet*, 352, 1433–1437.

11 Merrill, J. (1996) Ecstasy and neurodegeneration. *British Medical Journal*, 313, 423.

12 Anonymous (1995) Khat chewing as a cause of psychosis. *British Journal of Hospital Medicine*, 54, 322–326.

13 Bowers, M. (1987) The role of drugs in the production of schizophreniform psychoses and related disorders. In *Psychopharmacology: The Third Generation of Progress* (ed. H. Meltzer), pp. 819–823. New York: Raven Press.

14 Advisory Council on the Misuse of Drugs (1995) *Volatile Substance Abuse: A Report by the Advisory Council on the Misuse of Drugs*. London: HMSO.

Chapter 2

1 Harrison, L. (1984) *Tobacco battered and the pipes shattered: the fate of the first British campaign against tobacco smoking.* Paper presented at the Centennial Symposium of the Society for the Study of Addictions, The Royal Society, London, October 1984.

2 Gossop, M. (1982) *Living with Drugs.* London: Temple Smith.

3 Edwards, G. (1971) *Unreason in an Age of Reason.* London: Royal Society of Medicine.

4 Anslinger, H. J. & Tompkins, W. F. (1953) *The Traffic in Narcotics.* New York: Fisk & Wagnalls.

5 Berridge, V. (1977) Opium and the historical perspective. *Lancet*, ii, 78–80.

Chapter 3

1 Joint Working Group, Royal College of Physicians, Royal College of Psychiatrists & Royal College of General Practitioners (1995) *Alcohol and the Heart in Perspective; Sensible Limits Reaffirmed.* A report of a joint working group. London: Royal College of Physicians.

2 Office of National Statistics (1999) Smoking Among Secondary School Children Survey. In: *Social Trends*, vol. 29, p. 126.

3 Berridge, V. (1999) *Opium and the People.* London: Free Association Books.

4 Quoted in Stimson, G. & Oppenheimer, E. (1982) *Heroin Addiction: Treatment and Control in Britain.* London: Tavistock.

5 Parker, H., Bury, C. & Egginton, R. (1998) *New Heroin Outbreaks Amongst Young People in England and Wales.* Crime Detection and Prevention Series. Paper 92. London: Home Office.

Chapter 4

1 Mackesy, M. E., Fendrich, M. & Goldstein, P. J. (1997) Sequence of drug use among serious drug users: typical vs atypical progression. *Drug and Alcohol Dependence*, 45, 185–196.

2 Stimson, G. & Oppenheimer, E. (1982) *Heroin Addiction: Treatment and Control in Britain.* London: Tavistock.

3 Advisory Council on the Misuse of Drugs (1998) *Drug Misuse and the Environment.* London: The Stationery Office.

4 Parker, H., Bury, C. & Egginton, R. (1998) *New Heroin Outbreaks Amongst Young People in England and Wales.* Crime Detection and Prevention Series. Paper 92. London: Home Office.

5 Pearson, G. (1987) *The New Heroin Users.* Oxford: Basil Blackwell.

6 Grund, J-P. C., Stern, L. S., Kaplan, C. D., *et al* (1992) Drug use contexts and HIV-consequences: the effect of drug policy on patterns of everyday drug use in Rotterdam and the Bronx. *British Journal of Addiction*, 87, 381–392.

7 Townsend P., Davidson, N., & Whitehead M. (eds) (1992) *Inequalities in Health: The Black Report and The Health Divide.* London: Penguin. Black Report first published by the DHSS in 1980.

8 Auld, J., Dorn, N., & South, N. (1986) Irregular work, irregular pleasures: heroin in the 1980s. In *Confronting Crime* (eds R. Matthews & J. Young). London: Sage.

9 Marmot, M. G., Davey-Smith, G., Stansfield, S. *et al* (1991) Health inequalities among British civil servants: the Whitehall II study. *Lancet*, 337, 1387–1393.

10 McKeganey, N. (1989) Drug abuse in the community: needle sharing and the risk of HIV infection. In *Readings in Medical Sociology* (eds S. Cunningham-Birley & N. McKeganey), pp.113–137. London: Routledge.

11 McIntosh, J. & McKeganey, N. (2000) The recovery from dependent drug use: addicts' strategies for reducing the risk of relapse. *Drug Education, Prevention and Policy*, in press.

12 Inhelder, B. & Piaget, J. (1958) *The Growth of Logical Thinking.* New York: Basic Books.

13 Beyth-Marom, R., Austin, L., Fishchoff, B., *et al* (1993) Perceived consequences of risky behaviours: adults and adolescents. *Developmental Psychology*, 29, S49–63.

14 Shedler, J. & Block, J. (1990) Adolescent drug use and psychological health: A longitudinal inquiry. *American Psychologist*, 45, 612–630.

15 Robins L. & McEvoy L. (1990) Conduct problems as predictors of substance abuse. In *Straight and Devious Pathways from Childhood to Adulthood* (eds L. Robins & M. Rutter), pp. 182–204. Cambridge: Cambridge University Press.

16 McKee, M. (1999) Sex and drugs and rock and roll. *British Medical Journal*, 318, 1300–1301.

Chapter 5

1 Joint Working Party of the Royal College of Physicians and the British Paediatric Association (1995) *Alcohol and the Young.* London: Royal College of Physicians.

2 Hogan, D. M. (1998) Annotation: The psychological development and welfare of children of opiate and cocaine users: Review and research needs. *Journal of Child Psychology and Psychiatry*, **39**, 609–620.

3 Farrington, D. (1980) Truancy, delinquency, the home, and the school. In *Out of School* (eds L. Hersov & I. Berg), pp. 49–63. London: John Wiley and Sons.

4 Powis, B., Griffiths, P., Gossop, M., *et al* (1998) Drug use and offending behaviour among young people excluded from school. *Drugs: Education, Prevention and Policy*, **5**, 245–256.

5 Hough, M. (1996) *Drugs Misuse and the Criminal Justice System: A Review of the Literature*. Paper 15. London: Home Office.

6 Dorn, N., Baker, O., & Seddon, T. (1994) *Paying for Heroin: Estimating the Financial Cost of Acquisitive Crime Committed by Dependent Heroin Users in England and Wales*. London: Institute for the Study of Drug Dependence.

7 Healey, A., Knapp, M., Astin, J., *et al* (1998) Economic burden of drug dependency. Social costs incurred by drug users at intake to the National Treatment Outcome Research Study. *British Journal of Psychiatry*, **173**, 160–165.

8 Gossop, M., Marsden, J., Stewart, P., *et al* (1998) Substance use, health and social problems of service users at 54 drug treatment agencies. *British Journal of Psychiatry*, **173**, 166–171.

9 Goldstein, P. J. (1985) The drugs/violence nexus: a tripartite conceptual framework. *Journal of Drug Issues*, **15**, 493–506.

10 Burr, A. (1984) The ideologies of despair: a symbolic interpretation of punks' and skinheads' usage of barbiturates. *Social Science and Medicine*, **19**, 235–249.

11 Glaser, D. (1974) Interlocking dualities in drug use, drug control and crime. In *Drugs and the Criminal Justice System* (eds J. A. Inciardi & C. Chambers), pp. 39–56. Beverly Hills: Sage Publications.

12 Lewis, R. (1994) Flexible hierarchies and dynamic disorder – the trading and distribution of illicit heroin in Britain and Europe, 1970–90. In *Heroin Addiction and Drug Policy. The British System* (eds J. Strang & M. Gossop), pp. 42–54. Oxford: Oxford University Press.

13 Hamid, A. (1990) The political economy of crack-related violence. *Contemporary Drug Problems*, **17**, 31–78.

14 Dorn, N. & South, N. (1990) Drug markets and law enforcement. *British Journal of Criminology*, **30**, 171–188.

15 Biederman, J., Wilens, T., Mick, E., *et al* (1997) Is ADHD a risk factor for psychoactive substance use disorders? Findings from a four-year follow-up study. *Journal of the American Academy of Child and Adolescent Psychiatry*, **36**, 21–29.

16 Didcott, P., Reilly, D., Swift, W., *et al* (1997) *Long-term Cannabis Users on the New South Wales North Coast.* NDARC Monograph No. 30. Sydney: NDARC.

17 Institute of Medicine (1996) *Pathways of Addiction. Opportunities in Drug Abuse Research.* Washington D.C.: National Academy Press.

18 Mars, G., & Altman, Y. (1987) Alternative mechanism of distribution in a Soviet economy. In *Constructive Drinking* (ed. M. Douglas). Cambridge: Cambridge University Press.

CHAPTER 6

1 McCoy, A. W. & Block, A. A. (1992) *War on Drugs: Studies in the Failure of US Narcotics Policy.* Boulder and Oxford: Westview Press.

2 Lewis, R. (1998) Drugs, war and crime in the post-Soviet Balkans. In *The New European Criminology: Crime and Social Order in Europe* (eds V. Ruggiero, N. South & I. Taylor), pp. 216–229. London: Routledge.

3 Ruggiero, V. (1996) *Organised and Corporate Crime in Europe.* Aldershot: Dartmouth.

4 Stimson, G. V., & Choopanya, K. (1998) Global perspectives on drug injecting. In *Drug Injecting and HIV Infection: Global Dimensions and Local Responses* (eds G. V. Stimson, D. Des Jarlais & A. Ball). London: University College London Press.

5 Strang, J., Griffiths, P. & Gossop, M. (1997) Heroin in the United Kingdom: different forms, different origins, and the relationship to different routes of administration. *Drug and Alcohol Review,* 16, 329–337.

6 Frischer, M. (1998) Mobility and diffusion of drug injecting. In *Drug Injecting and HIV Infection: Global Dimensions and Local Responses* (eds G. V. Stimson, D. Des Jarlais & A. Ball). London: University College London Press.

7 Parker, H., Bury, C. & Egginton, R. (1998) *New Heroin Outbreaks Amongst Young People in England and Wales.* Crime Detection and Prevention Series. Paper 92. London: Home Office.

8 Dorn, N., Oette, L. & White, S. (1998) Drugs importation and bifurcation of risk. *British Journal of Criminology,* 38, 537–560.

9 United Nations Drug Control Programme (1996) *Money Laundering and Financial Investigators Manual.* Draft manual.

10 Quoted in Marks, J. (1997) *The Economic and Social Costs of Public Drug Dependence Policies.* Address to the European Cities' Drug Policy Forum, Paris-Montreuil, 27 October 1997.

11 Dunkerley, J. (1980) *Bolivia Coup d'Etat*. London: Latin America Bureau.

12 Lee III, R. W. (1989) *The White Labyrinth – Cocaine and Political Power*. New Brunswick and London: Transaction Publishers.

13 Sen, A. (1997) On corruption and organised crime. In *World Drug Report* (United Nations International Drug Control Programme), pp. 150–153. Oxford: Oxford University Press.

14 Rose-Ackerman, S. (1989) Which bureaucracies are less corruptible? In *Political Corruption: A Handbook* (eds A. J. Heidenheimer, M. Johnston & V. T. LeVine), pp. 803–826. London: Transaction Publishers.

CHAPTER 7

1 Botvin, G., Baker, E., Dusenbury, L., *et al* (1995) Long-term follow-up results of a randomized drug abuse prevention trial in a white middle-class population. *Journal of the American Medical Association*, **273**, 1106–1112.

2 Botvin, G., Schinke, S., Epstein, J., *et al* (1995) Effectiveness of culturally focused and generic skills training approaches to alcohol and drug abuse prevention among minority adolescents: Two year follow-up results. *Psychology of Addictive Behaviors*, **9**, 183–194.

3 Pentz, M. A., Dwyer, J., Mackinnon, D., *et al* (1989) A multicommunity trial for primary prevention of adolescent drug abuse. Effects on drug abuse prevalence. *Journal of the American Association*, **261**, 3259–3266.

4 McGurk, H. & Hurry, J. (1995) *Project Charlie: An evaluation of a life skills drug education programme for primary schools* (Drugs Prevention Initiative Publication, Paper 1). London: Home Office.

5 Hurry, J. & Lloyd, C. (1997) *A follow-up evaluation of Project Charlie: A life skills drug education programme for primary schools* (Drug Prevention Initiative Publication, Paper 17). London: Home Office.

6 White, D. & Pitts, M. (1997) *Health Promotion with Young People for the Prevention of Substance Misuse* (Health Promotion Effectiveness Review No. 5). London: Health Education Authority.

7 Tobler, N. S. (1986) Meta-analysis of 143 adolescent drug prevention programs: quantitative outcome results of program participants compared to a control or comparison group. *Journal of Drug Issues*, **16**, 537–567.

8 Tobler, N. S. (1992) Drug prevention programs can work: research findings. *Journal of Addictive Diseases*, **11**, 1–18.

9 Osterloh, J. (1990) Drug testing in the workplace. *Occupational Medicine*, **5**, 617–632.

10 Bray, R. M., Kroutil, L. A., Wheeless, S. C., *et al* (1992) *1992 Worldwide Survey of Substance Abuse and Health Behaviours Among Military Personnel.* RTI/5154/ 06-16FR. Research Triangle Park, NC: Research Triangle Institute.

11 Farrell, M., Macaulay, R. & Taylor, C. (1999) *An Analysis of the Random Mandatory Drug Testing Programme. A report to the Prisons Service Directorate of Health Care.* Research Findings. London: Home Office.

12 Rydell, C. & Everingham, S. (1994) *Controlling Cocaine: Supply Versus Demand Programs. MR-331-ONDCP/A/DPRC.* Santa Monica, CA: RAND Drug Policy Research Center.

CHAPTER 8

1 Department of Health, Scottish Office & Welsh Office (1991) *Drug Misuse and Dependence. Guidelines on Clinical Management.* London: HMSO.

2 Advisory Council on the Misuse of Drugs (1988) *AIDS and Drug Misuse. Part 1.* London: HMSO.

3 Lord President of the Council and Leader of the House of Commons, the Secretary of State for the Home Department, the Secretary of State for Health, the Secretary of State for Education & the Paymaster General (1995) *Tackling Drugs Together: A Strategy for England 1995–98.* London: HMSO.

4 Ministerial Drugs Task Force (1994) *Drugs in Scotland: Meeting the Challenge.* Scottish Home and Health Department, Edinburgh and London: HMSO.

5 Welsh Office (1998) *Forward Together. A Strategy to Combat Drug And Alcohol Misuse in Wales.* Cardiff: Welsh Office.

6 Task Force to Review Services for Drug Misusers (1996) *Report of an Independent Review of Drug Treatment Services in England.* London: Department of Health.

7 Gossop, M., Marsden, J., Stewart, D., *et al* (1997) The National Treatment Outcome Research Study in the United Kingdom: six-month follow-up outcomes. *Psychology of Addictive Behaviours,* **11**, 324–337.

8 H. M. Government (1998) *Tackling Drugs to Build a Better Britain: The Government's Ten-Year Strategy for Tackling Drug Misuse.* London: The Stationery Office.

9 UK Health Departments (1999) *Drug Misuse and Dependence – Guidelines on Clinical Management.* London: HMSO.

10 Seivewright, N. (1999) *Community Treatment of Drug Abuse: More than Methadone.* Cambridge: Cambridge University Press.

11 MacCarthy, J. & Borders, O. T. (1995) Limiting setting on drug abuse on methadone maintenance patients. *American Journal of Psychiatry,* **142**, 1419–1423.

12 Stitzer, M. L., Bickel, W. K., Bigelow, G., *et al* (1986) Effective methadone dose contingencies on urine analysis test results of poly-drug abusing methadone maintenance patients. *Drug and Alcohol Dependence*, **18**, 341–348.

13 Calsyn, D. A. & Saxon, A. J. (1987) A system for uniform application of contingencies for illicit drug use. *Journal of Substance Abuse Treatment*, **4**, 41–47.

14 Farrell, M., Ward, J., Mattick, R., *et al* (1994) Methadone maintenance treatment in opiate dependence: a review. *British Medical Journal*, **309**, 997–1001.

15 Ball, J. & Ross, A. (1991) *The Effectiveness of Methadone Maintenance Treatment*. New York: Springer-Verlag.

16 Strang, J., Sheridan, J. & Barber, N. (1996) Prescribing injectable and oral methadone to opiate addicts: results from the 1995 national postal survey of community pharmacies in England and Wales. *British Medical Journal*, **313**, 270–272.

17 Strang, J. & Sheridan, J. (1998) National and regional characteristics of methadone prescribing in England and Wales: local analyses of data from the 1995 National Survey of Community Pharmacies. *Journal of Substance Misuse*, **3**, 240–246.

18 Uchtenhagen, A., Gutzwiller, F. & Dobler-Mikola, A. (1997) *Programme for a Medical Prescription of Narcotics: Final Report of the Research Representatives. Summary of the Synthesis Report.* Zurich: University of Zurich.

19 Health Advisory Service (1996) *Children and Young People: Substance Misuse Services.* London: HMSO.

20 Weaver, T., Renton, A., Stimson, G. *et al* (1999) Severe mental illness and substance misuse. *British Medical Journal*, **318**, 137–138.

21 Edmunds, M., May, T., Hearnden, I. *et al* (1998) *Arrest Referral: Emerging Lessons from Research.* London: The Stationery Office.

22 Healey, A., Knapp, M., Astin, J., *et al* (1998) Economic burden of drug dependency. Social costs incurred by drug users at intake to the National Treatment Outcome Research Study. *British Journal of Psychiatry*, **173**, 160–165.

23 Gerstein, D. R., Johnson, R. A., Harwood, H. J., *et al* (1994) *Evaluating Recovery Services: The California Drug and Alcohol Treatment Assessment (CALDATA).* Sacramento, CA: California.

CHAPTER 9

1 Berridge, V. (1983) Britain: problems change with social change – opium and the nineteenth century. In *Drug Use and Misuse. Cultural Perspectives.* (eds G. Edwards, A. Arif & J. Jaffe). Beckenham, Kent: Croom & Helm and World Health Organization.

2   De Quincey, T. (1822) *Confessions of an English Opium-Eater*. London: Taylor & Hessey.

3   Berridge, V. & Edwards, G. (1987) *Opium and the People. Opiate Use in Nineteenth Century England* (first published by Allen Lane, 1981). New Haven and London: Yale University Press.

4   Clark, P. (1988) The 'Mother Gin' controversy in the early eighteenth century. *Transactions of the Royal Historical Society*, **38**, 63–84.

5   Clark, G. N. (1966) A History of the College of Physicians of London (vol. II). Oxford: Clarendon Press.

6   Warner, J. (1997) The naturalization of beer and gin in early modern England. *Contemporary Drug Problems*, **24**, 373–404.

7   Warner, J. & Ivis, F. (in press) 'Damn you, you informing Bitch.' Vox Populi and the unmaking of the Gin Act of 1736. *Journal of Social History*.

8   Smart, R. G. (1974) The effect of licencing restrictions during 1914–1918 on drunkenness and liver cirrhosis deaths in Britain. *British Journal of Addiction*, **64**, 109–121.

9   Tyrrell, I. (1997) The US prohibition experiment: myths, history and implications. *Addiction*, **92**, 1405–1409.

10 Fukui, S., Wada, K. & Iyo, M. (1990) History and current use of amphetamine in Japan. *Japan–US Scientific Sympozium '90 on Drug Dependence and Abuse*.

11 Brill, H. & Hirose, T. (1969) The rise and fall of a amphetamine epidemic: Japan 1945–55. *Seminars in Psychiatry*, **1**, 179–194.

12 McCoy, A. W. (1991) *The Politics of Heroin. CIA Complicity in the Global Drugs Trade*. New York: Lawrence Hill Books.

13 Robins, L. N. (1993) Vietnam veterans' rapid recovery from heroin addiction: a fluke or normal expectation? *Addiction*, **88**, 1041–1054.

14 Robins, L. N., Davis, D. H., Goodwin, D. W., *et al* (1974) Drug use by US Army enlisted men in Vietnam: a follow-up on their return home. *American Journal of Epidemiology*, **99**, 235–249.

15 Strang, J. (1992) The Fifth Thomas Okey Memorial Lecture: Research and practice: the necessary symbiosis. *British Journal of Addiction*, **87**, 967–986.

16 Ryan, M. (1995) Alcoholism and rising mortality in the Russian Federation. *British Medical Journal*, **310**, 646–648.

17 Bobak, M., McKee, M., Rose, R., *et al* (1999) Alcohol consumption in a national sample of the Russian population. *Addiction*, **94**, 857–866.

18 White, S. (1996) *Russia Goes Dry. Alcohol, State and Society*. Cambridge: Cambridge University Press.

19 Leon, D. A., Chenet, L., Shkolniknov, V. M., *et al* (1997) Huge variation in Russian mortality rates 1984–94: artefact, alcohol, or what? *Lancet*, **350**, 383–388.

20 Harrison, L. D. (1995) Trends and patterns of illicit drug use in the USA: implications for policy. *International Journal of Drug Policy*, **6**, 113–126.

21 Courtwright, D. T. (1995) The rise and fall and rise of cocaine use in the United States. In *Consuming habits. Drug history and anthropology* (eds P. E. Lovejoy & A. Sherratt). London and New York: Routledge.

22 McCoy, A. W. & Block, A. A. (1992) *War on Drugs: Studies in the failure of US Narcotics Policy*. Boulder and Oxford: Westview Press.

CHAPTER 10

1 Institute of Medicine (1996) *Pathways of Addiction. Opportunities in Drug Abuse Research*. Washington, DC: National Academy Press.

2 Lord President of the Council and Leader of the House of Commons, the Secretary of State for the Home Department, the Secretary of State for Health, the Secretary of State for Education & the Paymaster General (1995) *Tackling Drugs Together: A Strategy for England 1995–98*. London: HMSO.

3 H. M. Government (1998) *Tackling Drugs to Build a Better Britain: The Government's Ten-Year Strategy for Tackling Drug Misuse*. London: The Stationery Office.

4 Kraft, M. K., Rothbard, A. B., Hadley, T. R., *et al* (1997) Are supplementary services provided during methadone maintenance really cost-effective? *American Journal of Psychiatry*, **154**, 1214–1219.

5 Gossop, M., Marsden, J, Stewart, D., *et al* (1999) Methadone treatment practices and outcomes for opiate addicts treated in drug clinics and in general practice: results from the National Treatment Outcome Research Study. *British Journal of General Practice*, **49**, 31–34.

6 UK Health Departments (1999) *Drug Misuse and Dependence – Guidelines on Clinical Management*. London: HMSO.

7 Weaver, T., Renton, A., Stimson, G., *et al* (1999) Severe mental illness and substance misuse. *British Medical Journal*, **318**, 137–138.

8 Bammer, G., Dobler-Mikola, A., Fleming, P. M., *et al* (1999) The heroin prescribing debate: integrating science and politics. *Science*, **284**, 1277–1278.

9 Drucker, E. & Vlahov, D. (1999) Controlled clinical evaluation of diacetyl morphine for treatment of intractable opiate dependence. *Lancet*, **353**, 1543–1544.

10 Zwerling, C., Ryan, J. & Orav, E. J. (1990) The efficacy of pre-employment drug screening for marijuana and cocaine in predicting employment outcome. *Journal of the American Medical Association*, **264**, 2639–2643.

11 Normand, J. (1994) *Under the Influence? Drugs and the American Workforce*, Washington, D.C: National Academy Press.

12 Aldridge, J., Parker, H. & Measham, F. (1999) *Drug Trying and Drug Use Across Adolescence: A Longitudinal Study of Young People's Drug Taking in Two Regions of Northern England*. DPA Paper 1. London: Home Office.

13 Hibell, B., Andersson, B. & Bjarnason, T. (1997) *The 1995 ESPAD Report*. Stockholm: Swedish Council for Information on Alcohol and Other Drugs.

14 Hall, W., Solowij, N. & Lemon, J. (1994) *The Health and Psychological Effects of Cannabis*. National Drug Strategy Monograph Number 25. Canberra: Australian Government Publishing Service.

15 Swift, W., Hall, W. & Copeland, J. (1997) *Cannabis Dependence Among Long-Term Users in Sydney, Australia*. NDARC Technical Report No.47. Sydney: NDARC.

16 MacCoun, R. & Reuter, P. (1997) Interpreting Dutch cannabis policy: reasoning by analogy in the legalization debate. *Science*, **278**, 47–52.

17 Single, E. W. (1981) The impact of marijuana decriminalisation. In *Research Advances in Alcohol and Drug Problems*. (eds Y. Israel, F. B. Glaser, H. Kalant, *et al*) (vol. 6), pp. 405–424. New York: Plenum.

18 Institute of Medicine (1999) *Marijuana and Medicine. Assessing the Science Base* (eds J. E. Joy, W. J. Watson & J. A. Benson). Washington D C: National Academy Press.

19 Hansard, 4 February 1999.

Appendix I

Sir Peter Barclay, Chairman, Joseph Rowntree Foundation, York

Dr Claire Gerada, General Practitioner, London

Mr Roger Howard, Chief Executive, Standing Conference on Drug Abuse (SCODA)

Professor Philip Graham, Chair of the National Children's Bureau and Emeritus Professor of Child Psychiatry at the Institute of Child Health, London

Dr Laurence Gruer, Public Health Specialist and Director, HIV and Addictions Resource Centre, Greater Glasgow Health Board (member of the Working Party until January 1998)

Professor John Henry, Professor of Accident and Emergency Medicine, Imperial College of Science, Technology and Medicine, London (formerly at the Poisons Unit, Guy's Hospital)

Dr Jerome H. Jaffe, Clinical Professor of Psychiatry, University of Maryland School of Medicine and formerly Director, Office of Evaluation, Scientific Analysis and Synthesis, Center for Substance Abuse Treatment, USA Department of Health and Human Services

Dr Robert Kendell, formerly President of the Royal College of Psychiatrists and Chief Medical Officer for Scotland; Chairman of the Working Party

Professor David London, formerly Registrar of the Royal College of Physicians of London; and formerly Consultant Advisor in Medicine to the Chief Medical Officer, Department of Health

Ms Sarah Mars, Research Worker, Royal College of Psychiatrists and National Addiction Centre, Institute of Psychiatry

Dr John Merrill, Consultant in Drug Dependence, Drugs North West, Mental Health Services of Salford NHS Trust, Manchester

Mr Michael Peters, Director of Educational Services, City of York Council

Professor Gerry Stimson, Director, Centre for Research on Drugs and Health Behaviour, Imperial College School of Medicine, London

Professor John Strang, Director of the National Addiction Centre, Institute of Psychiatry and the Maudsley Hospital, London

Appendix II

Professor Virginia Berridge

Dr Peter Cohen

Professor Griffith Edwards

Dr Marcel de Kort

Dr Don Des Jarlais

Dr Nicholas Dorn

Professor David Grahame-Smith

Professor Christine Godfrey

Professor Wayne Hall

Sir Graham Hart

Professor David Hawks

Professor Mark Kleiman

Dr Dirk J Korf

Mr Roger Lewis

Dr John Marks

Mr Howard Marks

Dr Ethan Nadelman

Professor Peter Reuter

Dr Giel van Brussel

Professor Wim van den Brink

Mr Peter van Dilen

Mr Ian Wardle

Police Superintendent David Warren

Mr Paul Vasseur

Dr Brian Wells

Index

residential rehabilitation 162–163, 182
risk factors 59–82
risk-taking
  assessment by children and
    adolescents 76
  differing views of 72–73
road traffic accidents 4, 97
Rolleston Report (1926) 40–41, 149,
  159
Royal Commission on Opium 32
Russia and Soviet Union
  alcohol in 1980s and 90s 202–206
  economic upheaval and drugs trade
    103–104

schizophrenia 9, 17, 178, 181, 250
school-based prevention programmes
  128–129
school exclusion and truancy 87
secondary prevention 119, 124
sedatives 6–8
selective prevention 119
self-help support groups 164
'self-medication' 80
serotonin 11–12
sexually transmitted diseases 98, 144
shared care 166–167
sildenafil (Viagra) 57, 243
Single Convention on Narcotic Drugs
  (1961) 33
'skunk' 8, 248
sleeping tablets 7
smoking see tobacco
social deprivation and problem drug use
  in UK 66, 67–72, 77, 87, 132, 237–
    238
  in USA 94, 206–207, 208–209
social exclusion 13, 82, 237–238
socially tolerated substances 28, 67,
  138, 145
social support networks 68
solvents see volatile substance abuse

source country control 135–136
Soviet Union see Russia and Soviet
  Union
spirits 67
  gin and distilled spirits in England
    (1650 to 1760) 188–192
  in Russia 203, 204, 205
steroids, anabolic 6, 179
stigmatisation/marginalisation of users
  144
stimulants 35, 88, 96
  after 1945 in Japan 197–200
  in drinks 26
  treatment 174–176
  see also amphetamine, cocaine,
    ecstasy and nicotine
substitution model 159
suicide 93
supply and demand concept 119, 121–
  122
  and targeting of resources 219–224
Switzerland 139–140, 234–235
synthetic drugs
  development 34–36, 253
  production 108, 115

Taliban militia 104–105
targeting
  of deprived areas by dealers 68
  of prevention efforts 124–126
  of resources 219–224
  target populations for prevention
    122–124
tea 26, 27, 138, 192
technological innovations, effects of 34–
  36, 109, 113, 115
temazepam 7–8, 39, 52–53, 97, 177
tertiary prevention 119, 124
tetrahydrocannabinol (THC) 8, 141,
  248
theobromine 26, 138
therapeutic addicts 40–41